Ant Colony Optimization and Constraint Programming

Ant Colony Optimization and Constraint Programming

Christine Solnon

Series Editor
Narendra Jussien

First published 2010 in Great Britain and the United States by ISTE Ltd and John Wiley & Sons, Inc.
Adapted and updated from *Optimisation par colonies de fourmis* published 2008 in France by Hermes Science/Lavoisier © LAVOISIER 2008

ISTE Ltd
27-37 St George's Road
London SW19 4EU
UK

John Wiley & Sons, Inc.
111 River Street
Hoboken, NJ 07030
USA

www.iste.co.uk

www.wiley.com

Library of Congress Cataloging-in-Publication Data

Solnon, Christine.
   [Optimisation par colonies de fourmis. English]
   Ant colony optimization and constraint programming / Christine Solnon.
      p. cm.
   Includes bibliographical references and index.
   ISBN 978-1-84821-130-8
   1. Constraint programming (Computer science) 2. Mathematical optimization. 3. Swarm intelligence. 4. Ant algorithms. I. Title.
   QA76.612.S6513 2010
   005.1'16--dc22

                                                                                    2009050443

British Library Cataloguing-in-Publication Data
A CIP record for this book is available from the British Library
ISBN 978-1-84821-130-8

Printed and bound in Great Britain by CPI Antony Rowe, Chippenham and Eastbourne

Table of Contents

Foreword

Combinatorial optimization has a very special place in computer science. On the one hand, this field addresses fundamental problems such as scheduling, resource allocation and vehicle routing, which are central to our economies. On the other hand, combinatorial optimization problems are extremely hard from a computational complexity standpoint: it is very unlikely that an efficient algorithm able to solve all these problems efficiently exists and that a single approach would outperform all others in this field. Different combinatorial problems, or even different instances of the same application, may be solved by very different techniques or by a combination of some of them. Moreover, whatever the approach considered, solving a combinatorial optimization problem usually requires a significant amount of programming and experimentation work.

In this book, Christine Solnon focuses on Ant Colony Optimization (ACO), a relatively recent approach for solving combinatorial problems. The topic is relevant: during the last decade, ACO has gradually evolved from an intellectual curiosity to a metaheuristic that has obtained outstanding results on some applications. This is the case, for example, of scheduling in assembly lines: a particularly difficult application for which ACO is able to solve a large class of instances with a very impressive efficiency and success rate. The scientific article published by the author on this subject was, indeed, a true revelation for many researchers.

However, this book does not introduce ACO in an isolated way, but provides an overview of many approaches. The first part of the book provides a short but excellent summary of the state of the art, with a focus on constraint satisfaction problems. Not only does this presentation clearly identify ACO contributions, but it also highlights the similarities, differences and synergies between existing approaches and ACO. Indeed, a truly innovative contribution of this book is to show how ACO compares to approaches as varied as greedy algorithms, local search and constraint programming.

The second part is a very didactic presentation of ACO. It shows us that ACO is a metaheuristic which produces collective intelligence from individual behaviors and local interactions. It provides an intuitive presentation of the various ACO components and a detailed overview of diversification and intensification mechanisms used by ants to sample the search space and converge towards the best solutions.

The book is organized around a broad vision of constraint programming: the idea that constraint programming defines the combinatorial structure of an application in a declarative way, and that this structure can be exploited by different solution algorithms. This view allows the author to communicate the benefits of ACO in a much more general way than the existing literature; the last part of the book is a good illustration of this. The application chapters are a goldmine for readers interested in acquiring a deep understanding of ACO. The last chapter provides a glimpse of the future of this metaheuristic and allows us to imagine many other connections.

In brief, Christine Solnon has written an effective book which targets both students and researchers wishing to acquire a thorough knowledge of the principles underlying ACO as well as industrialists in search of new solutions for their combinatorial optimization problems. It also communicates a comprehensive approach for solving combinatorial problems based on constraint programming, and allows us to establish judicious connections between several areas. This book is short, well written and full of ideas. It makes us curious to learn even more.

Pascal Van Hentenryck
Professor of Computer Science
Brown University

Acknowledgements

This book is the result of many interactions with many different people; it is impossible to mention them all here. Each of them have laid trails that have influenced me. At the moment of writing these acknowledgements, it is difficult to put these trails into order.

However, I would like to express my particular gratitude to Narendra Jussien who encouraged me to write this book; Pascal van Hentenryck who wrote the preface; Patrick Albert for his moral support; the IBM/Ilog society for its financial support; Pierre-Antoine Champin, Yves Deville and Serge Fenet who read preliminary versions of this book; and the Master and PhD students Inès Alaya, Madjid Khichane, Olfa Sammoud, Sébastien Sorlin and Arnaud Stuber. Each of them will recognize their trails.

Many thanks to Lucas, Léo and Lison, who train me to juggle with constraints every day of my life!

Chapter 1

Introduction

The ability of ant colonies to form paths for carrying food is rather fascinating. When considering the scale of ants, this path-finding problem is complex: ants only have a local perception of their environment, they do not have maps and they do not use GPS. The problem is solved collectively by the whole colony: paths actually emerge from a huge number of elementary interactions.

This collective problem-solving mechanism has given rise to a meta-heuristic – that is, a generic approach for solving problems – referred to as *ant colony optimization* (ACO). The first ACO algorithm was initially proposed by Dorigo in 1992 to solve the traveling salesman problem, the goal of which is to find the shortest tour that passes through a given set of cities. Since this pioneering work, ant colony optimization has been used to solve many complex combinatorial optimization problems.

These combinatorial problems are challenging for computer scientists since solving them may involve the review of a huge number (usually exponential) of combinations. Most people will be familiar with the combinatorial explosion phenomenon, which transforms an apparently simple problem into a tricky brain teaser as soon as the size of the problem to be solved is increased.

For example, let us consider pentamino puzzles. The goal of such puzzles is to tile a figure with a given set of pentaminoes (shapes composed of five adjacent squares) without overlapping, as illustrated in Figure 1.1.

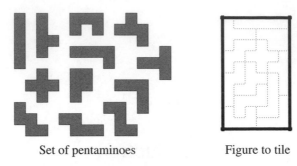

Set of pentaminoes   Figure to tile

Figure 1.1. *Example of pentamino puzzle; the solution is displayed in dashed lines*

When the number of pentaminoes is small enough, these problems are rather easily solved by a systematic review of all possible combinations. However, when the number of pentaminoes is slightly increased, the number of different combinations to review increases so drastically that the problem can no longer be solved by a simple enumeration. For larger problems, even the most powerful computer cannot enumerate all combinations within a reasonable amount of time.

The challenge of solving these problems clearly goes beyond puzzles. This combinatorial explosion phenomenon also occurs in many industrial problems such as scheduling activities, planning a production or packing objects of different volumes into a finite number of bins. It is therefore highly important to design algorithms that are actually able to solve these difficult combinatorial problems.

This book examines the ability of ant colony optimization for solving these complex combinatorial problems. This study is carried out within the context of constraint programming, which allows us to describe combinatorial problems in a declarative way by means of constraints.

1.1. Overview of the book

The book comprises three parts, described in the following sections.

As a preamble to these three parts, we introduce combinatorial problems and discuss computational complexity issues in Chapter 2. The goal is to provide a clear understanding of the challenge: as the combinatorial explosion cannot be avoided, we have to design intelligent approaches which are able to restrain or get around it.

1.1.1. *Constraint programming*

The first part of this book provides an overview of different existing approaches for solving combinatorial problems within the context of constraint programming.

We introduce *constraint satisfaction problems* in Chapter 3, which provide a framework for modeling combinatorial problems in a declarative way by means of constraints.

We then describe three main types of approaches that may be used to solve constraint satisfaction problems.

Exact approaches are described in Chapter 4, where we explore the space of combinations in a systematic way until either a solution is found or inconsistency is proven. In order to (try to) restrain combinatorial explosion, these approaches structure the set of all combinations in a tree and use pruning techniques to reduce the search space and ordering heuristics to define the order in which it is explored.

Heuristic approaches get around combinatorial explosion by deliberately ignoring some combinations. We discuss the two main types of heuristic approaches:

– *Perturbative heuristic approaches* (Chapter 5) build new combinations by modifying existing combinations by applying cross-over and mutation operators for genetic algorithms, applying elementary transformations for local searches or moving with respect to a given velocity for particle swarm optimization.

– *Constructive heuristic approaches* (Chapter 6) use a stochastic model to generate new combinations in an incremental way. This model is static for greedy (randomized) algorithms. It is dynamic and evolves with respect to previous experience for estimation of distribution algorithms and ant colony optimization.

In Chapter 7 we introduce some constraint programming languages. These languages allow the user to describe a combinatorial problem in a declarative way by means of constraints. This problem can then be solved by embedded solving algorithms such as those described in Chapters 4, 5 and 6.

1.1.2. *Ant colony optimization*

The second part of this book describes ant colony optimization. As for other heuristic approaches described in Chapters 5 and 6, ant colony optimization only explores part of the space of all combinations and uses (meta-) heuristics to guide the search towards the most promising areas while deliberately ignoring others.

Ant colony optimization borrows its features from the collective behavior of ant colonies and, more particularly, from their collective ability to find the shortest path between two points. We therefore begin the second part in Chapter 8 with a description of mechanisms which allow ant colonies to converge towards the shortest paths. We then describe the *Ant System*, the first ant-based algorithm introduced by Dorigo in 1992 to solve the traveling salesman problem, and we describe the generic framework of ant colony optimization for solving static combinatorial optimization problems.

Beyond the ant metaphor, we describe the mechanisms which allow artificial ants to converge towards solutions in Chapter 9 and, more particularly, those used to balance diversification and intensification:

– Diversification aims to ensure a good sampling of the search space and therefore reduce the risk of ignoring an area which actually contains a solution. This is mainly ensured by use of a stochastic model to construct new combinations.

– Intensification aims to guide the search towards the best combinations. It is ensured by a reinforcement mechanism which exploits past constructions to progressively bias the stochastic model.

In Chapter 10, we describe some extensions of ACO that have recently been proposed to solve continuous problems (where some variables may be defined over continuous numerical intervals), dynamic problems (where data may change during the solution process) and multi-objective optimization problems (where several objective functions require to be optimized).

We conclude this second part with Chapter 11, where we provide hints for implementing ACO algorithms.

1.1.3. *Constraint programming with ant colony optimization*

Algorithms based on ant colony optimization have proven to be very effective for solving many combinatorial optimization problems. In this book we focus on their ability to solve constraint satisfaction problems, which constitute a generic class of combinatorial problems.

We first illustrate (Chapter 12) the abilities of ant colonies in the car sequencing problem, a real-world industrial problem that is very often used to evaluate constraint programming languages. This problem involves scheduling cars along an assembly line, while satisfying capacity constraints which ensure that the different work units on the assembly line are not overloaded. We show that ant colony optimization obtains very competitive results for this challenging problem.

We study the abilities of ant colonies to solve generic constraint satisfaction problems, for which we do not have any specific knowledge of the constraints used, in Chapter 13. Again, we show that ant colony optimization is able to resolve complex problems in an efficient manner.

We show how to integrate ant colony optimization into a constraint programming library in Chapter 14. This integration allows us to benefit from existing procedures for modeling, verifying and propagating constraints. The tree-based exploration of the search space, usually employed in constraint programming languages, is however replaced by a stochastic exploration guided by previous experiments using the basic principles of ant colony optimization.

Chapter 15 concludes with details of future research which could be carried out for a better integration of ant colony optimization into a constraint programming language.

Chapter 2

Computational Complexity

A problem is said to be combinatorial if it can be resolved by the review of a finite set of combinations. Most often, this kind of solving process is met with an explosion of the number of combinations to review. This is the case, for example, when a timetable has to be designed. If there are only a few courses to schedule, the number of combinations is rather small and the problem is quickly solved. However, adding a few more courses may result in such an increase of the number of combinations that it is no longer possible to find a solution within a reasonable amount of time.

This kind of combinatorial explosion is formally characterized by the theory of computational complexity, which classifies problems with respect to the difficulty of solving them. We introduce *algorithm complexity* in section 2.1, which allows us to evaluate the amount of resources needed to run an algorithm. In section 2.2, we introduce the main *complexity classes* and describe the problems we are interested in within this classification. We show that some instances of a problem may be more difficult to solve than others in section 2.3 or, in other words, that the input data may change the difficulty involved in finding a solution in practice. We introduce the concepts of *phase transition* and *search landscape* which may be used to characterize instance hardness. Finally, in section 2.4, we provide an overview of the main approaches that may be used to solve combinatorial problems.

2.1. Complexity of an algorithm

Algorithmic complexity utilizes computational resources to characterize algorithm scalability. In particular, the *time complexity* of an algorithm gives an order of magnitude of the number of elementary instructions that are executed at run time. It is used to compare different algorithms independently of a given computer or programming language.

Time complexity usually depends on the size of the input data of the algorithm. Indeed, given a problem, we usually want to solve different instances of this problem where each instance corresponds to different input data.

Example 2.1. *Let us consider the problem of searching for a value in an array. The input data of this problem are a value and an array in which to search for this value. This problem has an infinite number of instances, each instance being defined by a different couple (value, array).*

The time complexity gives an order of magnitude instead of the exact number of instructions. In addition, it may be difficult to compute this exact number. The goal is therefore to give an idea of the algorithm scalability, that is, the evolution of the increase in running time as the amount of input data increases. To this aim, we use the $\mathcal{O}$ notation: the time complexity of an algorithm is $\mathcal{O}(f(n))$ if there exist two constants c and n_0 such that the number of elementary instructions is lower than or equal to $c \times |f(n)|$ for any instance with input data size n greater than or equal to n_0. This $\mathcal{O}$ notation allows us to focus on growth rates when comparing algorithms.

Example 2.2. *Let us consider the functions displayed in Figure 2.1. The function $g_1(n) = 5n^2 + 3n + 10$ has a quadratic growth rate. When comparing g_1 with $f_1(n) = 6n^2$, we note that $g_1(n) < f_1(n)$ whenever $n > 4$ so that the order of g_1 is $\mathcal{O}(n^2)$. The function $g_2(n) = 15n + 30\log(n) + 50$ has a linear growth rate: when comparing g_2 with $f_2(n) = 20n$, we note that $g_2(n) < f_2(n)$ whenever $n > 30$ so that the order of g_2 is $\mathcal{O}(n)$. Finally, the function $g_3(n) = 20\log(n) + 10$ has a logarithmic growth rate: when comparing g_3 with $f_3(n) = 25\log(n)$, we note that $g_3(n) < f_3(n)$ whenever $n > 8$ so that the order of g_3 is $\mathcal{O}(\log(n))$.*

Let us assume that g_1, g_2 and g_3 give the exact number of instructions performed by three different algorithms: A_1, A_2 and A_3, respectively. Orders of magnitude give a good idea of the number of instructions executed and *therefore the time taken by each algorithm for a given value of n. For example, when n = 1000, A_1 performs a few million instructions; A_2 performs a few thousand instructions and A_3 performs a hundred or so instructions.*

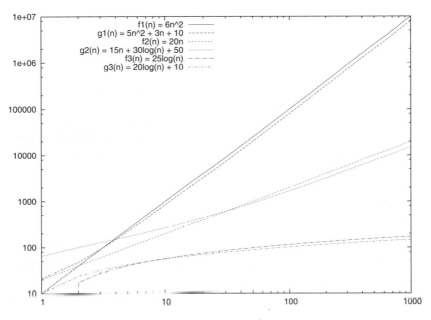

Figure 2.1. *Orders of magnitude: g_1 is in $\mathcal{O}(n^2)$, g_2 is in $\mathcal{O}(n)$ and g_3 is in $\mathcal{O}(\log(n))$ (note the logarithmic scales on both the x and y axes)*

Let us illustrate the interest in using orders of magnitude on a more concrete problem, i.e. the problem of searching for a value in a sorted array which contains n integer values.

We may design a first basic algorithm which sequentially scans the array until finding the relevant value. The time complexity of this first algorithm is $\mathcal{O}(n)$.

We may also design a second algorithm which performs a dichotomic search: the required value is compared to the value at the middle of the array, and the search process is iterated either on the left part of the array (if the searched-for value is smaller) or on the right part (if it is greater). The time complexity of this second algorithm is $\mathcal{O}(\log_2(n))$.

Even though we do not know the exact number of instructions performed by each algorithm, we know that the sequential algorithm will perform a few thousand instructions to find a value in an array of 1000 elements. The dichotomic algorithm will only perform a hundred or so instructions, however.

Refer to [COR 90] for more details on algorithmic complexity.

2.2. Complexity of a problem

The complexity of a problem is evaluated with respect to the complexity of the algorithms required to solve this problem. We always consider the best algorithm, the complexity of which is the lowest. This allows us to distinguish different classes of problems [PAP 94]. There actually exist many different classes of complexities; the *complexity zoo* (qwiki.stanford.edu/wiki/Complexity_Zoo) lists more than 400 different complexity classes. This section only briefly introduces the main classes, thus allowing us to formally characterize the class of problems which is of interest to us.

Complexity classes have been introduced for decision problems, i.e. problems which basically ask a question and the solution of which (the output data) is either *yes* or *no*. For these problems, we define the two classes $\mathcal{P}$ and $\mathcal{NP}$.

2.2.1. *The $\mathcal{P}$ class*

The $\mathcal{P}$ class contains all problems that may be solved in polynomial time by a Turing machine, which may be seen as a theoretical computer model. This implies in practice that any problem of this class may be solved by an algorithm, the time complexity of which is lower than or equal to $\mathcal{O}(n^k)$, where n is the size of the input data and k is a constant independent of the input data. This class actually contains all the problems that may be efficiently solved.

Some examples of problems in $\mathcal{P}$ are:

– searching for a value in an array;

– searching for the shortest path between two vertices in a weighted graph;

– searching for the maximum of a linear function satisfying a set of linear inequalities; and

– deciding if a given integer value is a prime number or not.

2.2.2. *The $\mathcal{NP}$ class*

The $\mathcal{NP}$ class contains all the problems that may be solved in polynomial time on a *non-deterministic* Turing machine. We may imagine such a non-deterministic machine as a computer, which is able to run a finite number of alternatives in parallel. Intuitively, this implies that solving a problem of $\mathcal{NP}$ may require the review of a large number (that may be exponential) of combinations, but that the review of each combination can be carried out in polynomial time on a deterministic machine. In other words, the problem of deciding if one given combination is actually a solution belongs to the $\mathcal{P}$ class.

Let us consider, for example, the satisfiability (SAT) of the Boolean formulae problem defined below.

PROBLEM 2.1.– *Given a set X of Boolean variables which may be assigned to* True *or* False*, a litteral is a variable of X or the negation of a variable of X, a clause is a disjunction of litterals and a Boolean formula is a conjunction of clauses. The goal of the SAT problem is to decide whether the satisfiability of a Boolean formula is met, i.e. to decide if there exists a truth assignment of the variables of X which satisfies the formula.*

The SAT problem belongs to $\mathcal{NP}$. Indeed, if there exists an exponential number (i.e. $2^{card(X)}$) of different truth assignments for the variables of X, we may check if a given truth assignment satisfies the formula in linear time with respect to the size of the formula.

Another example of a problem that belongs to $\mathcal{NP}$ is the clique problem defined below.

PROBLEM 2.2.– *Given a non-directed graph $G = (V, E)$ and a positive integer k, the goal of the clique problem is to decide if there exists a clique of size k, i.e. a subset of vertices $C \subseteq V$ such that $card(C) = k$ and all vertices of C are pairwise adjacent so that $\forall (i, j) \in C \times C, i \neq j \Rightarrow (i, j) \in E$.*

Indeed, given a subset of V, we may check in polynomial time with respect to the cardinality of this set if it is a clique of size k (even though there exists an exponential number of subsets of V).

Inclusion relationships between the two classes $\mathcal{P}$ and $\mathcal{NP}$ have given rise to a famous conjecture that may be summarized by $\mathcal{P} \neq \mathcal{NP}$. Indeed, though $\mathcal{P}$ is trivially included in $\mathcal{NP}$ (since any polynomial algorithm for a deterministic Turing machine is still polynomial for a non-deterministic Turing machine), the inverse relationship has never been proved nor refuted. Much research on this subject indicates that these two classes are actually different, however.

2.2.3. $\mathcal{NP}$-complete problems

Some problems in $\mathcal{NP}$ appear to be more difficult to solve than others because a polynomial algorithm to solve them (on a deterministic machine) has never been found. The most difficult problems of $\mathcal{NP}$ define the class of $\mathcal{NP}$-complete problems: a problem of $\mathcal{NP}$ is $\mathcal{NP}$-complete if it is at least as hard to solve as any other problem of $\mathcal{NP}$.

The first problem that has been shown to be $\mathcal{NP}$-complete is the SAT problem defined in problem 2.1 [COO 71]. Since then, many other problems have been shown to be $\mathcal{NP}$-complete such as graph coloring problems, traveling salesman problems or clique problems [PAP 94].

To show that a new problem P_{new} is $\mathcal{NP}$-complete, we first have to show that it belongs to $\mathcal{NP}$. This is usually done by showing that P_{new} may be solved by the review of a finite number of combinations and that there exists a polynomial algorithm for deciding if a given combination is actually a solution. We then have to show that P_{new} is at least as hard to solve as any other problem of $\mathcal{NP}$. This is usually done by showing that a problem P_{NPC}, already known to be $\mathcal{NP}$-complete (such as SAT), reduces to P_{new}. The idea is to show that P_{NPC} may be solved by transforming its instances into instances of P_{new}; if the transformation procedure has a polynomial time complexity then any polynomial algorithm for P_{new} may also be used to solve the problem in polynomial time P_{NPC}.

To illustrate this $\mathcal{NP}$-completeness proof by reduction, let us show that the clique problem defined in problem 2.2 is $\mathcal{NP}$-complete. We have already shown that this problem belongs to $\mathcal{NP}$. Let us now show that it is $\mathcal{NP}$-complete by reducing the SAT problem to it, thus showing that finding a clique of size k in a graph is at least as difficult as solving the SAT problem. Indeed, given a SAT instance defined by a set of variables X and a formula F composed of c clauses, we may define the non-directed graph $G = (V, E)$ such that:

- V associates a vertex with each litteral of each clause; and

– E associates an edge with every pair of vertices $(u, v) \in V \times V$ such that (1) u and v are associated with litterals that belong to different clauses and (2) the litteral associated with u is not the negation of the litteral associated with v.

We can trivially show that there exists a truth assignment which satisfies all clauses of F if and only if there exists a clique of c vertices in G.

Example 2.3. *Let us consider the Boolean formula*

$$F = (a \vee b \vee c) \wedge (\neg b \vee c) \wedge (\neg a \vee b).$$

The graph constructed from this formula is depicted in Figure 2.2. The three vertices a of C_1, c of C_2 and b of C_3 constitute a clique of size 3 and therefore correspond to a solution of the corresponding SAT instance.

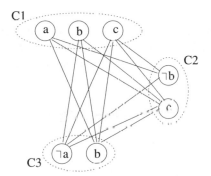

Figure 2.2. *Graph associated with the Boolean formula F*

The procedure used to transform any instance of the SAT problem into a clique problem has a polynomial time complexity. If we ever discover a polynomial algorithm to find a clique of a given size in a graph, then we could also use this algorithm to solve the SAT problem in polynomial time.

This equivalence by polynomial transformation between $\mathcal{NP}$-complete problems implies a very interesting property: if we ever find a polynomial algorithm for one of these problems (whatever the problem is), we could deduce polynomial algorithms to solve every other problem of $\mathcal{NP}$. We could then conclude that $\mathcal{P} = \mathcal{NP}$. The question of the existency of such an algorithm was considered in 1971 by Cook, but has not yet been resolved.

2.2.4. $\mathcal{NP}$-hard problems

$\mathcal{NP}$-complete problems are combinatorial problems since solving them implies the review of a finite (but exponential) number of combinations. However, some combinatorial problems are not $\mathcal{NP}$-complete. Indeed, to be $\mathcal{NP}$-complete, a problem must belong to the $\mathcal{NP}$ class. This implies that there must exist a polynomial algorithm to decide if one given combination is a solution. If we remove this constraint, we obtain the more general class of $\mathcal{NP}$-hard problems which contains all the problems that are at least as difficult as any problem of $\mathcal{NP}$, without necessarily belonging to $\mathcal{NP}$.

Example 2.4. *Let us consider the problem of the kth heaviest subset: given a set of n integers $S = \{i_1, i_2, \ldots, i_n\}$ and two integer values k and b, do there exist k different subsets $S_i \subseteq S$ such that the sum of the elements of each subset is greater than or equal to the bound b? Or, in other words, is the kth heaviest subset as heavy as b?*

This problem does not belong to $\mathcal{NP}$. Indeed, to solve this problem we have to review k combinations which are sets of subsets. There exist 2^n different subsets of S such that k (and therefore a combination) may have an exponential size with respect to n.

As this problem is at least as difficult as the hardest problems of $\mathcal{NP}$, we can conclude that it is $\mathcal{NP}$-hard.

2.2.5. Undecidable problems

Some decision problems cannot be solved. More precisely, it is impossible to design algorithms which can determine the answer in a finite time, even on a non-deterministic Turing machine. These problems are said to be undecidable.

A famous undecidable problem is the halting problem, which was proven to be undecidable by Turing in 1936. This problem may be stated as follows: given a program and a finite input, decide whether the program finishes running or will run forever for that input. If there exist programs for which it is easy decide if they finish or not, there also exist programs for which the only way to decide if they finish is to run them. However, if the program does not finish, we will never have an answer to the halting problem within a finite amount of time!

2.2.6. *Complexity of optimization problems*

The complexity classes $\mathcal{P}$ and $\mathcal{NP}$ are defined for decision problems, the goal of which is to decide if the answer to an input is *yes* or *no*. Many problems cannot be reduced to the decision of the validity of a proposition, but involve finding a solution which maximizes (or minimizes) a given objective function. These problems are called optimization problems.

We are able to define an associated decision problem for any optimization problem, the goal of which is to decide if there exists a solution such that the objective function is greater (or smaller) than or equal to a given bound. The complexity of an optimization problem is usually defined with respect to the complexity of its associated decision problem. In particular, if the decision problem is $\mathcal{NP}$-complete, then the optimization problem is said to be $\mathcal{NP}$-hard.

Example 2.5. *Let us consider the MaxSAT optimization problem, the goal of which is to find the largest number of clauses that may be satisfied in a given Boolean formula. The associated decision problem determines if it is possible to satisfy k or more clauses. As this problem is $\mathcal{NP}$-complete, the MaxSAT problem is said to be $\mathcal{NP}$-hard.*

The maximum clique problem, which involves finding the clique of maximum cardinality in a given graph, is also an $\mathcal{NP}$-hard problem as the associated decision problem is the $\mathcal{NP}$-complete clique problem defined in problem 2.2.

2.3. Where the most difficult instances can be found

Theoretical research on problem complexity is based on a worst-case evaluation of the complexity: the level of difficulty of a problem is defined with respect to its hardest instance. In practice, if we know that we will not be able to solve *all* instances of an $\mathcal{NP}$-hard problem within a reasonable amount of time, some instances may appear to be easier to solve than others.

Example 2.6. *Let us consider a timetabling problem involving assigning time slots to courses while satisfying exclusion constraints due to the fact that some courses cannot be taken simultaneously. This is a classical $\mathcal{NP}$-complete problem which basically corresponds to a graph coloring problem.*

However, the amount of time needed to find a solution to this problem depends highly on the input data, even if we consider input data of the same size and with the same number of courses and time slots. Typically, instances with very few exclusion constraints with respect to the number of available time slots are usually very easy to solve as they have a large number of solutions. Instances with many exclusion constraints are also usually easy to solve because we can trivially show that they are inconsistent. Intermediate instances – that have too many constraints to easily find a solution but not enough constraints to easily show that they are inconsistent – are often much harder to solve.

More generally, the hardness of an instance of a decision problem is related to a *phase transition* phenomenon which is introduced in the next section. We then introduce the concept of *search landscape* which characterizes the hardness of optimization problem instances.

2.3.1. *Phase transition*

Many $\mathcal{NP}$-complete decision problems are characterized by a control parameter such that the space of problem instances may be decomposed into two main areas: the underconstrained area where nearly all instances have a *yes* answer and the overconstrained area where nearly all instances have a *no* answer.

Example 2.7. *Let us consider the SAT problem defined in problem 2.1. For this problem, the control parameter is the ratio between the number of variables and the number of clauses. Instances for which this ratio is low (such that the number of clauses is low with respect to the number of variables) usually have many solutions; those for which this ratio is high are usually non-satisfiable.*

Most often, the transition between these two regions is sharp so that a very small variation of the control parameter value sperarates the two regions. This phenomenon is called *phase transition* by analogy with natural physical processes such as transitions between the solid, liquid and gaseous phases of a component due to the effects of temperature or pressure.

A very interesting property of this phenomenon is that the hardest instances are concentrated near the phase transition region, where instances are neither trivially solvable nor trivially inconsistent [CHE 91, HOG 96, MAC 98]. When plotting the evolution of the search cost with respect to the control parameter value, we observe a peak around the phase transition region such that a slight variation of the control parameter implies a transition from polynomial to exponential average search cost.

Figure 2.3 illustrates this on constraint satisfaction problems that have been randomly generated (see Chapter 3 for a detailed description of these problems). All instances have 20 variables, and each variable must be assigned to a value chosen within a domain which contains 20 values; each instance may therefore be solved by a review of 20^{20} combinations. For every pair of variables, a constraint forbids the simultaneous assignment of some pairs of values. These forbidden pairs of values are randomly chosen with respect to a tightness probability p_2. When $p_2 = 0$, no pair is forbidden so that constraints are empty and all assignments are solutions. When $p_2 = 1$, all pairs are forbidden and there is no solution. This tightness parameter p_2 is the control parameter which allows us to control constrainedness when generating instances.

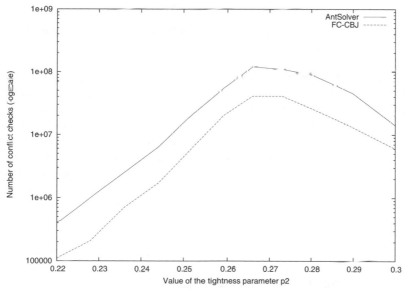

Figure 2.3. *Evolution of the search cost (number of conflict checks performed to find a solution) with respect to the tightness of constraint satisfaction problems. AntSolver is an algorithm based on ACO and FC-CBJ is an algorithm based on a tree search combined with forward-checking filtering and conflict-directed backjumping*

Figure 2.3 plots the evolution of the search cost with respect to this control parameter for two different algorithms (a heuristic ant-based approach and a complete tree search approach). This search cost is evaluated with respect to the number of conflict checks performed by each algorithm, i.e. the number of times an algorithm checks if a given pair of values is forbidden. This figure first shows us that a very slight variation of the control parameter p_2 results in a significant variation in the search cost (note the logarithmic scale on the y axis). It also shows us that the hardest instances are located around $p_2 = 0.27$. This corresponds to the phase transition region: when p_2 is smaller, generated instances are usually underconstrained; when it is greater, they are usually overconstrained. Interestingly, the location of the search cost peak does not depend on the approach used to solve problems [CLA 96, DAV 95].

Much research, both theoretical and experimental, has studied the location of this search cost peak with respect to the control parameter. In particular, [GEN 96] introduced the *constrainedness* of a class of instances, defined by

$$\kappa = 1 - \frac{\log_2(sol)}{\log_2(cand)}$$

where $cand$ is the number of candidate combinations and sol is the estimated number of combinations which are actually solutions.

Classes whose instances have a large number of solutions have a κ value close to zero. These instances belong to the underconstrained region and are usually easy to solve (even though very few instances of this region may appear to be very hard in practice [GEN 94]). On the contrary, classes whose instances have an estimated number of solutions close to zero have a κ value greater than 1. These instances belong to the overconstrained region and their infeasibility is usually easy to show. Between these two regions, classes whose instances have an estimated number of solutions close to 1 have a κ value close to 1. These instances belong to the phase transition region and are usually the hardest instances.

In particular, it has been shown that for the instances considered in Figure 2.3 the constrainedness κ is equal to 1 when the control parameter p_2 is equal to 0.266 [CLA 96]. This value actually corresponds to the observed search cost peak.

Previous research is useful in designing efficient approaches to solve combinatorial problems. In particular, it allows us to focus on the really hard instances when evaluating and comparing solving approaches. This kind of knowledge may also be used as heuristics to solve $\mathcal{NP}$-complete problems more efficiently [HOG 98].

However, let us note that studies on phase transition usually assume that instances are randomly and uniformly generated with respect to the control parameter, implying that constraints are uniformly distributed over the different variables of the problem. This assumption is not always realistic and real world problems are usually structured and exhibit non-uniform distributions of constrainedness.

2.3.2. Search landscape

Phase transition is defined for binary decision problems, such that we may partition the set of instances into two subsets with respect to their answer. For optimization problems, we may characterize the hardness of an instance with respect to different indicators.

Let us consider, for example, an instance of an optimization problem defined by a couple (S, f) such that S is the set of candidate combinations and $f : S \rightarrow \mathbb{R}$ is an objective function which associates a real cost with each combination. The goal is to find a combination $s^* \subset S$ such that $f(s^*)$ is maximal.

A first indicator of hardness of this instance is the state density [ROS 96] which evaluates the frequency of a cost c with respect to the total number of combinations: the denser a cost, the easier to find a combination with this cost.

This first indicator is independent of the approach used to solve the problem and does not take into account the way the combinations are explored. However, this point is very important in practice. If there is only one optimal combination but we have reliable heuristics to guide the search towards it, then this instance may appear to be easier to solve than another for which there are many optimal combinations hidden around bad combinations.

Hence, we often characterize the hardness of an instance with respect to the topology of its *search landscape* [FON 99, STA 95]. This topology is defined with respect to a neighborhood relationship $N \subseteq S \times S$ which depends on the approach used to solve the problem or, more precisely, on the way the set of combinations is explored. Two combinations s_i and s_j are neighbors if the considered search strategy is such that the combination s_j may be constructed from the combination s_i in one step of the search process.

This neighborhood relationship may be utilized to structure the set of combinations in a graph $G = (S, N)$ that may be represented as a landscape by defining the altitude of a vertex $s_i \in S$ by the value of the objective function $f(s_i)$. This value is called the *fitness* value in some solving approaches (e.g. genetic algorithms) and the search landscape is referred to as the *fitness landscape*.

We can use a metaphor to represent the search for a solution within a search landscape as the search for the highest mountain by a mountaineer who only has an altimeter (no map).

Within such a search landscape, mountain peaks are called *local optima* and correspond to combinations whose neighbors have lower or equal objective function values. If a local optimum is actually better than all the others, then it is a solution. Figure 2.4 displays an example of a search landscape which contains several local optima and two solutions.

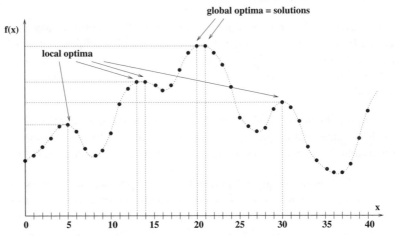

Figure 2.4. *Example of search landscapes for the maximization problem of a univariate function f whose variable takes an integer value ranging between 0 and 40, and for a neighborhood such that the neighbor combinations of $x = i$ are $x = i - 1$ and $x = i + 1$. For this neighborhood, $x = 5$ is a local optima as $f(4) \leq f(5)$ and $f(6) \leq f(5)$, but there also exist values of x for which $f(x) > f(5)$. $x = 13$, $x = 14$ and $x = 30$ are local optima and $x = 20$ and $x = 21$ are solutions*

The number of local optima and their distribution in the search landscape have a strong influence on the solution process:

– Hard instances usually have rough search landscapes, i.e. landscapes with many local optima (which are not solutions) which are rather uniformly distributed.

– When local optima are distributed in such a way that there is a rather high correlation between the objective function value of a combination and its distance (in the neighborhood graph) to a solution, the landscape is said to have a *Massif Central* shape. In this case, instances are usually easier to solve as we can use the objective function to guide the search [JON 95, MER 99].

– The easiest instances have search landscapes without plateaus such that all local optima are solutions. In this case, a simple greedy strategy – consisting of always moving to the best neighbor combination – is a winning strategy which always succeeds in finding a solution.

Figure 2.5 displays examples of both rough and *Massif Central* search landscapes.

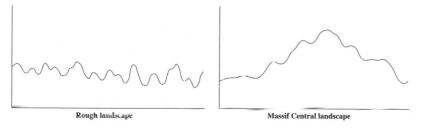

Rough landscape   Massif Central landscape

Figure 2.5. *Examples of search landscapes for a univariate function. The left-hand landscape is rough: it contains many local optima that are rather uniformly distributed and there is no correlation between the height of these local optima and their distance to the solution. The right-hand landscape has a* Massif Central *shape: local optima that are closer to the solution usually have better objective function values than those further away*

It is worth mentioning here that the search landscape depends both on the instance to be solved and the considered neighborhood; the landscape can be changed by changing the neighborhood.

2.4. Solving $\mathcal{NP}$-hard problems in practice

If some instances of $\mathcal{NP}$-hard problems appear to be easy to solve, there are also many hard instances for which combinatorial explosion cannot be avoided. However, we can easily design an algorithm to make the problem appear less tricky. To better understand the type of challenge we have to take up, let us consider a problem which may be solved by a simple review of 2^n combinations where n is the size of the input data.

Example 2.8. *To solve the SAT problem defined in problem 2.1, we may generate all possible truth assignments until finding an assignment which satisfies the formula. If the instance to be solved has n variables, there exist 2^n truth assignments as each variable may be assigned to either* true *or* false. *Hence, the SAT problem may be solved by the review of 2^n assignments in the worst case.*

Let us now assume that we have a computer which is able to review one billion combinations per second. In this case, the evolution of the time needed to solve our problem with respect to n is given in Table 2.1.

n	2^n	Time
30	$\sim 10^9$	~ 1 second
40	$\sim 10^{12}$	~ 16 minutes
50	$\sim 10^{15}$	~ 11 days
60	$\sim 10^{18}$	~ 32 years
70	$\sim 10^{21}$	~ 317 centuries

Table 2.1. *Evolution of the time needed to review 2^n combinations with respect to n*

This exercise shows us that, from a theoretical point of view, we cannot hope to design an algorithm that is able to solve all instances of an $\mathcal{NP}$-complete problem within a reasonable amount of time when n is greater than ~ 50.

However, many real world problems are $\mathcal{NP}$-hard such as timetabling, load balancing of assembly lines, vehicle routing and frequency assignment. Nearly 300 $\mathcal{NP}$-complete problems have been described in [GAR 79], the *compendium of $\mathcal{NP}$ optimization problems* (http://www.nada.kth.se/~viggo/problemlist/) reviews more than 200 $\mathcal{NP}$-hard optimization problems and the operational research (OR) library (http://people.brunel.ac.uk/~mastjjb/jeb/info.html) reviews more than 100 of these problems. It is therefore important to design approaches that are able to solve these problems in practice. To achieve this aim, we may consider the alternatives which are described in the following sections.

2.4.1. *Exploitation of particular cases*

Many $\mathcal{NP}$-complete problems become polynomial when the input data of the instance to solve satisfies some properties.

Example 2.9. *Let us consider the SAT problem defined by problem 2.1. This problem is $\mathcal{NP}$-complete in the general case. It is still $\mathcal{NP}$-complete when each clause contains at most three litterals (3-SAT). However, if each clause contains at most two litterals (2-SAT), then the problem may be solved in polynomial time.*

Similarly, some graph problems that are $\mathcal{NP}$-complete in the general case become easy to solve if the graph satisfies some properties such as planarity. Hence, if the clique problem defined in problem 2.2 is $\mathcal{NP}$-complete in the general case, it becomes polynomial when the graph is planar as the largest clique in a planar graph cannot have more than four vertices.

Hence, when we have to solve a problem which has been shown to be $\mathcal{NP}$-complete in the general case, we should first check if the instances that must be solved do not exhibit special features that have been ignored during the modeling step. In this case, we should check if these special features could be used to solve these special cases of the $\mathcal{NP}$-complete problem efficiently (in polynomial time).

2.4.2. *Approximation algorithms*

Another possibility of getting around combinatorial explosion when solving an $\mathcal{NP}$-hard problem is to accept a margin of error. Hence, ϵ-approximation algorithms are polynomial-time algorithms which compute a combination, the quality of which is bound by a factor ϵ with respect to the optimal solution. More precisely, let us denote the value of the objective function of the optimal solution by f^* and the value of the objective function of the combination found by the approximation algorithm by f'. This algorithm is an ϵ-approximation algorithm if we can show that, for every instance of the problem,

$$\frac{\mid f' - f^* \mid}{f^*} \leq \epsilon.$$

The approximation factor ϵ may be a constant. It may also be a function of the size of the input data.

All $\mathcal{NP}$-hard optimization problems are not equivalent by approximation. Some problems, such as bin packing for example, may be approximated with any ϵ factor (the time complexity of the ϵ-approximation algorithm increases when ϵ decreases). Other problems, such as maximum clique, cannot be approximated with a constant factor or even with a polynomial factor (unless $\mathcal{P} = \mathcal{NP}$).

These ϵ-approximation algorithms are not described in this book. We refer the interested reader to [SHM 95] for more details.

2.4.3. Heuristics and metaheuristics

A third possibility of avoiding combinatorial explosion is to partially explore the search space by deliberately choosing to ignore some parts of it. These approaches are therefore said to be *incomplete* and use heuristics and metaheuristics to guide the search when choosing the combinations to be explored:

– heuristics are empirical rules which depend on the problem to be solved; and

– metaheuristics are generic strategies that may be used to solve any combinatorial optimization problem.

For decision problems, these approaches may not find the solution of feasible instances (if they have made wrong choices), and they cannot be used to prove that an infeasible instance has no solution. For optimization problems, these approaches may not find the optimal solution and, of course, they cannot prove the optimality of the combination found even if it is actually optimal. Unlike ϵ-approximation algorithms, there is no theoretical guarantee of the quality of the computed combination with respect to the optimal combination.

However, in practice, these (meta-) heuristic approaches have shown to be very effective for many combinatorial problems and are able to quickly compute good combinations that are often optimal. These approaches are described in Chapters 5 and 6. Ant colony optimization, which is more widely described in the second part of the book, is also a heuristic approach.

2.4.4. Structuring and filtering the search space

If we cannot accept approximate solutions or if it is necessary to prove the optimality of the solution found, then we must face combinatorial explosion and design an algorithm which explores the set of all combinations in an exhaustive way.

This systematic enumeration is usually carried out by structuring the set of all combinations in a search tree. The goal is to allow the search process to prune some branches of the search tree, corresponding to subsets of combinations that do not contain solutions. This pruning is carried out in an *a priori* way without enumerating all the combinations by using bounding techniques, or by propagating constraints.

These pruning techniques are usually combined with ordering heuristics that aim to develop the most promising branches first.

These approaches are said to be *exact* as they are always able to find the optimal solution or prove inconsistency if there is no solution. However, the time needed to solve a problem depends on the efficiency and the relevance of the pruning techniques and the ordering heuristics, and is exponential in the worst case. These approaches are described in Chapter 4.

Constraint Programming

Introduction to Part I

Problem solving is a major quest of artificial intelligence. Constraint programming contributes to this quest by providing high-level languages that allow us to describe a problem in a declarative way by means of constraints, i.e. properties of the solution to be found. These constraint satisfaction problems are then automatically solved by generic algorithms. The constraint programming challenge has been well summarized by Freuder [FRE 97]: "Constraint programming represents one of the closest approaches computer science has yet made to the Holy Grail of programming: the user states the problem, the computer solves it."

Part I presents this constraint programming paradigm which will be implemented with ant colony optimization in Part III.

In Chapter 3, we introduce *constraint satisfaction problems* and illustrate this class of problems through four classical examples: the n-queens problem, the stable marriage problem, randomly generated binary problems and the car sequencing problem.

We then describe the main existing approaches that may be used to solve constraint satisfaction problems. In Chapter 4, we first describe *exact approaches* which explore the space of all combinations in an exhaustive way by structuring it as a search tree. In order to try to restrain combinatorial explosion, this tree search is combined with filtering techniques (which aim to prune subsets of combinations) and ordering heuristics (which aim to guide the search towards the best branches first).

When filtering techniques and ordering heuristics are not able to prevent combinatorial explosion, we have to give up exhaustivity and use *heuristic approaches* that explore the space of all combinations in an incomplete way. We use (meta-) heuristics to guide the search towards the most promising areas while deliberately ignoring other areas. In Chapter 5, we describe perturbative heuristic approaches that iteratively modify existing combinations to build new combinations. In Chapter 6, we describe constructive heuristic approaches that iteratively build new combinations from scratch.

Finally, we show in Chapter 7 how these different solving algorithms may be integrated within constraint programming languages, allowing us to describe a problem in a declarative way by means of constraints.

Chapter 3

Constraint Satisfaction Problems

Constraints are ubiquitous in everyday life and many real-life activities – e.g. constructing a timetable, packing boxes into a van, planning air traffic or designing a healthy meal – may be reduced to the problem of finding a solution which satisfies some constraints (or properties). Constraint Satisfaction Problem (CSP) refers to this set of problems.

We first introduce constraints in section 3.1 and then define constraint satisfaction problems in section 3.2. We then discuss the extension of the CSP framework to optimization problems in section 3.3. Finally, in sections 3.4–3.7, we describe some classical constraint satisfaction problems, i.e. the n-queens problem, the stable marriage problem, randomly generated binary problems and the car sequencing problem.

All of these problems are $\mathcal{NP}$-hard in the general case and we shall describe the main approaches that may be used to solve them in the next three chapters.

3.1. What is a constraint?

A constraint is a logical relation (a property that must be satisfied) among a set of unknowns, referred to as *variables*. Hence, a constraint defines the set of all authorized combinations of values for its variables or, conversely, restricts the values that may be assigned simultaneously to these variables.

Example 3.1. *The constraint* $x + 3y = 12$ *restricts the values that may be assigned simultaneously to the variables* x *and* y.

3.1.1. *Definition of a constraint*

A constraint may be defined by a simple enumeration of the tuples of values that belong to the relation.

Example 3.2. *The constraint*

$$(x, y) \in \{(0, 1), (0, 2), (1, 2)\}$$

constrains x *to be assigned to* 0 *or* 1 *and* y *to be assigned to* 1 *or* 2 *if* $x = 0$, *and to* 2 *if* $x = 1$.

In a dual way, we may define a constraint by enumerating the tuples of values that do not belong to the relation; this is usually the case when there are less tuples that do not belong to the relation than tuples that do.

We may also define a constraint by using well-known mathematical properties. There exist different kinds of constraints, depending on the type of values that may be assigned to the variables.

In particular, numerical constraints hold between numerical variables, i.e. variables that should be assigned numerical values. A numerical constraint is either an equality ($=$), a disequality ($\neq$) or an inequality ($\leq, \geq, <, >$) between two arithmetic expressions. These arithmetic expressions may be linear or non-linear functions which may contain variable products or logarithmic functions, exponentials, etc.

Set constraints hold between set variables, i.e. variables that should be assigned to sets of values. A set constraint may be an equality ($=$), a disequality ($\neq$), an inclusion ($\subset, \subseteq$) or a membership ($\in$) relation between set expressions that may be defined with set operators such as $\cup$ and $\cap$.

Boolean constraints hold between Boolean variables, i.e. variables that should be assigned to *true* or *false*. They are defined with logical operators such as $\wedge, \vee, \neg$ or $\Rightarrow$.

There exist other types of constraints, and each constraint programming language provides its own language to define constraints. Depending on the language considered, the set of operators and functions that may be used to define constraints may vary.

3.1.2. *Arity of a constraint and global constraints*

The *arity* of a constraint is the number of variables involved in the constraint. We say that a constraint is binary if its arity is two, i.e. it involves two variables.

Some constraints involve a subset of variables, the cardinality of which is not fixed in advance. In this case, the constraint is said to be global.

For example, the global constraint *'allDiff'* constrains a given set of variables to be assigned to different values.

Note that any constraint whose arity is greater than two may be transformed into an equivalent set of binary constraints. For example, the global constraint *'allDiff(x,y,z)'* is semantically equivalent to the three binary constraints: $x \neq y$, $x \neq z$ and $y \neq z$.

The interest in global constraints does not only rely on their expressiveness, however. Indeed, a global constraint may be exploited more efficiently than an equivalent set of binary constraints (with respect to algorithmic complexity but also with respect to the amount of information that may be deduced from it) in most cases [BES 03]. The interested reader may refer to [BEL 07] for the description of a large number of global constraints.

3.2. What is a constraint satisfaction problem?

A CSP is a problem modeled by means of constraints over variables. More formally, a CSP is defined by a triple (X, D, C) such that:

– X is a finite set of variables (corresponding to the unknowns of the problem);

– D is a function which associates a domain $D(x_i)$ with each variable $x_i \in X$, i.e. $D(x_i)$ is the set of values that may be assigned to x_i;

– C is a finite set of constraints and each constraint $c_j \in C$ is a relation between some variables of X; we denote this set of variables by $var(c_j)$.

CSPs are also referred to as *constraint networks*.

Solving a CSP (X, D, C) involves assigning values to variables in such a way that all constraints are satisfied. More formally, we introduce the following notation and definitions:

– An *assignment* is a set of variable/value couples, denoted

$$A = \{(x_1, v_1), (x_2, v_2), \ldots, (x_r, v_r)\}$$

such that the same variable is not assigned to different values, i.e.

$$\forall((x_i, v_i), (x_j, v_j)) \in A \times A, x_i = x_j \Rightarrow v_i = v_j$$

and the value assigned to a variable in a pair belongs to its domain, i.e.

$$\forall(x_i, v_i) \in A, v_i \in D(x_i).$$

We denote the set of variables assigned to a value in an assignment A as $var(A)$, i.e.

$$var(A) = \{x_i \mid (x_i, v_i) \in A\}.$$

– An assignment is *complete* if it assigns all the variables of the problem, i.e. if $var(A) = X$; it is *partial* otherwise.

– An assignment A *satisfies* a constraint c_k such that $var(c_k) \subseteq var(A)$ if the relation defined by c_k is true for the values of the variables of c_k defined in A; otherwise, the assignment *violates* the constraint.

– A (complete or partial) assignment is *consistent* if it satisfies all the constraints and it is *inconsistent* if it violates one or more constraint.

– A *solution* is a complete and consistent assignment, i.e. an assignment of all the variables which satisfies all the constraints.

Example 3.3. *Let us consider the CSP* (X, D, C)*:*

$$\begin{aligned} X &= \{x_1, x_2, x_3, x_4\} \\ D(x_i) &= \{0, 1\}, \forall x_i \in X \\ C &= \{x_1 \neq x_2, \quad x_3 \neq x_4, \quad x_1 + x_3 < x_2\}. \end{aligned}$$

The partial assignment $A_1 = \{(x_1, 0), (x_2, 0)\}$ *is inconsistent because it violates the constraint* $x_1 \neq x_2$.

On the other hand, the assignment $A_2 = \{(x_1, 0), (x_2, 1), (x_3, 0), (x_4, 1)\}$ *is complete and consistent: it is a solution.*

3.2.1. *Complexity of CSPs*

Since domains may be continuous numerical intervals, all CSPs are not combinatorial problems. The theoretical complexity of a CSP depends on the domains of the variables and on the type of constraints used.

In some cases, the problem may be polynomial. This is the case, for example, when all constraints are linear equations and inequations and all domains are continuous numerical intervals.

In some other cases, the problem may be undecidable. This is the case, for example, when constraints may be any arbitrary mathematical formula and variable domains are continuous numerical intervals.

However, in many cases the problem is $\mathcal{NP}$-complete. In particular, CSPs over finite domains (such that each domain is a finite set of values) are $\mathcal{NP}$-complete in the general case.

3.3. Optimization problems related to CSPs

Constraint satisfaction problems involve finding one solution that satisfies all the constraints or else proving inconsistency if no solution exists. However, we also have to deal with optimization issues in many cases. In particular, solving overconstrained problems often evolves into maximizing constraint satisfaction. Constrained optimization problems also involve optimizing some objective function while satisfying constraints.

3.3.1. *Maximizing constraint satisfaction*

When the constraints of a CSP are such that they cannot all be satisfied (that is, the problem has no solution), the CSP is said to be *overconstrained*. In this case, we usually want to find a complete assignment which satisfies as many constraints as possible or, conversely, violates as few constraints as possible. This problem is called partial CSP or MaxCSP [FRE 92].

In many real-life problems, constraints may not all be equally important. Some constraints may be *hard*, implying that they should not be violated; others may be *soft*, allowing them to be violated at some given cost. In this case, we associate a weight to each soft constraint (thus defining its violation cost) and the goal is to find the complete assignment which satisfies all hard constraints and minimizes the weighted sum of the violated soft constraints. This problem is called a valued CSP (VCSP) or a weighted CSP (WCSP) [SHI 95].

More generally, we may express preferences among the constraints of a CSP by using the generic semi-ring CSP framework (or SCSP) which generalizes maxCSPs and WCSPs [BIS 97]. An SCSP is defined over a semi-ring structure which mainly defines how to aggregate the weights of the constraints to define the objective function.

For all these overconstrained CSPs, the search space is defined by the set of all possible complete assignments and the goal is to find the assignment which maximizes the satisfaction level of the assignment: the number of satisfied constraints for maxCSPs, the weighted sum of satisfied constraints for WCSPs or an aggregation function for SCSPs. In the general case, these problems are $\mathcal{NP}$-hard as the associated decision problems are usually $\mathcal{NP}$-complete.

It should be noted that maxCSPs, WCSPs and SCSPs are generalizations of CSPs; an algorithm designed to solve any of these problems may therefore also be used to solve a CSP.

3.3.2. *Constrained optimization*

When the constraints of a CSP are such that there exist many different solutions that all satisfy them, the CSP is said to be *underconstrained*. In this case, some solutions may be preferred to others. These preferences may be expressed by the user by adding an objective function to be maximized (or minimized), thus defining a *constrained optimization problem*.

More formally, a constrained optimization problem is defined by a CSP (X, D, C) and an objective function $f : X \rightarrow \mathbb{R}$. The goal is to find a solution of the CSP which maximizes (or minimizes) f. For many of these constrained optimization problems, the difficulty is not in finding a solution but in finding the optimal solution with respect to f.

A classical example of constrained optimization problem is the multi-dimensional knapsack problem (MKP) defined below.

PROBLEM 3.1.– *Given:*

– a knapsack whose capacity is defined with respect to k dimensions and such that a maximal capacity c_j is associated with every dimension $j \in [1; k]$; and

– a set of n objects such that each object $i \in [1; n]$ has a profit p_i and a volume in k dimensions $d_{i,1} \times d_{i,2} \times \ldots \times d_{i,k}$,

the goal is to fill the knapsack with a subset of the n objects such that the sum of the profits of the selected objects is maximized while the capacity of the knapsack is not exceeded in any dimension.

To model this problem, we may define the CSP (X, D, C) such that

– X associates a variable x_i with each object $i \in [1; n]$;

– the domain of each variable x_i is defined by $D(x_i) = \{0, 1\}$ so that $x_i = 1$ if the object i is selected and $x_i = 0$ otherwise; and

– C contains a capacity constraint C_j for each dimension $j \in [1; k]$:

$$C_j \equiv \sum_{i=1}^{n} d_{i,j} x_i \leq c_j.$$

The objective function to maximize is $f(X) = \sum_{i=1}^{n} p_i x_i$.

Note that it is very easy to find a solution to any instance of this CSP: we just have to assign all variables to zero. However, it is much more difficult ($\mathcal{NP}$-hard) to find the solution which maximizes f.

It should also be noted that CSPs with soft constraints such as WCSP may be transformed into constrained optimization problems by integrating the violation costs of soft constraints into the objective function.

3.4. The n-queens problem

3.4.1. *Description of the problem*

The n-queens problem involves placing n queens on an $n \times n$ chessboard (with n rows and n columns) so that no queen may be captured by any other queen in one move. Recall that a queen may be captured by another queen in one move if they share a same row, column or diagonal. For example, a solution to the 4-queens problem is displayed in Figure 3.1.

It should be noted that this problem is not $\mathcal{NP}$-complete. Indeed, there exist polynomial algorithms which use predefined patterns to build solutions [HOF 69]. However, this problem is an ideal one to introduce and discuss CSP models.

To model a problem as a CSP, we must first identify the set X of variables (the unknowns of the problem) together with their domains (the values they

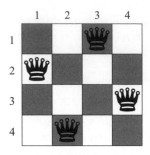

Figure 3.1. *Solution to the 4-queens problem*

may be assigned). We then have to identify the constraints that hold between the variables. This modeling step is essential to any problem-solving process; CSPs simply provide a structuring framework.

The same problem may often be modeled by different CSPs. For example, for the n-queens problem we can define the three different CSPs described in the following sections.

3.4.2. *First CSP model*

To model the n-queens problem as a CSP, we may choose to associate a variable with every square of the chessboard. Let us assume that rows and columns are numbered from 1 to n and let us denote the variable associated with the square on row i and column j as $x_{(i,j)}$. Each variable may be assigned to 0 (if no queen is placed on the square) or 1 (if a queen is placed on the square).

The CSP (X, D, C) corresponding to this first model is formally defined:
– the set of variables is

$$X = \{x_{(i,j)} \mid i, j \in \{1, \ldots, n\}\};$$

– the domain of each variable $x_{(i,j)} \in X$ is

$$D(x_{(i,j)}) = \{0, 1\};$$

– the set of constraints C is decomposed into four subsets of constraints:
  - there must be exactly one queen in each row:

$$\forall i \in \{1, \ldots, n\} : \sum_{j=1}^{n} x_{(i,j)} = 1;$$

- there must be exactly one queen in each column:

$$\forall j \in \{1, \ldots, n\} : \sum_{i=1}^{n} x_{(i,j)} = 1;$$

- there must not be more than one queen in the same rising diagonal (note that two squares share a same rising diagonal if and only if their sum of row and column numbers are equal):

$$\forall k \in \{2, \ldots, 2n\} \qquad \sum_{(i,j) \text{ such that } i+j=k} x_{(i,j)} \leq 1;$$

- there must not be more than one queen in the same falling diagonal (note that two squares share a same falling diagonal if and only if their difference of row and column numbers are equal):

$$\forall k \in \{1 - n, \ldots, n - 1\} : \qquad \sum_{(i,j) \text{ such that } i-j=k} x_{(i,j)} \leq 1.$$

When considering this model, the solution depicted in Figure 3.1 for four queens corresponds to the assignment:

$$\begin{aligned} A = \quad & \{(x_{(1,1)}, 0), (x_{(1,2)}, 1), (x_{(1,3)}, 0), (x_{(1,4)}, 0), \\ & (x_{(2,1)}, 0), (x_{(2,2)}, 0), (x_{(2,3)}, 0), (x_{(2,4)}, 1), \\ & (x_{(3,1)}, 1), (x_{(3,2)}, 0), (x_{(3,3)}, 0), (x_{(3,4)}, 0), \\ & (x_{(4,1)}, 0), (x_{(4,2)}, 0), (x_{(4,3)}, 1), (x_{(4,4)}, 0)\}. \end{aligned}$$

3.4.3. *Second CSP model*

To model the n-queens problem as a CSP, we may also choose to associate variables with queens. Since we know in advance that there is exactly one queen in each column, the problem is to determine on which row we should place the queen of column i. Let us denote the variable associated with the queen of column i as x_i: the value of this variable gives the row in which this queen should be placed.

The CSP (X, D, C) corresponding to this second model is formally defined:

– the set of variables is

$$X = \{x_i \mid i \in \{1, \ldots, n\}\};$$

– the domain of each variable $x_i \in X$ is

$$D(x_i) = \{1, \ldots, n\};$$

– the set of constraints C is decomposed into three subsets of constraints:
  - queens must be in different rows:

$$\forall i \in \{1, \ldots, n\}, \forall j \in \{1, \ldots, n\}, i \neq j \Rightarrow x_i \neq x_j;$$

  - queens must be in different rising diagonals:

$$\forall i \in \{1, \ldots, n\}, \forall j \in \{1, \ldots, n\}, i \neq j \Rightarrow x_i + i \neq x_j + j;$$

  - queens must be in different falling diagonals:

$$\forall i \in \{1, \ldots, n\}, \forall j \in \{1, \ldots, n\}, i \neq j \Rightarrow x_i - i \neq x_j - j.$$

When considering this model, the solution depicted in Figure 3.1 for four queens corresponds to the following assignment:

$$A = \{(x_1, 2), (x_2, 4), (x_3, 1), (x_4, 3)\}.$$

3.4.4. *Third CSP model*

The second model ensures that no queen may be captured by three subsets of binary difference constraints: the first subset ensures that all queens are in different rows, the second that they are in different rising diagonals and the third that they are in different falling diagonals. Each of these subsets could be replaced by a single global constraint expressing that a set of variables must be assigned to different values.

Hence, a third model for the n-queens problem may be defined by extending the second model in order to introduce new variables associated with rising and falling diagonals of the queens and to replace the three sets of binary difference constraints by three global difference constraints.

The CSP (X, D, C) corresponding to this third model is formally defined:
– the set of variables is

$$X = \{x_i, rd_i, fd_i \mid i \in \{1, \ldots, n\}\}$$

where x_i, rd_i and fd_i represent the row number, the rising diagonal number and the falling diagonal number of the queen of column i, respectively;

– for each $i \in \{1, \ldots, n\}$, the domains of the variables are:

$$D(x_i) = \{1, \ldots, n\}$$
$$D(rd_i) = \{2, \ldots, 2n\}$$
$$D(fd_i) = \{1 - n, \ldots, n - 1\};$$

– the set of constraints C contains a first subset of constraints to describe the relationships between row and diagonal variables:

$$\forall i \in \{1, \ldots, n\} : rd_i = x_i + i$$
$$\forall i \in \{1, \ldots, n\} : fd_i = x_i - i$$

and there are also three global difference constraints:

$$allDiff(\{x_i \mid i \in \{1, \ldots, n\}\})$$
$$allDiff(\{rd_i \mid i \in \{1, \ldots, n\}\})$$
$$allDiff(\{fd_i \mid i \in \{1, \ldots, n\}\}).$$

When considering this model, the solution depicted in Figure 3.1 for four queens corresponds to the following assignment:

$$A = \quad \{(x_1, 2), (x_2, 4), (x_3, 1), (x_4, 3),$$
$$(rd_1, 3), (rd_2, 6), (rd_3, 4), (rd_4, 7),$$
$$(fd_1, 1), (fd_2, 2), (fd_3, \quad 2), (fd_4, -1)\},$$

3.4.5. *Influence of the model on the solution process*

The three CSPs defined above all model the same problem and all have the same set of solutions, even though solutions may be formulated differently. It is therefore worth debating if some models are better than others.

There are different criteria for assessing the quality of a model, such as its relevancy and accuracy with respect to the original problem or its readability. A major criterion – probably the most important one due to the combinatorial nature of the problem in the general case – is the efficiency of the solution process, i.e. the time required to find a solution in the search space of the problem. This search space is composed of the set of all possible complete assignments that may be built, and different models of a same problem may lead to different search spaces.

Indeed, the first model introduces n^2 variables and each variable may be assigned to two values, so that the search space is composed of 2^{n^2} complete assignments. The second model introduces n variables and each variable may be assigned to n different values; the search space is therefore composed of n^n complete assignments. The third model introduces $3n$ variables. The first n variables may be assigned to n different values whereas the last $2n$ variables may be assigned to $2n - 1$ different values. The search space is therefore composed of n^{5n} complete assignments.

The size of the search space clearly influences the time needed to find a solution. However, to solve a CSP, we use constraints to *prune* this search space. More precisely, we use constraints to infer that some subsets of assignments do not contain solutions *without enumerating assignments*. This is a basic principle of constraint programming. Consider, for example, the third model. It contains three times as many variables as the second model. However, the constraints holding between these variables are such that, as soon as one variable associated with a queen i (x_i, rd_i or fd_i) is assigned to a value, we can easily deduce the values of the two other variables by a simple *propagation* of the two constraints $rd_i = x_i + i$ and $fd_i = x_i - i$. This simple propagation allows us to prune the search space by removing in an *a priori* way any complete assignment which does not satisfy these constraints. Hence, a solution algorithm based on this simple pruning principle explores the same number of combinations both with the second and the third model.

Moreover, the third model introduces three global difference constraints (which express the fact that a subset of variables must be assigned to different values) whereas the second model only uses binary difference constraints. By grouping a set of binary difference constraints into a single global constraint, we give knowledge to the solving algorithm. This knowledge may be used to prune the search space more drastically.

Example 3.4. *Consider the following CSP:*
- $X = \{x_1, x_2, x_3\}$;
- $D(x_1) = \{a, b\}$, $D(x_2) = \{a, b\}$, $D(x_3) = \{a, b, c\}$;
- $C = \{x_1 \neq x_2, x_1 \neq x_3, x_2 \neq x_3\}$.

When considering each difference constraint separately, we cannot reduce the search space. However, if we consider the global constraint 'x_1, x_2 and x_3 must be assigned to different values', then we can infer that x_3 must be assigned to c (as otherwise either x_1 or x_2 could not be assigned to a value different from that of x_3).

As well as being used to prune more values, a global difference constraint may also be processed more efficiently than the equivalent set of binary constraints. Indeed, checking that an allDiff constraint is globally consistent may be reduced to a matching problem in the bipartite graph. This bipartite graph associates a vertex with every variable of the allDiff constraint and every value in the domains of these variables and an edge is associated with every couple (x_i, v_i) such that v_i is a value in the domain of the variable x_i. Régin has shown that this matching problem may be very efficiently solved by using the algorithm of Hopcroft and Karp [RÉG 94].

The constraints therefore have a greater influence on the solving process than the number of variables and the size of their domains. This will be discussed in more detail in Chapter 4.

3.5. The stable marriage problem

3.5.1. *Description of the problem*

A marriage bureau would like to propose stable marriages to its clients. To this aim, it asks them to rank candidates in preference lists. These preference lists may be incomplete, i.e. if Paul does not want to marry Isabelle, he may not rank her. Also, preference lists may contain *ex aequo*: if Paul is still debating between Mary and Jane, he may rank them at the same level.

From these preference lists the goal is to constitute stable couples. By stable, we mean that breaking two couples to constitute a new couple should not lead to increased satisfaction for this new couple.

For example, if Romeo marries Isabelle and Paul marries Juliet, and if Romeo prefers Juliet to Isabelle and Juliet prefers Romeo to Paul, then these marriages are not stable as both Romeo and Juliet would be better married to each other.

More formally, two couples (M_1, W_1) and (M_2, W_2) are stable if

$$\neg((M_1 \text{ prefers } W_2 \text{ to } W_1) \wedge (W_2 \text{ prefers } M_1 \text{ to } M_2))$$
$$\wedge \quad \neg((M_2 \text{ prefers } W_1 \text{ to } W_2) \wedge (W_1 \text{ prefers } M_2 \text{ to } M_1))$$

and a set S of couples is stable if every pair of couples of S is stable.

Example 3.5. *Consider the instance introduced in [GEN 02]. There are six men (referred to as* 1, 2, 3, 4, 5 *and* 6 *so that they remain anonymous) and six women (referred to as* 7, 8, 9, 10, 11 *and* 12 *for the same reason). Their preferences are expressed in Tables 3.1 and 3.2.*

When considering these preference lists, we can see that if 3 *marries* 9 *and* 6 *marries* 7, *then* 3 *and* 7 *will be tempted to divorce in order to marry each other as* 3 *prefers* 7 *to* 9 *and* 7 *prefers* 3 *to* 6.

The following set of couples is stable and is therefore a solution:

$$\{(1, 10), (2, 8), (3, 7), (4, 9), (5, 11), (6, 12)\}.$$

1 prefers: 8, (12 and 10 *ex aequo*)
2 prefers: (8 and 11 *ex aequo*), 12
3 prefers: 7, 9, 12
4 prefers: 12, 9
5 prefers: 8, 7, 11
6 prefers: 12, (10 and 8 *ex aequo*), 11, 7

Table 3.1. *Male rankings*

7 prefers: (5 and 3 *ex aequo*), 6
8 prefers: 2, 5, 1, 6
9 prefers: (3 and 4 *ex aequo*)
10 prefers: 6, 1
11 prefers: 5, 2, 6
12 prefers: 1, (4 and 6 *ex aequo*), 2, 3

Table 3.2. *Female rankings*

This problem may seem artificial but we obtain a more realistic problem if we replace, for example, men by students looking for work experience placements and women by companies looking for trainees.

If incomplete lists and *ex aequo* are forbidden, so that preference lists define strict and total orders, the stable marriage problem may be solved in polynomial time. However, the problem becomes $\mathcal{NP}$-complete [GEN 02] as soon as lists become incomplete and contain *ex aequo*.

3.5.2. *CSP model*

To model this problem as a CSP, we first have to identify the set X of variables and their associated domains. The goal here is to guess who marries who. To express this, we may associate a variable x_i with every man i and a variable y_j with every woman j. However, as these relations are symmetrical, we may only keep one of these two sets of variables.

From the previous example, we define $X = \{x_1, x_2, x_3, x_4, x_5, x_6\}$.

For each variable x_i, the corresponding domain contains every woman ranked by i and who has ranked i.

From the previous example, we define

$$D(x_1) = \{8, 10, 12\} \qquad D(x_4) = \{9, 12\}$$
$$D(x_2) = \{8, 11, 12\} \qquad D(x_5) = \{7, 8, 11\}$$
$$D(x_3) = \{7, 9, 12\} \qquad D(x_6) = \{7, 8, 10, 11, 12\}.$$

We then have to specify that there must not be several men married to the same woman. This may be carried out by adding a binary difference constraint for every pair of variables. As for the n-queens problem, it is both more elegant and efficient to post a global difference constraint on the whole set of variables X

Finally, we have to specify that marriages must be stable. This may be achieved by adding a binary constraint for every couple of men (i, j) which ensures that either i does not prefer the wife of j to his wife, or that the spouse of j does not prefer i to her husband. These binary constraints may be defined in extension by enumerating all couples of women (k, l) such that the two couples (i, k) and (j, l) are stable.

From the previous example, we define

$$(x_1, x_2) \in \{(8, 11), (10, 8), (10, 11), (10, 12), (12, 8), (12, 11)\}$$
$$(x_1, x_3) \in \{(8, 7), (8, 9), (8, 12), (10, 7), (10, 9), (10, 12), (12, 7), (12, 9)\}$$
$$(x_1, x_4) \in \{(8, 12), (8, 9), (10, 12), (10, 9), (12, 9)\}$$
etc.

A solution to this problem is

$$\{(x_1, 10), (x_2, 8), (x_3, 7), (x_4, 9), (x_5, 11), (x_6, 12)\}$$

or, in other words, 1 marries 10, 2 marries 8, 3 marries 7, etc.

3.6. Randomly generated binary CSPs

The n-queens problem and the stable marriage problem may be modeled with binary CSPs, i.e. CSPs defined with binary constraints only. These binary constraints may be defined by listing, for every pair of variables, the set of pairs of values that may be assigned to these variables. Such CSPs may be randomly generated. This may initially seem futile as there already exist many real-world problems that have not yet been solved. However, randomly generated instances are very useful to evaluate scaled-up properties of solution algorithms; the number of variables, size of domains, number of constraints or the tightness of the constraints can be easily changed.

A class of randomly generated binary CSPs is usually characterized by a quadruple $< n, m, p_1, p_2 >$ where:

 – n is the number of variables of the CSP;

 – m is the size of the domains;

 – $p_1 \in [0, 1]$ is a measure of the density of the constraints and determines the number of constraints; and

 – $p_2 \in [0, 1]$ is a measure of the tightness of the constraints and determines the number of pairs of values which are forbidden for each constraint.

Given a class $< n, m, p_1, p_2 >$, we may consider different generation models as described in [MAC 98]. In particular, when generating an instance, we may either consider p_1 and p_2 as probabilities or as ratios.

A very interesting property of randomly generated binary CSPs is that the phase transition region has been clearly located [CLA 96]: the constrainedness κ introduced in section 2.3.1 is defined by the formula:

$$\kappa = \frac{n-1}{2} p_1 \log_m \left(\frac{1}{1 - p_2} \right).$$

The hardest instances (and therefore those that interest us most when evaluating a solution algorithm) are those for which κ is equal to 1.

Let us return to Figure 2.3 which plots the evolution of the search cost when increasing the tightness p_2 from 0.22 to 0.3 for instances of class $< 20, 20, 1, p_2 >$. This figure shows us that the hardest instances are those for which $p_2 \sim 0.27$. For this class of instances, κ equals 1 when $p_2 = 0.266$.

3.7. The car sequencing problem

3.7.1. *Description of the problem*

The car sequencing problem was first described by Parello *et al.* [PAR 86], and was first introduced to the constraint programming community in 1988 by Dincbas *et al.* [DIN 88]. It is a classical benchmark for constraint programming languages and it is the first problem of CSPLib, the library of test problems for constraint solutions [GEN 99].

This problem involves scheduling cars along an assembly line in order to install options (e.g. sunroof, radio or air conditioning). Each option is installed by a different station, designed to handle at most a certain percentage of the cars passing along the assembly line. The cars requiring this option must be spaced such that the capacity of every station is never exceeded.

This requirement may be formalized by ratio constraints: each option i is associated with a p_i/q_i ratio such that, for any subsequence of q_i consecutive vehicles, p_i vehicles at most may require option i. More precisely, an instance of the car sequencing problem is defined by a tuple (V, O, p, q, r), where

   $- V = \{v_1, \ldots, v_n\}$ is the set of vehicles to be produced;

   $O - \{o_1, \ldots, o_m\}$ is the set of different options;

   $- p : O \rightarrow \mathbb{N}$ and $q : O \rightarrow \mathbb{N}$ define the capacity constraint associated with each option $o_i \in O$; this capacity constraint imposes that, for any subsequence of $q(o_i)$ consecutive cars on the line, at most $p(o_i)$ of them may require option o_i; and

   $- r : V \times O \rightarrow \{0,1\}$ defines options requirements, i.e. for each vehicle $v_i \in V$ and for each option $o_j \in O$, $r(v_i, o_j) = 1$ if o_j must be installed on v_i and $r(v_i, o_j) = 0$ otherwise.

Example 3.6. *The instance introduced in [DIN 88] is defined by the tuple (V, O, p, q, r) such that:*

  – There are 10 cars to schedule:

$$V = \{v_1, v_2, v_3, v_4, v_5, v_6, v_7, v_8, v_9, v_{10}\}.$$

  – There are 5 options to install:

$$O = \{o_1, o_2, o_3, o_4, o_5\}.$$

– *Capacity constraints associated with options are defined as:*

$$p(o_1) = 1, \quad p(o_2) = 2, \quad p(o_3) = 1, \quad p(o_4) = 2, \quad p(o_5) = 1$$
$$q(o_1) = 2, \quad q(o_2) = 3, \quad q(o_3) = 3, \quad q(o_4) = 5, \quad q(o_5) = 5$$

or, in other words, there must not be more than one car requiring option o_1 every two consecutive cars or more than two cars requiring option o_2 every three consecutive cars, etc.

– *Required options are defined by the array r:*

	o_1	o_2	o_3	o_4	o_5
v_1	1	0	1	1	0
v_2	0	0	0	1	0
v_3	0	1	0	0	1
v_4	0	1	0	0	1
v_5	0	1	0	1	0
v_6	0	1	0	1	0
v_7	1	0	1	0	0
v_8	1	0	1	0	0
v_9	1	1	0	0	0
v_{10}	1	1	0	0	0

or, in other words, we should install options o_1, o_3 and o_4 on car v_1, option o_4 on car v_2, etc.

Note that two different cars of V may require the same configuration of options; all cars requiring the same configuration of options (e.g. cars v_3 and v_4) are clustered within the same *car class*.

The car sequencing problem involves finding a sequence of the vehicles of V, thus defining the order in which they will pass along the assembly line. The *decision problem* consists of determining if it is possible to find a sequence that satisfies all capacity constraints, whereas the *optimization problem* involves finding a minimum cost sequence where the cost function usually evaluates constraint violations.

A solution to the instance described previously is the sequence

$$< v_1, v_2, v_9, v_3, v_7, v_5, v_6, v_8, v_4, v_{10} > .$$

We may check in the table below that all capacity constraints are actually satisfied:

	o_1	o_2	o_3	o_4	o_5
v_1	1	0	1	1	0
v_2	0	0	0	1	0
v_9	1	1	0	0	0
v_3	0	1	0	0	1
v_7	1	0	1	0	0
v_5	0	1	0	1	0
v_6	0	1	0	1	0
v_8	1	0	1	0	0
v_4	0	1	0	0	1
v_{10}	1	1	0	0	0

The decision problem has been shown to be $\mathcal{NP}$-hard by a transformation from the Hamiltonian path problem [GEN 98] and by a transformation from the exact cover by 3-sets problem [KIS 04].

Kis also showed that the problem is $\mathcal{NP}$-hard in the strong sense and does not belong to $\mathcal{NP}$ in the general case. This comes from the fact that an instance of the car sequencing problem may be encoded by giving, for each different car class, the number of cars belonging to this class and the subset of options required by these cars.

With such an encoding, and provided that the number of cars within a same car class can be arbitrarily large, the length of a solution (which is a sequence of $|V|$ car classes) is not bound by a polynomial in the length of the instance.

A more general problem which introduces paint batching constraints and priority levels for capacity constraints has been proposed by Renault for the ROADEF (Société Française de Recherche Opérationnelle et d'Aide à la Décision) challenge in 2005 [SOL 08].

3.7.2. *CSP model*

The CSP model of the car sequencing problem usually introduces the concept of car classes: all cars requiring the same set of options are grouped into the same car class. The goal here is to reduce the search space. Indeed, let us consider an instance such that there are k different car classes. Let us partition V into k disjoint subsets $V = V_1 \cup V_2 \cup \ldots V_k$ such that all vehicles within the same subset V_i require the same configuration of options. In this case, the number of different combinations of the vehicles of V in a sequence is

$$\frac{card(V)!}{card(V_1)! \cdot card(V_2)! \cdot \ldots card(V_k)!}.$$

The CSP formulation of the car sequencing problem usually introduces two different kinds of variables:

– A *slot variable* X_i is associated with each position i in the sequence of cars. This variable corresponds to the class of the ith car in the sequence and its domain is the set of all car classes.

– An *option variable* O_i^j is associated with each position i in the sequence and each option j. This variable is assigned to 1 if option j has to be installed on the ith car of the sequence and 0 otherwise, so that its domain is $\{0, 1\}$.

There are usually three different kinds of constraints:

– *Link constraints* specify the link between slot and option variables, i.e. $O_i^j = 1$ if and only if option j has to be installed on X_i.

– *Capacity constraints* specify that station capacities must not be exceeded, i.e. for each option j and each subsequence of q_i cars, a linear inequality specifies that the sum of the corresponding option variables must be smaller than or equal to p_i.

– *Demand constraints* specify, for each car class, the number of cars of this class that must be sequenced.

3.8. Discussion

The CSP formalism introduced here provides a structuring framework to model problems by means of constraints, useful for describing many combinatorial problems.

For example, the CSP library described in [GEN 99] (see website http://www.csplib.org/) reviews a large number of problems that have been modeled as CSPs. These problems belong to different application fields such as scheduling, design, configuration, frequency assignment or bio-informatics.

The constraint programming paradigm is based on this formalism and provides high-level languages that allow the user to describe the CSP to be solved in a declarative way. These CSPs are solved by embedded solvers that are able to solve CSPs in a generic way.

In the following chapters, we describe the main approaches that may be used to solve CSPs in a generic way.

Chapter 4

Exact Approaches

We describe a first generic approach for solving combinatorial problems modeled as CSPs. The idea is to explore the set of all possible assignments in a systematic way until either finding a solution (if the CSP is consistent) or demonstrating that there is no solution (if the CSP is inconsistent).

The basic algorithm, which builds a search tree to enumerate assignments, is called *simple backtrack* and is introduced in section 4.1. As the number of assignments to explore may be huge (exponential), this tree-based exploration is combined with filtering techniques which propagate constraints to reduce the number of assignments to explore. These techniques are introduced in section 4.2.

We may also use ordering heuristics to (try to) start the enumeration with the most promising assignments. These heuristics are introduced in section 4.3. In section 4.4, we briefly show how to solve optimization problems related to CSPs with tree-search approaches. Finally, in section 4.5, we discuss the efficiency of this kind of generic approach with respect to dedicated approaches.

4.1. Construction of a search tree

We may solve a finite domain CSP by a simple enumeration of all possible complete assignments until finding a solution which satisfies all constraints, or proving inconsistency. Such a *generate-and-test* approach cannot be used within a reasonable limit of time when the problem has more than ∼30 variables: for a CSP with n variables such that each domain contains k values, there exist k^n different complete assignments.

We may reduce the number of assignments to explore by using constraints to eliminate sets of complete assignments which share the same partial inconsistent assignment. The idea is to build assignments in an incremental way starting from an empty assignment, instantiating a new variable at each step and checking at each step that the current partial assignment is actually consistent. If this is not the case it is not completed, thus eliminating all complete assignments that contain this partial assignment.

This basic solving principle is called *simple backtrack*, and is detailed in algorithm 4.1. The *simpleBacktrack* function is recursive and must be initially called with an empty assignment $A = \emptyset$. It returns a solution to the CSP (X, D, C) or $\emptyset$ if the CSP does not have a solution.

We usually say that the *simpleBacktrack* function builds a *search tree*. Each node of this tree corresponds to a consistent assignment: the root corresponds to the empty assignment; internal nodes correspond to partial assignments; and leaves correspond either to partial assignments which cannot be consistently extended or to complete assignments, i.e. solutions. Edges of the search tree correspond to recursive calls: a node corresponding to an assignment A is the father of a node corresponding to an assignment A' if *simpleBacktrack*$((X, D, C), A)$ has called *simpleBacktrack*$((X, D, C), A')$.

Example 4.1. *Figure 4.1 displays the search tree built by* simpleBacktrack *for the second CSP model of the 4-queens problem introduced in section 3.4, when variables and values are chosen in increasing order.*

The *simpleBacktrack* function builds the search tree in depth first with respect to a chronological backtracking principle: when a partial assignment A cannot be completed without violating constraints, the function continues the search by backtracking to the last choice point. This depth-first exploration is very easy to implement with a recursive function. However, it may explore many unnecessary assignments when failure is due to a poor choice made much higher in the search tree.

Example 4.2. *Let us consider the CSP such that:*
  – there are n variables, i.e. $X = \{x_1, x_2, \ldots, x_n\}$;

Algorithm 4.1: simpleBacktrack$((X, D, C), A)$

Input:
a CSP (X, D, C)
a (partial or complete) assignment A for (X, D, C)
Precondition:
A is consistent
Postrelation:
If A cannot be extended to a solution of (X, D, C) then return $\emptyset$,
otherwise return a solution A' of (X, D, C) such that $A \subseteq A'$

1 **begin**
2   **if** $var(A) = X$ **then**
        /* All variables are assigned $\Rightarrow$ A is a solution
        */
3   **return** A
4   **else**
5   Choose a variable $x_i \in X$ such that $x_i \notin var(A)$
6   **for** *each value $v \in D(x_i)$* **do**
7   **if** $A \cup \{(x_i, v)\}$ *is consistent* **then**
8                  $Sol \leftarrow$ simpleBacktrack$((X, D, C), A \cup \{(x_i, v)\})$
9   **if** $Sol \neq \emptyset$ **then return** Sol
        /* No value of $D(x_i)$ allows A to be extended to a
        solution   */
10   **return** $\emptyset$

11 **end**

– *domains are defined by*

$$\begin{aligned}
D(x_1) &= \{n, n+1\} \\
D(x_i) &= \{i, i+1\}, \forall i \in \{2, \ldots, n-2\} \\
D(x_{n-1}) = D(x_n) &= \{n-1, n\};
\end{aligned}$$

– *all variables must have different values, i.e.*

$$\forall (x_i, x_j) \in X \times X, i \neq j \Rightarrow x_i \neq x_j.$$

Let us assume that simpleBacktrack *chooses the next variable to assign in increasing order, i.e. from x_1 to x_n, and that it also chooses the values to be assigned in increasing order. In this case, it first assigns x_1 to n. Then for*

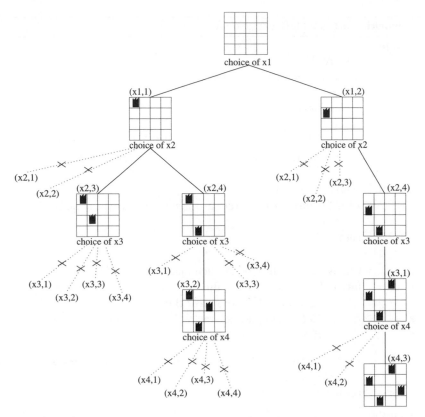

Figure 4.1. *Search tree constructed by* simpleBacktrack *for the 4-queens problem when variables and values are chosen in increasing order*

$i \in \{2, \ldots, n-1\}$ *it assigns* x_i *to* i. *Finally, it tries to assign* x_n *and realizes that there is no consistent value for* x_n *as* $x_{n-1} = n-1$ *and* $x_1 = n$.

In this example, the inconsistency comes from the first choice $x_1 = n$. *However, instead of directly* backjumping *to this bad choice,* simpleBacktrack *tries all other* 2^{n-1} *possible assignments with* $x_1 = n$ *before choosing another value for* x_1.

Different techniques such as *backjumping* and *intelligent backtracking* have been proposed to avoid this kind of search trashing. The interested reader may refer to [BAK 95] for more details.

4.2. Constraint propagation

To improve the *simpleBacktrack* function, we may propagate constraints to filter domains of non-assigned variables by removing inconsistent values, i.e. values that do not belong to any solution. If this filtering removes all values in the domain of a variable, then we can conclude that the current partial assignment cannot be extended to a solution and the search can backtrack to a previous choice.

This constraint propagation step may be carried out after each new variable assignment before recursively calling *simpleBacktrack* to extend the current partial assignment (before line 8 of algorithm 4.1). Note that a value removed from a domain must be restored in the domain when the assignment which causes its removal is changed by a backtrack.

Pioneering work for constraint propagation was carried out by Waltz in 1972 [WAL 72] for a scene drawing application. Since then, many different constraint propagation algorithms have been proposed. These algorithms achieve different partial consistencies and also have different time and space complexities.

In this section, we do not aim to describe all of the existing propagation algorithms. We briefly describe two basic and well-known techniques: *forward checking* and *maintaining arc consistency*. The reader may refer to [DEB 01] for a more thorough presentation and comparison of different constraint propagation algorithms.

4.2.1. *Forward checking*

The basic idea of forward checking is to propagate all constraints involving a given variable x_i just after the assignment of this variable to a value v_i. This removes any value which is not consistent with the assignment of x_i to v_i from the domains of the non-assigned variables.

More precisely, after the assignment of x_i to v_i, we propagate binary constraints between x_i and any non-assigned variable x_j by removing from the domain of x_j any value v_j such that the assignment $\{(x_i, v_i), (x_j, v_j)\}$ violates the constraint between x_i and x_j.

Example 4.3. *Consider the second CSP model of the 4-queens problem introduced in section 3.4. Once x_1 has been assigned to 1, the propagation* *of the constraint* $x_1 \neq x_2$ *removes the value 1 from the domain of* x_2. *The propagation of the constraint* $1 - x_1 \neq 2 - x_2$ *removes the value 2 from the domain of* x_2.

Figure 4.2 displays the search tree constructed by simpleBacktrack *when it is combined with forward checking for the second CSP model of the 4-queens problem introduced in section 3.4.*

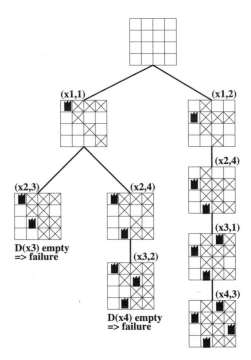

Figure 4.2. *Search tree constructed by* simpleBacktrack *when combined with forward checking for the 4-queens problem (variables and values are chosen in increasing order); values removed by forward checking are crossed out*

When constraints have arities greater than 2, we may propagate constraints such that all variables but one assigned. More precisely, once a variable x_i has been assigned to a value v, we propagate each constraint c_j such that $x_i \in var(c_j)$ and all other variables of $var(c_j)$ but one are assigned. Let x_k be the non-assigned variable of $var(c_j)$. The propagation of c_j removes any value v_k from the domain of x_k such that the assignment $A \cup \{(x_i, v), (x_k, w)\}$ violates the constraint c_j.

This forward checking filtering may be combined with other filtering which ensures higher level partial consistencies, e.g. such as that introduced in the next section. This is referred to as extended forward checking in [BES 02].

Note that if we filter domains each time a variable is assigned to a value, then it is no longer necessary to check that a value is consistent with the current partial assignment A before recursively calling *simpleBacktrack* (line 7 of algorithm 4.1).

4.2.2. *Maintaining arc consistency*

A stronger filtering technique, but also a more computationally expensive method, is obtained by maintaining *arc consistency* (also referred to as 2-consistency).

Roughly speaking, a binary CSP is arc consistent if each value v_i in the domain of a non-assigned variable x_i has at least one *support* in the domain of every other non-assigned variable, thus ensuring that if x_i is assigned to v_i then every other variable will still have at least one consistent value in its domain.

More precisely, given two variables x_i and x_j and a value $v_i \in D(x_i)$, a value $v_j \in D(x_j)$ is a support of v_i if the partial assignment $\{(x_i, v_i), (x_j, v_j)\}$ is consistent. A binary CSP (X, D, C) is arc consistent if every value in every domain has at least one support in the domain of every other non-assigned variable.

To maintain arc consistency while constructing a partial assignment A, we filter the domain of each non-assigned variable x_i by removing any value v_i such that there exists a non-assigned variable x_j whose domain does not contain a support of (x_i, v_i). In other words, we remove v_i from $D(x_i)$ if there exists x_j such that, for each value $v_j \in D(x_j)$, the partial assignement $\{(x_i, v_i), (x_j, v_j)\}$ is inconsistent.

Example 4.4. *Let us consider again the second CSP model of the 4-queens problem introduced in section 3.4. Once x_1 has been assigned to 1, we may remove 3 from the domain of x_2 (as well as the values 1 and 2 which violate the constraints $x_1 \neq x_2$ and $1 - x_1 \neq 2 - x_2$, respectively). Indeed, if $x_2 = 3$, then x_3 cannot be assigned consistently:*

– if $x_3 = 1$, the constraint $x_3 \neq x_1$ is violated;

– if $x_3 = 2$, the constraint $x_3 + 3 \neq x_2 + 2$ is violated;

– if $x_3 = 3$, the constraint $x_3 \neq x_2$ is violated; and

– if $x_3 = 4$, the constraint $x_3 - 3 \neq x_2 - 2$ is violated.

Figure 4.3 displays the search tree constructed by simpleBacktrack *when arc consistency is maintained for the second CSP model of the 4-queens problem.*

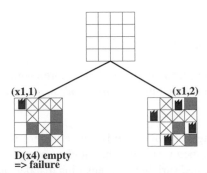

Figure 4.3. *Search tree constructed by* simpleBacktrack *when arc consistency is maintained (variables and values are chosen in increasing order) for the 4-queens problem; values removed by forward checking are crossed out and those removed by maintaining arc consistency are depicted in gray*

Note that such a filtering must be repeated until domains can no longer be reduced: as soon as a value v_i is removed from the domain of a variable x_i, we must check that v_i is not the only support of a value v_j of another variable x_j. If this is the case, we have to remove v_j from $D(x_j)$. There exist many different algorithms for ensuring arc consistency, which exhibit different time and space complexities. Refer to [ROS 06] for more details.

Arc consistency may also be generalized to non-binary CSPs. In this case, it is referred to as generalized arc consistency [BES 97].

4.3. Ordering heuristics

The order in which *simpleBacktrack* builds assignments depends on the order in which it chooses variables (line 5 of algorithm 4.1) and on the order in which it chooses values (line 6 of algorithm 4.1). Of course, these two orders have a strong influence on the time spent solving the problem. Let us imagine that *simpleBacktrack* could take advice from an *oracle* which always knows the right choice to make. In this case, the solution can be found without backtracking. Unfortunately, as CSPs are $\mathcal{NP}$-complete problems, it is most probable that such an oracle will never be programmed. However, we may use *heuristics* to guide the search when choosing variables and values (heuristics are approximate guidelines and are not 100% reliable).

4.3.1. Heuristics for choosing variables

The order in which variables are instantiated has an influence on the number of nodes of the search tree built by *simpleBacktrack*.

Example 4.5. *Consider a CSP with three variables x_1, x_2 and x_3 such that $card(D(x_1)) = card(D(x_2)) = 4$ and $card(D(x_3)) = 2$. If we instantiate x_1 and x_2 before x_3, then in the worst case (if constraint propagation does not prune any branches) the search tree may have $1+4+(4\times4)+(4\times4\times2) = 53$ nodes. However, if we instantiate x_3 before x_1 and x_2, then the search tree may have (in the worst case) $1+2+(2\times4)+(2\times4\times4) = 43$ nodes. The number of leaves is of course equal for both cases, i.e. $4 \times 4 \times 2 = 32$ leaves.*

The order in which variables are instantiated also influences the depth of the search tree. Indeed, by assigning a critical variable (the domain of which only contains values that violate constraints with non-assigned variables) sooner, we prune the corresponding branch in the search tree sooner.

Finally, when *simpleBacktrack* is combined with filtering techniques such as forward checking or maintaining arc consistency, the order in which variables are instantiated influences the breadth of the search tree. Indeed, the assignment of a highly constrained variable may allow filtering algorithms to drastically reduce some domains and, therefore, reduce the number of sons of the corresponding node in the search tree.

A classical heuristic to choose the next variable to assign is called *first-fail* or *min-domain*. The idea is to choose the variable that has the smallest domain. For example, when designing a timetable, is it usually best to assign the most critical courses first (those for which the number of available time slots is the smallest) in order to prevent other (less constrained) courses using these time slots.

When *simpleBacktrack* is not combined with filtering techniques, the size of the domains does not change. This order may be computed before starting to solve the problem, by sorting variables by increasing domain size. However, when filtering techniques are used to reduce domains during the search process, the order becomes dynamic.

When several variables have smallest domains, a classical heuristic to break ties consists of choosing the most constraining variable, i.e. the one which is involved in the largest number of constraints. This heuristic is referred to as *max-degree* as it corresponds to the degree of the variable in the graph defined by constraints (when constraints are binary).

4.3.2. *Heuristics for choosing values*

Given the next variable to assign, the order in which values are assigned to this variable also has a great influence on the time taken to find a solution (if the problem actually has a solution and if the goal is to find just one solution). However, if the goal is to compute all the solutions, or if the problem does not have any solution, then the search will have to try all possible values for each variable.

In this case, the order in which they are considered does not influence the solution process. Indeed, in this case the search tree always has the same branches and the only thing that changes is the order in which these branches are built.

Note that the above remark is no longer true if we consider a solution process based on binary branching rules such that, at each step, we choose a variable x_i and a value v_i and then successively explore the two branches corresponding to the two subproblems obtained by adding the constraints $x_i = v$ and $x_i \neq v$, respectively.

A generic heuristic which is often used consists of choosing the most promising values, i.e. those which have the smallest number of conflicts with values in domains of non-assigned variables. When the tree search is combined with a filtering algorithm which maintains arc consistency, we usually maintain (for each value v) the set of values of other variables for which v is a support. In this case, we may choose the value which maximizes the number of such supports.

Some value-ordering heuristics are problem-dependent. In particular, when the problem involves finding a permutation of values for a set of variables, a good heuristic is to assign the most critical values first. For example, for the car sequencing problem described in section 3.7, a good value-ordering heuristic is to assign cars which require critical options first, i.e. options which are required by a large number of cars with respect to the capacity of the station [SMI 96].

4.3.3. *Randomized restart*

Given a CSP instance, there usually exist good variable and value-ordering heuristics that allow us to quickly solve it. However, good heuristics for a particular instance may happen to be very bad heuristics for others.

This remark has given rise to *randomized restart* approaches [KAU 02]. The idea is to introduce a small amount of randomness in ordering heuristics (for example, by choosing variables and values with respect to probabilities), and to limit the number of recursive calls to *simpleBacktrack* (or to limit the CPU time). If the current search has not found a solution within the given limit, then it is stopped and a new search is started. This new search will make different choices (as some randomness has been introduced in ordering heuristics) and may find the solution quicker.

A similar idea is found in *algorithm portfolios* [GOM 01], which run different algorithms concurrently on a sequential machine so that the solution time is shared between the different algorithms. Indeed, from one instance to another, different algorithms need very different times to find a solution: an algorithm which may be very fast for a particular instance may be very slow for another. By running these different algorithms concurrently, we decrease the average time spent on finding a solution.

Randomized restart is considered a special case of algorithm portfolios: instead of running different algorithms concurrently, we sequentially perform different runs of the same algorithm while introducing randomness in choices. The different runs therefore develop different search trees.

It should be also mentioned that these approaches are no longer exact approaches as they may fail to find a solution for a feasible instance (unless a time limit is not imposed).

4.4. From satisfaction to optimization problems

The *simpleBacktrack* procedure may be adapted to solve optimization problems related to CSPs introduced in section 3.3.

In particular, to solve constrained optimization problems we may simply add a new constraint each time a solution is found in order to force the search to look for better solutions with respect to the objective function. More precisely, let A be a solution that has just been found by *simpleBacktrack* and let b be the value of the objective function f corresponding to the assignment A. Instead of returning the solution A, we simply add the constraint $f(X) < b$ if the objective function must be minimized, or $f(X) > b$ if the objective function must be maximized. This forces *simpleBacktrack* to continue its search for solutions better than b.

In this case, *simpleBacktrack* usually builds larger search trees as the search is not stopped when a first solution has been found, but continues to find better solutions or to prove that the last solution found is the best one. To restrain combinatorial explosion, a first key point is to use ordering heuristics that allow the search to find better solutions quicker: the better the solution, the more branches are pruned by the new constraint on the objective function. This may be done, for example, by using *greedy* ordering heuristics that choose the variable/value assignment that most increases the objective function to be optimized.

Example 4.6. *For the MKP defined in problem 3.1, a greedy ordering heuristic consists of choosing the non-assigned variable corresponding to the object with the highest profit and assigning this variable to 1 first.*

Another important point in restraining combinatorial explosion when solving constrained optimization problems is to propagate constraints to reduce variable domains, as described in section 4.2. We may also combine constraint propagation with dedicated bounding techniques. In particular, some $\mathcal{NP}$-hard optimization problems become polynomial when relaxing some constraints. In this case, we may use the solution to the polynomial relaxed problem as a boundary to the original $\mathcal{NP}$-hard problem.

Example 4.7. *We consider linear programming problems which involve maximizing a linear function while satisfying some linear inequations (such as the MKP). When some variables must be assigned to integer values, the problem is $\mathcal{NP}$-hard. However, when relaxing the constraints that enforce variables to be assigned to integer values to allow them to be assigned to real values, the problem becomes polynomial. In this case, we may use the solution of the relaxed problem over the reals to add a new constraint on the objective function since the solution of the relaxed problem is greater than or equal to the solution of the original problem.*

Tree-search-based approaches may also be used to solve optimization problems that aim to maximize constraint satisfaction such as MaxCSPs, WCSPs or SCSPs. In this case, we may use specific constraint propagation algorithms that extend local consistencies such as arc consistency to deal with soft constraints. These propagation algorithms compute lower bounds of the violation cost of the solutions associated with nodes of the search tree, thus allowing the search to prune branches that do not contain better solutions than the best computed so far. The interested reader may refer to [ROS 06] for more details.

4.5. Discussion

We have described a generic approach for solving finite domain CSPs. The idea is to explore the search space in a systematic way by partitioning it into smaller subspaces and using constraint propagation (to prune subspaces that do not contain solutions) and ordering heuristics (to explore the most promising subspaces first). This *branch and propagate* solution approach is an instantiation of the well-known *branch and bound* approach often used in operation research to solve combinatorial optimization problems.

The *branch and propagate* solving approach has an exponential time complexity in the worst case, i.e. if filtering techniques are not strong enough to restrain the combinatorial explosion or if ordering heuristics are misleading the search. However, experimental results have shown that it is able to solve many CSP instances in a reasonable amount of time. This is corroborated by the industrial success of constraint programming, most languages of which integrate constraint solvers based on *branch and propagate* approaches as we shall see in Chapter 7.

The *branch and propagate* solving approach is generic, that is, it may be used to solve any finite domain CSP provided that it is defined by a triple (X, D, C). This approach may therefore be used to solve a very large number of combinatorial problems. As a counterpart, this generic approach may be less efficient than a dedicated algorithm which has been designed to solve a specific combinatorial problem. Indeed, dedicated approaches may take advantage of knowledge of the problem to be solved to reduce the search space.

Example 4.8. *Consider the graph isomorphism problem, the goal of which is to decide if two given graphs are structurally equivalent, i.e. if there exists a bijection between their vertices such that all edges are matched. The* *theoretical complexity of this problem is still not clearly stated: if it belongs to $\mathcal{NP}$, then no-one has ever found a polynomial algorithm for it. Alternatively, it has not been proven to be $\mathcal{NP}$-complete. This problem may be very efficiently solved by dedicated approaches such as Nauty [MCK 81], even though their worst case complexities are exponential.*

The graph isomorphism problem may be easily modeled as a constraint satisfaction problem. However, CSP models lose the global semantics of the problem which is decomposed into a set of binary constraints (which separately check that edges are matched). Hence, a generic CSP solver is not at all competitive with a dedicated approach for this problem.

To give domain-dependent knowledge to CSP solvers, we may introduce *global constraints* and design dedicated filtering algorithms for these global constraints. There exist a large number of global constraints [BEL 07] which often allow constraint programming to compete with (and, in some cases, to outperform) dedicated approaches.

Example 4.9. *Let us consider the global* allDiff *constraint which constrains a set of variables to be assigned to all different values. This global constraint is more efficiently propagated than an equivalent set of binary constraints by using the matching algorithm of Hopcroft and Karp [HOP 73], as proposed by Régin in [RÉG 94].*

Note that this dedicated filtering is not only more quickly performed, but is also stronger (i.e. it removes more values) than propagating each binary constraint separately.

More generally, the efficiency of the solution process depends greatly on the chosen CSP model. For example, we have introduced in section 3.4 three different CSP models for the n-queens problem. Each model induces a different search space, but constraint propagation also reduces these search spaces differently. Hence, the third CSP model induces a larger search space than the second (as it introduces three times as many variables), but it also makes use of global difference constraints which reduce the search space more efficiently and more strongly. The solution process is therefore more efficient for the third model than for the second.

We could propose even more efficient models for the n-queens problem by integrating knowledge on symmetries, for example. Indeed, different assignments may be equivalent with respect to symmetry operations on the chessboard such as rotations and reflections. We may *break symmetries* in a CSP model by adding constraints. In the n-queens problem, we may constrain the queen in the first column to be above the queen in the last column, i.e. $x_1 < x_n$. Any solution that the additional constraint invalidates can be turned into a valid solution through reflection in the y axis of the chessboard. The propagation of such symmetry breaking constraints allows us to prune the search space and, therefore, to solve the problem more efficiently.

These last remarks appear to be contradictory to the declarativity aim of constraint programming. Indeed, if the user simply has to model their problem by means of constraints and then asks generic constraint solvers to automatically solve it, the efficiency of the solving process (and therefore its practicability) greatly depends on the CSP model chosen. In practice, finding a good CSP model is an art which requires a deep understanding of the solving mechanisms.

Chapter 5

Perturbative Heuristic Approaches

The exact approaches described in Chapter 4 are able to solve many constraint satisfaction problems. However, constraint propagation techniques and ordering heuristics are not always able to restrain combinatorial explosion; some instances cannot be solved by these approaches within a reasonable amount of time.

In this case we may use heuristic approaches. These approaches do not explore the search space exhaustively, but deliberately ignore some parts of it. As a consequence, they may fail to find a solution and, of course, they cannot be used to prove that an instance does not have a solution (or prove the optimality of a solution in the case of optimization problems). As a counterpart, these approaches have polynomial time complexities so that they always end within a reasonable amount of time, even for very large instances.

We describe perturbative heuristic approaches which explore the search space of a combinatorial optimization problem by iteratively perturbating combinations in order to build new combinations.

It should be noted that perturbative approaches are usually designed to solve optimization problems and not satisfaction problems. We have shown in section 3.3 that CSPs are closely related to two different kinds of optimization problems. These problems either aim to maximize constraint satisfaction (for overconstrained CSPs) or to optimize some additional objective function (for underconstrained CSPs).

In this chapter, we shall assume that the problem to solve is defined by a couple (S, f) such that S is a set of candidate combinations corresponding to the search space and $f : S \rightarrow \mathbb{R}$ is an objective function which associates a numerical value with each combination of S. In this case, the goal is to find an optimal combination $s^* \in S$ which maximizes (or minimizes) f.

The most popular perturbative approaches are genetic algorithms (see section 5.1), local search (section 5.2) and particle swarm optimization (section 5.3). All of these approaches combine intensification mechanisms (which guide the search around the best combinations found so far) with diversification mechanisms (which allow the search to move away from these best combinations in order to discover new areas which may contain even better combinations). In section 5.4 we study these mechanisms and their influence on the solution process of perturbative approaches.

5.1. Genetic algorithms

5.1.1. *Basic principles*

Genetic algorithms (GAs) draw their inspiration from the evolutionary process of biological organisms in nature and, more particularly, from three main mechanisms which allow them to better fit their environment:

– *Natural selection* implies that individuals that are well fitted to their environment usually have a better chance of surviving and, therefore, reproducing.

– *Reproduction by cross-over* implies that an individual inherits its features from its two parents so that two well-fitted individuals tend to generate new individuals that are also well fitted (and hopefully better fitted).

– *Mutation* implies that some features may randomly appear or disappear, allowing nature to introduce new abilities that are spread to the next generations thanks to natural selection and cross-over if these new abilities better fit the individual to its environment.

Genetic algorithms combine these three mechanisms above to define a metaheuristic for solving combinatorial optimization problems. The idea is to let a population of combinations evolve (by applying selection, cross-over and mutation) in order to find better fitted combinations. The fitness of a combination is evaluated with respect to the objective function to optimize. Algorithm 5.1 describes this basic principle, the main steps of which are briefly described in the following sections.

Algorithm 5.1: Genetic algorithm (GA)

Input: a combinatorial optimization problem (S, f)
Postrelation: returns a combination of S
1 **begin**
2   Initialize the population
3   **while** *stopping criteria not reached* **do**
4   Select combinations from the population
5   Create new combinations by recombination and mutation
6   Update the population
7   **return** *the best combination that ever occurred within the population*
8 **end**

5.1.1.1. *Representation of combinations*

Each individual in the population corresponds to a combination in the search space S. When designing a genetic algorithm, a key point is to choose a suitable representation for combinations. This point is closely related to the choice of recombination operators: the representation should be such that individuals that are created by recombination should inherit features of their parents.

5.1.1.2. *Initialization of the population*

In most cases, the initial population is randomly generated with respect to a uniform distribution in order to ensure a good diversity of the combinations. The size of the population depends on the problem to be solved and on the size of the search space to explore. It should be large enough to provide a representative sampling of the search space.

5.1.1.3. *Selection of combinations*

This step involves choosing the combinations of the population that will be used to generate new combinations (by recombination and mutation). Selection procedures are usually stochastic and designed so that the selection of the best combinations is favored, while leaving a small chance that poorer combinations be selected.

There exist several different ways to implement this selection step. For example, *tournament selection* consists of randomly selecting a small number of combinations in the population and keeping the best combination (or randomly selecting one with respect to a probability proportional to the objective function).

5.1.1.4. *Recombination and mutation of combinations*

Recombination has the aim of generating new combinations from selected combinations. When two combinations are recombined, the operation is usually called a *cross-over*. There exist many different cross-over operators. For example, *one-point cross-over* randomly chooses a cross-over point on the combination of each parent, and swaps all data beyond that point in order to generate two child combinations.

Mutation aims to slightly modify combinations. It is usually implemented by randomly selecting combination components and choosing new values for these components.

New combinations obtained by recombination and/or mutation may not satisfy some problem-dependent constraints; they may not belong to the search space S any longer. In this case, they may be repaired by a greedy local search procedure.

5.1.1.5. *Population updating step*

This step replaces some combinations of the population with some of the new combinations (generated by applying recombination and mutation operators) in order to create the next generation population.

Once again, there exist many different replacement strategies that may or may not favor diversity and that may or may not be elitist. For example, we may choose to keep the best combinations in the next generation population, whether they belong to the previous population or have just been generated. Alternatively we may choose to keep only the new combinations, whatever their fitness.

5.1.1.6. *Stopping criteria*

The evolution process is iterated, from generation to generation, either until it finds a solution whose quality reaches some given bound or a fixed number of generations or a CPU time limit has been reached. We may also use diversity indicators such as the resampling rate or the average pairwise distance to restart a new search when the population becomes too uniform.

5.1.2. *Using GAs to solve CSPs*

Genetic algorithms for solving CSPs usually involve a population of complete assignments; the fitness function evaluates the number of violated constraints. Different mechanisms dedicated to CSPs have been proposed such as dedicated cross-over operators or repair mechanisms.

Craenen *et al.* [CRA 03] have experimentally compared eleven GAs for solving binary CSPs. They have shown that three algorithms (Heuristics GA version 3, Stepwise Adaptation of Weights and Glass-Box) exhibit very similar performances and clearly outperform the other eight algorithms. However, these three best GAs are not at all competitive with exact branch and propagate approaches or with other heuristic approaches such as local search and ant colony optimization. In particular, GAs often fail to find a solution to the hardest instances which are close to the phase transition region. We have shown in [VAN 04] that for these instances GAs are not able to diversify the search. They suffer from a resampling phenomenon, where a small subset of assignments are often recomputed.

Other GAs have been proposed to solve specific constraint satisfaction problems. These dedicated GAs take advantage of knowledge of the problem to be solved in order to design better cross-over and mutation operators, allowing the search to generate better combinations. For example, [ZIN 07] introduces a GA dedicated to the car sequencing problem which obtains very competitive results.

GAs may also achieve very good performance on constrained optimization problems such as the multidimensional knapsack problem [CHU 98].

5.2. Local search

5.2.1. *Basic principles*

Local search (LS) explores the search space by modifying a combination in an iterative way. Beginning with an initial combination, it iteratively moves from the current combination to a neighbor combination by applying some transformation. LS may be viewed as a very particular case of GA, such that the population is composed of only one combination.

Algorithm 5.2 describes this basic principle, the main steps of which are briefly described in the following sections.

Algorithm 5.2: Local search (LS)

Input:
  a combinatorial optimization problem (S, f)
  a neighborhood function $n : S \rightarrow \mathcal{P}(S)$
Postrelation:
  returns a combination of S

1 **begin**
2 | Generate an initial combination $s \in S$
3 | $s^* \leftarrow s$
4 | **while** *stopping criteria not reached* **do**
5 | | Choose $s' \in n(s)$
6 | | $s \leftarrow s'$
7 | | **if** $f(s') > f(s^*)$ **then**
8 | | | $s^* \leftarrow s'$

9 | **return** s^*
10 **end**

5.2.1.1. *Neighborhood function*

The LS algorithm is parameterized by a neighborhood function $n : S \rightarrow \mathcal{P}(S)$ which defines the set of combinations $n(s)$ that may be obtained by applying some transformation operators to a given combination $s \in S$. We may consider different kinds of transformation operators such as changing the value of one variable or swapping the values of two variables. Each different transformation operator induces a different neighborhood, the size of which may vary. The choice of the transformation operators therefore has a strong influence on the solution process.

A strongly desirable property of the transformation operator is that it must allow the search to reach the optimal combination from any initial combination. In other words, the directed graph which associates a vertex with each combination of S, and an edge (s_i, s_j) with each couple of combinations such that $s_j \in n(s_i)$, must contain a path from any of its vertices to the vertex associated with the optimal combination.

5.2.1.2. *Generation of the initial combination*

The search begins from a combination which is often randomly generated. The initial combination may also be generated with a greedy approach such as those introduced in section 6.1. When a local search is hybridized with another metaheuristic such as genetic algorithms or ant colony optimization, the initial combination may be the result of another search process.

5.2.1.3. *Choice of a neighbor*

At each iteration of LS, a combination s' in the neighborhood of the current combination s must be chosen. There exist many different strategies for choosing a neighbor.

Greedy strategies always choose a neighbor which is better than the current combination or the best neighbor if no neighbor is better. The *best improvement* greedy strategy scans the whole neighborhood and selects the best neighbor, i.e. the one which most improves the objective function. The *first improvement* greedy strategy selects the first neighbor which improves the objective function.

These greedy strategies may be compared to hill climbers that always choose a raising path. This kind of strategy usually allows the search to quickly improve the initial combination. However, once the search has reached a locally optimal combination, i.e. a combination whose neighbors all have worse objective function values, it becomes stuck with it.

To avoid these local optima, we may consider different metaheuristics such as those described in section 5.2.2.

5.2.1.4. *Stopping criteria*

Moves are iterated until either the search has found a solution of sufficient quality or a fixed number of moves has been reached (or a CPU time limit has been reached). LS may then be iterated as discussed in the following.

5.2.2. *Metaheuristics based on LS*

There exist many different metaheuristics that are based on LS. We briefly describe some of them in this section; the interested reader may refer to [STÜ 04] for more details. Metaheuristics usually define strategies for allowing LS to escape from local optima.

For instance, *variable neighborhood search* changes the neighborhood function n when the current combination is locally optimal [MLA 97]. Indeed, a combination which is locally optimal with respect to some neighborhood n

may not be locally optimal with respect to some other neighborhood n', such that $n' \nsubseteq n$.

Some metaheuristics iterate LS several times to escape from local optima, starting from different initial combinations. Initial combinations are chosen randomly and independently, as proposed in *multistart local search*. Initial combinations may also be obtained by applying a perturbation operator to the best combination that has previously been computed, as proposed in *iterated local search* [LOU 02]. Different LSs may also be performed in parallel, starting from different initial combinations and regularly redistributing current combinations by suppressing the worst and duplicating the best, as proposed in *go with the winner* [DIM 96].

Another way to escape from local optima is to allow the search to move to poorer combinations, until reaching a new hill to climb on. A very simple way to implement this idea is to introduce a parameter $p_{\text{noise}} \in [0; 1]$ to control the probability of moving to worse combinations, thus leading to *random walk* [SEL 94]. Before choosing the next combination $s' \in n(s)$, a real value v is randomly chosen within $[0; 1[$. If $v < p_{\text{noise}}$ then s' is randomly chosen within $n(s)$, otherwise s' is chosen with respect to a greedy strategy.

Simulated annealing [AAR 89] may be viewed as a refinement of random walk. It introduces a temperature parameter T to control the probability of moving to worse combinations. This is carried out in such a way that this probability is progressively decreased during the search process. More precisely, at each iteration, a combination s' is randomly chosen in $n(s)$. If s' is better than s then the search moves to s'; otherwise it either rejects s' and tries another combination, or moves to s' with respect to an acceptance probability defined by $\exp([f(s') - f(s)]/T)$. Temperature T is initialized to a high value so that the acceptance probability is close to 1 at the beginning of the search. It is slightly decreased after each move so that it progressively converges towards 0, thus progressively forbidding the search to move to poorer combinations.

Tabu search [GLO 93] does not introduce a probability of deteriorating move acceptance and always chooses to move to the best neighbor. It makes backward moves tabu in order to avoid cycling around local optima. More precisely, it memorizes the last k operations that have been carried out in order to move from a combination to a neighbor combination, and marks the backward operations as tabu. At each iteration, the best neighbor $s' \in n(s)$ is chosen such that the operation that transforms s into s' is not tabu.

5.2.3. *Using LS to solve CSPs*

Local search has been very widely and successfully applied to solve CSPs. To illustrate this success, we mention the 2005 ROADEF challenge, the goal of which was to solve a car sequencing problem. Among the 18 finalist teams, 17 (including the winners) had proposed an approach based on LS [SOL 08].

5.2.3.1. *Neighborhood*

The search space is, in general, composed of all possible complete assignments and a move consists of modifying the value of a variable. The neighborhood of a complete assignment contains all complete assignments obtained by changing the value of one variable. Depending on the kind of constraints used, other neighborhoods may be considered e.g. swapping the values of two variables when these variables are involved in a permutation constraint which constrains a set of variables to be assigned to a permutation of a set of values.

It may also be possible to consider neighborhoods not only between complete assignments, but between partial assignments. In particular, the *decision repair* approach proposed by Jussien and Lhomme [JUS 02] combines constraint propagation techniques (such as those described in Chapter 4) with an LS over the space of partial assignments. Given a current partial assignment A, if constraint propagation detects an inconsistency then the neighborhood of A is the set of all assignments that may be obtained by suppressing a variable/value couple from A. Otherwise, the neighborhood of A is the set of assignments that may be obtained by adding a variable/value couple to A.

5.2.3.2. *Strategies for choosing moves*

Many different strategies have been proposed. The *min-conflict* strategy proposed by Minton *et al.* [MIN 92] consists of randomly choosing a variable involved in at least one constraint violation and changing the assignment of this variable to the value which minimizes the number of violations. This greedy strategy is famous because it has allowed Minton *et al.* to solve the n-queens problem for a million queens. However, on many other CSPs, it may be stuck in local minima. A simple way to escape from these local minima is to combine *min-conflict* with *random walk* [WAL 96].

Galinier and Hao [GAL 97] proposed a LS algorithm based on the tabu metaheuristic and have experimentally shown that this strategy obtains very good results on a large number of randomly generated binary CSP instances.

Starting from a randomly generated complete assignment, the idea is to choose, at each iteration, the move which most increases the number of satisfied constraints and which is not tabu. A move involves changing the value of a variable, and is marked as tabu if the variable/value couple has already been chosen since the last k moves. An aspiration criteria has been added, which allows the search to select a tabu move if it results in an assignment which satisfies more constraints than the best assignment found previously.

5.3. Particle swarm optimization

5.3.1. *Basic principles*

Particle swarm optimization (PSO) borrows some of its features from the collective behavior of bird flocks or fish schools. The birds or fish collectively converge towards an objective such as a source of food, while only having a local perception of their environment [KEN 95]. The idea is to let a set of particles evolve. Each particle i is associated with a combination s_i of the search space, which defines the position of i in this space. Each particle i also has a velocity v_i which is used to determine the position of i at the next step of the search process, i.e. the next combination explored by i. This velocity evolves at each iteration with respect to the best combination found by the particle and the best combination found by neighbor particles.

Algorithm 5.3 describes this basic principle, the main steps of which are briefly described in the following sections.

5.3.1.1. *Initialization of the particles of the swarm*

The combination s_i and the velocity v_i initially associated with a particle i are usually randomly generated with respect to a uniform distribution. The number of particles depends on the problem and the size of the instance. It must be large enough to provide a representative sampling of the search space.

5.3.1.2. *Neighborhood of a particle*

At each iteration, each particle i modifies its velocity with respect to (among other variables) the best combination $best_{N(i)}$ found by one of its neighbors since the start of the search. The set $N(i)$ of neighbor particles may be dynamically defined with respect to some geographical criteria if there exists a way of measuring the distance between two particles. It is usually easier to consider a static neighborhood, defined at the beginning of the search process. In this case, different neighborhood topologies such as a ring topology

Algorithm 5.3: Particle swarm optimization (PSO)

Input: a combinatorial optimization problem (S, f)
Postrelation: returns a combination of S
1 **begin**
2   **for** *each particle i of the swarm W* **do**
3   choose an initial combination $s_i \in S$
4      $best_i \leftarrow s_i$
5   choose an initial velocity v_i
6   **while** *stopping criteria not reached* **do**
7   **for** *each particle i of the swarm W* **do**
8   let $N(i) \subseteq W$ be the neighborhood of i in the swarm
9       $best_{N(i)} \leftarrow best_k$ with $k = argmax_{j \in N(i)} f(best_j)$
10   modify v_i with respect to $best_i$ and $best_{N(i)}$
11   modify s_i with respect to v_i
12   **if** $f(s_i) > f(best_i)$ **then** $best_i \leftarrow s_i$
13   **return** *the best combination found by a particle of the swarm*
14 **end**

(where each particle has exactly two neighbors) may be considered. Note that a particle i is usually assumed to belong to its neighborhood.

5.3.1.3. *Update of particle velocities*

The velocity v_i of a particle i is updated at each iteration with respect to:

$$v_i \leftarrow \omega v_i + c_1 f_1(best_i - s_i) + c_2 f_2(best_{N(i)} - s_i)$$

where ω is a parameter which defines the particle inertia, c_1 and c_2 are coefficients of acceleration and define the influence of the particle (*cognitive* component) and of its neighborhood (*social* component), respectively, f_1 and f_2 are two numbers which are randomly chosen in $[0; 1]$ with respect to a uniform distribution, $best_i$ is the best combination found by i since the beginning of the search and $best_{N(i)}$ is the best combination found by a neighbor of i since the start of the search.

This formula assumes that velocities and combinations may be combined in a linear way. If this is straightforward for problems over continuous domains, this is not obvious for problems over finite domains. In this case, we may round up the obtained real value to the closest integer value. However, this may not be meaningful when finite domains contain symbolic values. Note also that the velocity of particles is usually bound by a parameter.

5.3.1.4. *Update of combinations associated with particles*

Once the velocity has been updated, it is used to modify the current combination s_i according to:

$$s_i \leftarrow s_i + v_i.$$

It may occur that the new combination does not belong to the search space S. In that case, a repair procedure to transform it into a combination of S must be implemented.

5.3.1.5. *Stopping criteria*

As for genetic algorithms, the particle evolution process is iterated until either a good enough combination has been found, some time limit has been reached or the combinations of the swarm have become too similar (indicating search stagnation).

5.3.2. *Using PSO to solve CSPs*

PSO has not often been used to solve finite domain CSPs. Indeed, this approach was initially proposed to solve problems over continuous domains. If it has since been extended to solve problems over finite symbolic domains, it is not (yet) competitive for solving CSPs. However, see [YAN 06] in which PSO is hybridized with simulated annealing to solve binary CSPs.

5.4. Discussion

All of the perturbative approaches described in this chapter build new combinations by applying transformation operators to existing combinations: at each step, one or more combinations are chosen (within a pool of combinations that have already been built). Some transformation operators are applied to these combinations in order to build new combinations. Perturbative approaches mainly differ in two points:

– The way they choose the combinations to be perturbated: GAs use selection rules that are borrowed from biological evolution. LS usually chooses the last generated combination (but some LS-based metaheuristics may consider different strategies). PSO chooses the current combinations associated with particles.

– The way they choose the transformation operators that are applied to build new combinations: GAs apply mutation and cross-over operators. Greedy LS applies operators that improve the quality of the current combination whereas LS-based metaheuristics often have strategies to favor the application of improving operators while allowing the application of deteriorating operators. PSO first updates velocities with respect to the best combinations found so far and then modifies combinations with respect to these velocities.

The success of perturbative approaches relies on their ability to determine the correct balance between two goals: *intensification* (also called *exploitation*) and *diversification* (also called *exploration*).

Intensification aims at building better combinations. This first goal is achieved by favoring the selection of the best combinations built so far when choosing the combinations to be perturbated and/or by favoring the application of operators that improve the quality of combinations:

– In GAs, elitist selection strategies favor the reproduction of the best combinations and cross-over operators try to keep the best features of both parents in order to generate better offspring.

– In LS, intensification is achieved by favoring the choice of moves towards better combinations. When different LSs are performed (either concurrently as for *go with the winners* or sequentially as for *iterated local search*), intensification is achieved by choosing starting points of new LSs in the neighborhood of the best combinations found so far.

– In PSO, velocities are updated with respect to the best combinations found so far.

Intensification mechanisms allow the search to quickly converge towards combinations that are locally optimal, i.e. that cannot be improved by the application of a single transformation operator. These intensification mechanisms must therefore be counterbalanced by diversification mechanisms in order to allow the search to move away from local optima and discover new areas (which may contain better combinations). This second goal is usually achieved by introducing randomness:

– In GAs, random mutation enables the search to generate new combinations.

– In LS, diversification is ensured by allowing the search to choose worse neighbors with a small probability.

– In PSO, diversification is ensured by the two random numbers f_1 and f_2.

A balance between intensification and diversification is achieved by setting parameters appropriately, for example: mutation rate, selection policies or size of the population for GAs; the length of the tabu list for tabu search; the initial temperature and the speed of cooling for simulated annealing; and the coefficients of acceleration and inertia for PSO.

This balance should be chosen carefully. Indeed, the more the search is intensified, the quicker it converges towards better combinations. However, if the search is over-intensified, the algorithm may stagnate around local optima. This concentrates all the search effort within a small subarea without being able to explore other areas. On the contrary, if the search is over-diversified so that it behaves like a random search, the algorithm may spend most of its time exploring poor quality combinations.

It should be noted here that the correct balance between intensification and diversification clearly depends on the goal of the user and the CPU time available to spend on the solution process. When CPU time is limited or if the user simply wants a good solution whether optimal or not, it is best to favor intensification. On the contrary, if CPU time is not limited or if the user needs the best solution possible, diversification should be favored in order to ensure a good sampling of the search space and limit the probability of missing the optimal solution.

The correct balance between intensification and diversification also depends on the instance to be solved or, more precisely, on the topology of its search landscape (see section 2.3.2). In particular, if there is a good correlation between the quality of a locally optimal combination and its distance to the closest optimal combination (such as *Massif Central* landscapes), then the best results are usually obtained with a strong intensification of the search. On the contrary, if the search landscape contains many local optima which are uniformly distributed in the search space independently of their quality, the best results are usually obtained with a strong diversification of the search.

Different approaches have been proposed to dynamically adapt parameters that balance intensification and diversification during the search process. This is usually referred to as *reactive search* [BAT 08].

For example, the reactive tabu search approach [BAT 01] dynamically adapts the length of the tabu list by increasing it when combinations are recomputed (indicating that it is turning around a local optima), and decreasing it when the search has not recomputed combinations for a while. Also, the *IDwalk* local search of [NEV 04] dynamically adapts the number of neighbors considered at each move.

Chapter 6

Constructive Heuristic Approaches

Perturbative heuristic approaches described in the previous chapter explore the search space of a problem in an opportunistic and incomplete way by locally modifying combinations. They use (meta-) heuristics to attempt to move towards the best combinations.

Constructive heuristic approaches described in this chapter also explore the search space in an opportunistic and incomplete way, but they iteratively build new combinations from scratch. Each combination is constructed in an incremental way: starting from an empty combination, combination components are added iteratively until a complete combination is obtained. Each construction corresponds to a branch of the search tree developed by complete approaches introduced in Chapter 4. However, in the heuristic approaches described in this chapter, the different constructions are independent in the sense that we never backtrack on choices made during the construction and the same combination may be constructed more than once.

As for perturbative approaches, constructive approaches are designed to solve optimization problems and not satisfaction problems. We shall therefore assume in this chapter that the problem to solve is defined by a couple (S, f). S is a set of candidate combinations corresponding to the search space and $f : S \to \mathbb{R}$ is an objective function which associates a numerical value with each combination of S. In this case, the goal is to find an optimal combination $s^* \in S$ which maximizes (or minimizes) f.

In section 6.1, we first describe greedy randomized approaches which build combinations in a greedy way. These approaches choose the components to be added to combinations with respect to some problem-dependent heuristics that locally evaluate the interest of adding a component to a partial combination. We then describe two constructive approaches that refine this greedy randomized construction process by using probabilistic models to build combinations. These models progressively bias probabilities of choosing combination components with respect to past constructions in order to build better combinations:

– *estimation of distribution algorithms* (section 6.2) defines these probabilities with respect to probability distributions of the best combinations built so far;

– *ant colony optimization* (section 6.3) defines these probabilities with respect to pheromone trails which compile past constructions.

Finally, we discuss issues related to intensification and diversification in section 6.4.

6.1. Greedy randomized approaches

6.1.1. *Basic principles*

A greedy algorithm builds a combination in an incremental way. It starts from an empty combination and incrementally completes it by adding components to it. At each step, the component to be added is chosen in a greedy way: we choose the component which maximizes some problem-dependent heuristic function which locally evaluates the interest of adding the component with respect to the objective function.

Example 6.1. *A greedy algorithm for the MKP defined in problem 3.1 may be defined as follows. Starting from an empty set, objects are iteratively added to this set until no more objects may be added without violating a capacity constraint. At each step, we choose the object to be added from the set of objects which do not violate capacity constraints with respect to a greedy heuristic. For example, the object with the highest profit or ratio of profit to volume is chosen.*

These algorithms are able to build combinations very quickly as the search never backtracks to a previous choice. The quality of the constructed combinations depends on the reliability of the heuristic. Some optimization problems (that belong to the $\mathcal{P}$ complexity class) are solved to optimality by such greedy algorithms. For example, Dijkstra's algorithm finds a shortest path in a weighted graph provided that all weights are positive values. Prim's or Kruskall's algorithms find a minimum spanning tree in a weighted graph [COR 90]. However, for $\mathcal{NP}$-hard problems, greedy algorithms build suboptimal combinations.

If the greedy heuristic function is not deterministic (in particular, if it randomly breaks ties when there are several best components), different runs may build different combinations. In this case, we may iterate greedy constructions several times and return the best constructed combination over all runs.

Greedy randomized algorithms deliberately introduce randomness into greedy algorithms in order to diversify the constructed combinations when iterating greedy constructions.

For example, we may randomly choose the next component from the k best components or from the set of components whose quality is bounded by a given ratio with respect to the best component [FEO 89]. Another possibility is to choose the next component with respect to probabilities which are defined proportionally to component qualities [JAG 01].

The Greedy Randomized Adaptive Search Procedure (GRASP) hybridizes a greedy randomized algorithm with a local search [RES 03]. At each iteration, one or more combinations are constructed by a greedy randomized procedure. Some of these combinations are then improved by a local search procedure.

Some mechanisms may be used to benefit from past constructions when building new combinations. For example, a hash table may be used to memorize the previously constructed combinations so that local search is applied only to new combinations. We may also dynamically adapt the value of the parameter (usually called α) which determines the degree of randomness of the greedy construction in order to diversify the search when the constructed combinations are too similar. We may also keep track of the number of times each component has been selected in order to bias the probabilities of choosing these components when building new combinations (for example, decreasing the probability of choosing components that have been used often in order to diversify the search).

6.1.2. *Using greedy randomized algorithms to solve CSPs*

We may construct a complete assignment for a CSP by using the following greedy principle. Starting from the empty assignment, a non-assigned variable is chosen at each iteration and a value is assigned to this variable until all variables have been assigned. To choose variables and values, ordering heuristics introduced in section 4.3 for exact tree-search approaches may be considered.

A well-known implementation of this greedy principle is provided by the DSATUR (degree saturation) algorithm introduced in 1979 by Brélaz to solve the graph coloring problem [BRÉ 79]. The goal of this problem is to assign colors to vertices so that all adjacent vertices are assigned to different colors.

The DSATUR algorithm builds a color assignment in a greedy way by choosing, at each step, the non-colored vertex which has the largest number of adjacent vertices of different colors (the most saturated vertex). Ties are broken by choosing the vertex which has the highest degree in the subgraph induced by the non-colored vertices (the most constraining vertex). The chosen vertex is then colored with the smallest color (with respect to some given order over the set of colors) which has not been assigned to an adjacent vertex.

Greedy randomized algorithms may be iterated several times in order to return the best constructed assignment at the end. We have shown in [GOT 03] that such a greedy randomized algorithm is able to very quickly solve many instances of the car sequencing problem introduced in section 3.7. This greedy randomized algorithm is a building block of an ant colony optimization algorithm and is detailed in Chapter 12.

Note that a greedy randomized algorithm may be considered as a very special case of the random restart strategy introduced in section 4.3, where the tree search is restarted at the end of each assignment construction.

6.2. Estimation of distribution algorithms

6.2.1. *Basic principles*

Estimation of distribution algorithms (EDAs) may be considered as a refinement of greedy randomized algorithms. At each iteration, a set of combinations is generated according to a greedy randomized principle as described in the previous section. However, EDAs take advantage of previously computed combinations to bias the construction of new combinations. This is possible thanks to a probabilistic model: at each step, the probabilistic model is used to generate new combinations. It is then updated with respect to the best constructed combinations in order to increase the probability of generating better combinations [LAR 01].

EDAs are also called *probabilistic model-building genetic algorithms*, and they may be viewed as evolutionary approaches. In GAs, a population of combinations is evolved by using selection and recombination operators. In EDAs, a probabilistic model is evolved to reflect the probability distribution of the best constructed combinations. However, in genetic algorithms, new combinations are built by modifying combinations of the population. For EDAs, new combinations are built in a greedy randomized way using the probabilistic model.

Algorithm 6.1 describes this basic principle, the main steps of which are briefly described in the following sections.

Algorithm 6.1: Estimation of distribution algorithm (EDA)

Input: a combinatorial optimization problem (S, f)
Postrelation: returns a combination of S

1 **begin**
2 | Generate an initial population of combinations $P \subseteq S$
3 | **while** *stopping criteria not reached* **do**
4 | | use P to construct a probabilistic model M
5 | | use M to generate new combinations
6 | | update P with respect to these new combinations
7 | **return** *the best combination that has been built during the search process*
8 **end**

6.2.1.1. *Generation of the initial population*

In most cases, the initial population is randomly generated with respect to a uniform distribution. Only the best constructed combinations are kept in the population.

6.2.1.2. *Construction of a probabilistic model*

Different kinds of probabilistic models may be considered. The simplest type, population-based incremental learning (PBIL) [BAL 94], is based on the probability distribution of each combination component (independently of other components). In this case, we compute the occurrence frequency of each component in the population. The probability of selecting this component is defined proportional to its frequency. Other models may take into account dependency relationships between components by using Bayesian networks [PEL 99]. In this case, the dependency relationships between components are modeled by edges in a graph, and conditional probability distributions are associated with these edges. Such models usually allow the search to build better combinations. However, they are also more expensive to compute.

6.2.1.3. *Generation of new combinations*

New combinations are built in a greedy randomized way, using the probabilistic model to choose components.

6.2.1.4. *Update of the population*

In most cases, only the best combinations are kept in the population for the next iteration of the search process, regardless of whether they belong to the current population or to the set of new generated combinations. However, it is also possible to keep lower quality combinations in order to maintain a good diversity in the population, thus ensuring a representative sampling of the search space.

6.2.2. *Using EDAs to solve CSPs*

Using EDAs to solve CSPs has not been investigated much until now, with the exception of [HAN 03] who hybridized an EDA with a greedy local search based on the *min-conflict* heuristic of [MIN 92] for solving binary CSPs.

6.3. Ant colony optimization

There is a strong similarity between ACO and EDAs [ZLO 04]. Both approaches use a probabilistic model to build new combinations. In both approaches, this probabilistic model evolves during the search process with respect to previously built combinations in an iterative learning process.

The originality and the main contribution of ACO are that it borrows features from the collective behavior of ants to update the probabilistic model. Indeed, the probability of choosing a component depends on a quantity of pheromone which represents the past experience of the colony with respect to the choice of this component. This quantity of pheromone evolves by combining two mechanisms. The first mechanism is a pheromone laying step: pheromone trails associated with the best combinations are reinforced in order to increase the probability of selecting these components. The second mechanism is pheromone evaporation: pheromone trails are uniformly and progressively decreased in order to progressively forget older experiences.

This approach is described in more detail in Part II of this book; its application to CSPs is described in Part III.

6.4. Discussion

EDA and ACO are *model-based* approaches which use probabilistic models to generate combinations [ZLO 04]. As for perturbative heuristic approaches described in Chapter 5, the success of model-based approaches relies on their ability to balance the intensification of the search around the most promising areas with the diversification of the search towards new areas.

Intensification and diversification are achieved by different mechanisms, however. As combinations are built with respect to a probabilistic model, the goal is to let this model evolve in such a way that the probability of building good combinations increases (thus intensifying the search around these good combinations) while the probability of building new combinations does not become too small (thus ensuring diversification of the search). More precisely, intensification is achieved by increasing the probability of selecting components that belong to the best combinations built so far, while diversification is ensured by preventing the probability of selecting a component from becoming too small.

ACO has borrowed simple and efficient mechanisms from real ant colonies for balancing intensification and diversification. This will be discussed in Chapter 9.

Chapter 7

Constraint Programming Languages

Algorithms for solving CSPs described in the previous chapters are usually called constraint solvers. Some of these solvers have been embedded into programming languages, giving rise to a new programming paradigm referred to as *constraint programming (CP)*. To solve a CSP with CP we simply specify the problem and it is is solved automatically by embedded solvers.

The success of CP approaches depends mainly on the following points:

– the language must allow the user to easily describe the problem without having to enter into details related to the solution process; and

– the embedded solvers must be able to efficiently solve the modeled problems (which are often highly combinatorial).

These two points are difficult to reconcile: a solution process is usually much more efficient if it has some knowledge of the specifics of the problem to guide the search.

The first system to integrate a constraint solver into a modeling language in order to automatically solve problems modeled by means of constraints is Alice, designed in 1976 by Laurière [LAU 78]. Pioneering work has also been carried out based on Prolog, which is a logic programming language that integrates a solving engine based on a tree search. The extension of logic programming to constraint logic programming has been carried out in a straightforward way by adding a constraint propagation mechanism to this solving engine. We introduce constraint logic programming in section 7.1.

Since these very first languages, many other CP languages that embed exact tree search-based solvers have been proposed. Many of them are designed as libraries within object-oriented languages such as Java or C++. We introduce one of these libraries (Choco) in section 7.2.

There exist fewer CP languages based on heuristic approaches such as those introduced in Chapters 5 and 6. The most familiar is Comet which is more particularly dedicated to constraint-based local search. This language is introduced in section 7.3.

7.1. Constraint logic programming

The embedding of tree search-based constraint solvers in Prolog is straight-forward. Indeed, Prolog may be viewed as a CP language itself: the domain of the variables is the Herbrand universe (i.e. the set of terms, also called trees, that may be built from the functional symbols of the program) while the constraints are equalities between terms (unifying two Prolog terms requires an equality constraint between these two terms).

The operational semantic of Prolog has therefore been extended in a very straightforward way in order to handle constraints over domains other than the Herbrand universe. This is done by replacing the unification mechanism of Prolog by a more general constraint satisfaction mechanism. For more information on the abstract machine shared by constraint logic programming languages, see [COL 90].

Generally speaking, a constraint logic programming (CLP) language which allows the user to post constraints defined over a domain X is referred to as $CLP(X)$. $CLP(H)$ corresponds to Prolog (H stands for Herbrand universe), $CLP(R)$ extends Prolog to numerical constraints over the reals and $CLP(FD)$ extends Prolog to constraints over finite domains.

For example, Gnu-Prolog (www.gprolog.org) belongs to the $CLP(FD)$ family and integrates a finite domain constraint solver. An example of a Gnu-Prolog program for the n-queens problem (section 3.4) is depicted in Figure 7.1. The queens/2 predicate succeeds if Vars is a list of N values corresponding to the positions of the queens in a solution of the n-queens problem.

For example, when asking

```
?- queens(8,Vars)
```

the first answer of the Prolog interpreter is:

```
Vars = [1,5,8,6,3,7,2,4]
```

or, in other words, $x_1 = 1$, $x_2 = 5$, $x_3 = 8, \ldots$.

```
1   queens(N,Vars) :-
2       length(Vars,N),
3       fd_domain(Vars,1,N),
4       fd_all_different(Vars),
5       allDiffDiag(1,Vars),
6       fd_labeling(Vars).
7   allDiffDiag(_,[]).
8   allDiffDiag(I,[XI|Vars]) :-
9       Iplus1 is I + 1,
10      allDiffDiagForXI(I,XI,Iplus1,Vars),
11      allDiffDiag(Iplus1,Vars).
12  allDiffDiagForXI(_,_,_,[]).
13  allDiffDiagForXI(I,XI,J,[XJ|Vars]) :-
14      I+XI #\= J+XJ,
15      I-XI #\= J-XJ,
16      Jplus1 is J + 1,
17      allDiffDiagForXI(I,XI,Jplus1,Vars).
```

Figure 7.1. *Gnu-Prolog program corresponding to the second CSP model of the n-queens problem*

The second answer of the Prolog interpreter is

```
Vars = [1,6,8,3,7,4,2,5]
```

and so on, for the 92 solutions of the 8-queens problem.

The main part of the program defines the problem in a declarative way. We first declare that Vars is a list of N variables (line 2), and that variables of Vars must be assigned to integer values between 1 and N (line 3). It is then declared that values assigned to Vars must all be different (line 4), and the predicate allDiffDiag is called to declare constraints that ensure there is at most one queen in each diagonal (line 5). The predicate allDiffDiag/2 calls the predicate allDiffDiagForXI/2 for each couple (I,XI) such that

XI is the variable associated with the queen in line I (line 10). The predicate allDiffDiagForXI/4 posts the constraints I+XI $\neq$ J+XJ and I-XI $\neq$ J-XJ (lines 14 and 15) for each couple (J,XJ) such that J>I and XJ is the variable associated with the queen in line J.

Once variables, domains and constraints have been declared, Gnu-Prolog searches for a solution (line 6). Constraints on finite domains are solved by Gnu-Prolog using propagation techniques such as arc consistency (see Chapter 4).

Gnu-Prolog can use variable and value-ordering heuristics due to options of the predicate fd_labeling. For example, Gnu-Prolog can assign variables with respect to the *min-domain* heuristic by replacing line 6 with

$$\text{fd\_labeling}(\text{Vars}, [\text{variable\_method}(\text{first\_fail})]).$$

7.2. Constraint programming libraries

Many CP languages are defined as libraries of classical programming languages such as, for example, C++ or Java. Well-known examples of such libraries are ILOG Solver (www.ilog.fr), GECODE (www.gecode.org) and Choco (choco-solver.net). To model and solve a constraint satisfaction problem with these languages, we simply call methods defined in these libraries.

An example of modeling and solving the n-queens problem with the Java Choco library is displayed in Figure 7.2. As for Prolog, the main part of the program corresponds to the declaration of the CSP model. We first declare a new CSP model m (line 1) and an array of n integer variables (line 2). Each of these variables, queens[i], may be assigned to a value between 1 and n (lines 3 and 4) and is added to m (line 5). For each couple (i,j), we define the constraints queens[i] $\neq$ queens[j], queens[i] $\neq$ queens[j]+j-i and queens[i] $\neq$ queens[j]-j+i and add them to m (lines 6 to 14).

Once the model m is completed, a solver s is created (line 15) and initialized with the model (line 16). Finally, the solver searches for all solutions (line 17). (Alternatively, we could simply search for just one solution and print this.)

7.3. Constraint-based local search

CP languages can also integrate heuristic-based solvers which do not explore the search space in an exhaustive way. This integration may appear to

```
1  Model m = new CPModel();
2  IntegerVariable[] queens = new IntegerVariable[n];
3  for(int i = 0; i< n; i++)
4    queens[i] = makeIntVar("Q_"+i, 1, n);
5  m.addVariables(queens);
6  for(int i = 0; i < n; i++){
7    for(int j = i+1; j < n; j++){
8      int k = j - i;
9      Constraint c1 = neq(queens[i], queens[j]);
10      Constraint c2 = neq(queens[i], plus(queens[j], k));
11      Constraint c3 = neq(queens[i], minus(queens[j], k));
12      m.addConstraints(c1, c2, c3);
13   }
14 }
15 Solver s = new CPSolver();
16 s.read(m);
17 s.solveAll();
```

Figure 7.2. *Choco program corresponding to the second CSP model of the*
n-queens problem

be tricky to achieve, however, because of the duality of the goals of CP. (Note that this duality is also observed in CP languages that embed exact tree search-based solvers. Indeed, an efficient solution process usually requires that the search be programmed, i.e. ordering heuristics specified. This may not be so straightforward to implement and often reduces the readability of the model.)

A CP language must allow the user to define their problem in a declarative way, without entering into details of the solution process. However, the efficiency of heuristic approaches relies on the use of appropriate incremental data structures which allow the search to quickly evaluate candidates before making a decision (i.e. incremental evaluation of the neighborhood before each move for local search approaches and of combination components before adding them to a partial combination for greedy randomized constructive approaches).

Van Hentenryck and Michel have designed a programming language referred to as Comet [VAN 05] which aims to achieve these two goals for local search. In particular, they introduce *incremental variables* which allow the user to specify incremental data structures to efficiently evaluate neighborhoods.

An example of a Comet program for the n-queens problem (section 3.4) is depicted in Figure 7.3 (see [VAN 05] for more details).

```
1   include "LocalSolver";
2   LocalSolver m();
3   range Pos = 1...n;
4   UniformDistribution distr(Pos);
5   var{int} queen[i in Pos](m,Pos) := distr.get();
6   ConstraintSystem S(m);
7   S.post(alldifferent(queen));
8   S.post(alldifferent(all(i in Pos) queen[i] + i));
9   S.post(alldifferent(all(i in Pos) queen[i] - i));
10  m.close();

11  while (S.violations() > 0) {
12   selectMax(q in Pos)(S.getViolations(queen[q]))
13     selectMin(v in Pos)(S.getAssignDelta(queen[q],v))
14         queen[q] := v;
15  }
```

Figure 7.3. *Comet program corresponding to the second CSP model of the n-queens problem*

As for other CP languages described in this chapter, the main part of the program corresponds to the description of the problem. We first declare a new solver (line 2) and a number generator, which randomly generates integer values within Pos with respect to a uniform distribution (line 4). We then declare an array of variables. Each element of this array is a variable which may be assigned to a value that belongs to Pos, initialized by the random number generator (line 5). These variables are incremental variables, i.e. constraints, invariant properties and objective functions dependent on these variables are updated automatically in an incremental way each time their values are modified.

The second part of the program declares constraints holding between incremental variables, i.e. global difference constraints within the values of the queen array and the values associated with diagonals (lines 7 to 9). Comet then builds and initializes incremental data structures used to maintain constraint violation counters, invariant properties and objective function values (line 10).

The final part of the program specifies the local search procedure that should be used to solve the problem. In this example, it is a greedy local search based on the *min conflict* heuristic of [MIN 92]. At each iteration, the search first selects the variable which is involved in the largest number of constraint violations (line 12) and then chooses the value which minimizes the number of constraint violations for this variable (line 13). Note that evaluations of constraint violations are carried out in constant time by incremental variables. The selected move is then performed (line 14) and Comet propagates constraints to incrementally update constraint violations. This local search is iterated until all constraints have been satisfied (the user may also add a condition regarding the maximum number of moves).

Comet may be utilized to solve combinatorial problems with heuristic approaches other than local search such as ACO. Van Hentenryck and Michel [VAN 05] give an example of a Comet program for solving the car sequencing problem with ACO. However, Comet invariants have been designed for an efficient incremental evaluation of invariant properties within a local search context. If they may be used to evaluate candidates at each step of a greedy construction, they are less efficient than *ad hoc* data structures. Indeed, they usually maintain more information than necessary as choices made during a greedy construction are never modified (whereas local search iteratively modifies variable assignments).

7.4. Discussion

There exist a large number of CP languages based on the exact approach described in Chapter 4 and a number of languages based on the perturbative heuristic approaches described in Chapter 5. However, there does not exist a CP language based on the constructive heuristic approaches described in Chapter 6. This remark has motivated the work described in Part III of this book. In particular, the integration of ACO within a CP language is discussed in Chapter 14.

Ant Colony Optimization

Introduction to Part II

Despite the fact that a single ant has very simple abilities, a colony of ants is able to accomplish rather astonishing tasks. Everyone has observed the fascinating ability of ant colonies to find a food source in a cupboard and to form a path to bring it back to the nest, as well as finding new alternative paths when the first path has been destroyed. This ability to collectively find paths is the inspiration for the *ant colony optimization (ACO)* metaheuristic which is described in this second part.

In Chapter 8, we introduce swarm intelligence and study some mechanisms used by real ant colonies to find shortest paths. In particular, we show that this collective ability is based on an indirect communication means, i.e. via the deposit of pheromone trails within the environment. We then describe *Ant System*, the first algorithm that uses this indirect communication means to solve the traveling salesman problem. Artificial ants iteratively build Hamiltonian tours in a greedy randomized way, and pheromone is used to bias probabilities with respect to past experience in order to progressively guide the colony towards better tours. Finally, we describe the ACO metaheuristic which generalizes this principle to combinatorial optimization problems.

As for other heuristic approaches described in Chapters 5 and 6, exploring a search space with ACO raises the question of finding the right balance between intensification and diversification. This issue is more particularly discussed in Chapter 9, where we introduce different indicators which may be used to measure the intensification and diversification of an ACO search.

The basic ACO framework introduced in Chapter 8 is designed for solving static combinatorial optimization problems. In Chapter 10, we describe some extensions of this framework that have been introduced to deal with optimization problems over continuous problems (such that some variables take their values within continuous numerical intervals), dynamic optimization problems (such that instance data may change during the solving process) and multi-objective optimization problems (such that several objectives should be optimized).

Finally, in Chapter 11 we discuss some technical issues related to an efficient implementation of ACO algorithms.

Chapter 8

From Swarm Intelligence to Ant Colony Optimization

A colony of ants is a complex system whose global behavior is the result of local and elementary interactions. This global behavior appears as intelligent when observing it from an upper scale. In section 8.1, we briefly introduce these notions of complex systems and swarm intelligence. We describe the basic mechanisms which actually allow a colony of ants to find a shortest path between two points in section 8.2.

In section 8.3 we describe Ant System, the first algorithm which borrows features from the collective behavior of ant colonies to solve a combinatorial optimization problem. (Other previously proposed algorithms borrowed such features but were not however designed for solving combinatorial optimization problems.) This algorithm has been designed for solving the traveling salesman problem, which exhibits some similarities to the shortest path problem solved by real ant colonies.

Improvements on this first algorithm have been proposed, the goal of which is to better control the balance between the intensification and the diversification of the search. Ant-based algorithms have also been used to solve many different combinatorial optimization problems. The ACO metaheuristic has evolved from these different research projects, and is described in section 8.4.

8.1. Complex systems and swarm intelligence

The complexity of systems is different from the complexity of algorithms and problems introduced in Chapter 2. An $\mathcal{NP}$-hard problem, which is said to be complex with respect to computational complexity, is simply said to be 'complicated'.

A complex system is composed of a large number of interacting entities and exhibits a global behavior which cannot be reduced to the sum of the behaviors of all entities, even though the behavior of each entity is well known and defined. This agrees with *holism*, i.e. 'The whole is more than the sum of its parts'.

Example 8.1. *Let us consider the life game proposed by Conway in 1970. Cells are positioned in a 2D grid and each cell is either living or dead. Interactions between cells are limited to the perception of the number of living cells in the neighborhood. At each iteration, the state (living or dead) of each cell is determined by the number of cells which are alive in its neighborhood (composed of its eight adjacent cells):*

– A living cell with two or three living neighbors survives; otherwise it dies (either by loneliness if the number of living neighbors is lower than two or by overpopulation if it is greater than three).

– A dead cell becomes alive if it has exactly three living neighbors (otherwise, it stays dead).

By simulating the life game from an initial configuration, we can observe patterns emerging from these simple interactions as illustrated in Figure 8.1. Starting from the configuration of iteration 0, we observe that the system enters an oscillating phase at iteration 7 such that it endlessly repeats the two states of iterations 7 and 8.

Interactions between entities of a complex system may be *direct*, from one entity to another, or *indirect*, through local modifications of the environment in which entities evolve. In particular, many social insects communicate by laying trails of a chemical substance called *pheromone* on the ground. These trails have an influence on their behavior. This kind of worker stimulation through the performance they accomplish has been called *stigmergy* by Grassé in 1959 [GRA 59].

Complex systems often exhibit fascinating auto-organization capabilities such that sophisticated structures may be observed at the scale of the global

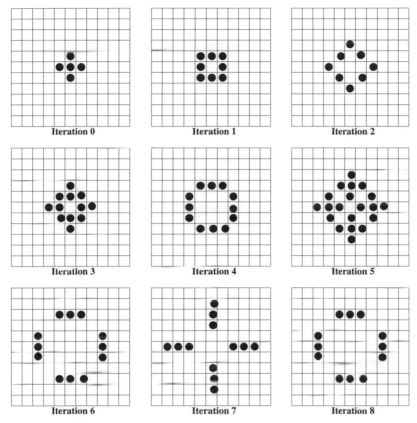

Figure 8.1. *Example of emergent patterns in the life game. Living cells are represented by black dots; other cells are dead*

system. These structures are the result of a large number of elementary interactions and *emerge* at the level of the global system without having been explicitly programmed at the level of the entities: entities are not conscious of the task achieved at the level of the system.

There exist many examples of complex systems whose emergent structures (often quite impressive) may be observed in nature such as swarms of bees or colonies of ants or termites. In particular, termites are able to build nests which may reach several metres high which maintain an optimal temperature (African countries have high temperature gradients between day and night). This collective ability to achieve global tasks is called *swarm intelligence*.

As well as this ability to build complex structures from simple interactions, natural complex systems often exhibit interesting properties of robustness (e.g. the elimination of some entities does not prevent the complex system from achieving its global task) and adaptation to changes which may occur in the environment.

Natural complex systems are therefore a rich source of inspiration for the problem-solving community. For example, particle swarm optimization (section 5.3) borrows features from the collective behavior of swarms of insects or flocks of birds to solve optimization problems; genetic algorithms (section 5.1) borrow features from species evolution to solve optimization problems; artificial immune systems borrow features from the immune system of vertebrates to solve anomaly detection problems [DAS 99]; and artifical neural networks borrow features from brains to solve pattern recognition problems.

8.2. Searching for shortest paths by ant colonies

ACO borrows its features from the ability of some ant species to find, collectively, the shortest path between two points. This ability is explained by the fact that ants communicate in an indirect way, i.e. through their environment by laying trails of pheromone. Ants randomly choose their path, but the probability of choosing a direction depends on pheromone trails on the ground. The higher the pheromone trail within a particular direction, the higher the probability of choosing this direction.

This indirect communication via the environment allows ant colonies to converge towards a shortest path in an autocatalytic reinforcement process.

This process has been highlighted by the *double bridge experiment*, which was designed by Deneubourg *et al.* [DEN 90]. In this experiment, the nest of a colony is connected to a food source by a bridge. This bridge separates into two branches such that ants may travel between the nest and the food source via either of these.

In a first configuration, the two branches have the same length (see Figure 8.2a). In a second configuration, one of the two branches is significantly longer than the other (Figure 8.2b). For each of these two configurations, different experiments are achieved. For each experiment, we observe the evolution of the percentage of ants passing through each branch with respect to time.

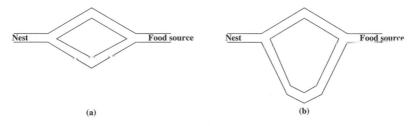

Figure 8.2. *Double bridge experiment*

In the configuration displayed in Figure 8.2a (where the two branches have the same length), we observe that the colony often converges on one of the two branches at the end of the experiment. About 80% of the ants use this branch (the chosen branch may change from one experiment to another). This convergence phenomenon, which is observed in about 90% of the experiments, may be explained as follows.

The first ants that leave the nest randomly choose one of the two branches with respect to a uniform distribution, as pheromone has not yet been laid. However, it may occur that one of the two branches is chosen slightly more often than the other. In this case, the branch which has been preferred receives a slightly higher amount of pheromone so that the probability of choosing this branch further increases slightly. This probability continuously increases in an autocatalytic way until almost all the ants use this branch. Note that there is always a small number of ants (about 20%) that do not follow the highest pheromone trail but use the other branch.

In the configuration depicted in Figure 8.2b (one branch significantly longer than the other), we observe that the large majority of ants use the smallest of the two branches at the end of the experiment. This convergence towards the smallest branch is observed for each experiment, and may be explained as follows.

The first ants that leave the nest randomly choose one of the two branches with respect to a uniform distribution, as pheromone has not yet been laid. However, ants which have chosen the shortest path reach the food source earlier. When arriving at the intersection point, the shorter branch has allowed more ants to reach this intersection and the pheromone trail laid on it is therefore higher. Hence, more ants choose this shortest branch to come back to the nest, starting the autocatalytic process which allows the colony to converge towards the shortest branch. Note finally that some ants may not follow the highest pheromone trail but use the longer branch, thus exhibiting an exploratory behavior.

Deneubourg *et al.* [DEN 90] have proposed a mathematical continuous model of this double bridge experiment. This model uses differential equations to model the evolution of pheromone trail intensities with respect to time. In this model, the probability of an ant choosing a branch depends on the quantity of pheromone on this branch. This quantity of pheromone is proportional to the number of ants which have passed along this branch.

Dorigo and Stützle have adapted this continuous model to a discrete model, thus bridging the gap to use this autocatalytic process for solving combinatorial problems [DOR 04]. Artificial ants walk in a multigraph that contains two vertices v_1 and v_2. These two vertices are connected by two edges e_1 and e_2. Time is discretized ($t \in \mathbb{N}$), and ants need l_1 (respectively, l_2) time units to cross edge e_1 (respectively, e_2).

Initially, all ants are positioned on one of the two vertices. Each time an ant reaches a vertex, it leaves this vertex to reach the other one, using one of the two edges that connect these two vertices. Ants randomly choose one of the two edges with respect to probabilities defined as follows. Let v be the vertex on which an ant is located and let v' be the other vertex. This ant chooses to move to v' by using the edge e_1 with the probability

$$p_{ve_1}(t) = \frac{[\phi_{ve_1}(t)]^\alpha}{[\phi_{ve_1}(t)]^\alpha + [\phi_{ve_2}(t)]^\alpha},$$

whereas it chooses to move to v' by using the edge e_2 with the probability

$$p_{ve_2}(t) = \frac{[\phi_{ve_2}(t)]^\alpha}{[\phi_{ve_1}(t)]^\alpha + [\phi_{ve_2}(t)]^\alpha}$$

where $\phi_{ve_1}(t)$ (respectively, $\phi_{ve_2}(t)$) is the quantity of pheromone laying on the endpoint v of edge e_1 (respectively, e_2), defined by the number of ants that have left or reached vertex v using edge e_1 (respectively, e_2) and α is a parameter which represents the sensitivity of ants to pheromone trails, thus determining the speed of convergence of the colony.

When simulating this discrete model and measuring at each time unit the number of ants on each edge, we observe that ants progressively converge towards the shortest edge in a very similar way to the continuous model of [DEN 90]. As for real ant colonies, this convergence is explained by the combination of the two points:

– the probability of choosing an edge depends on the quantity of pheromone on it, i.e. on the number of ants that have previously walked on this edge; and

– the shortest edge is crossed more quickly so that the quantity of pheromone on it increases faster.

These two mechanisms underly the ACO metaheuristic. They are combined with a third mechanism, i.e. pheromone evaporation. Indeed, pheromone trails laid by real ants are volatile so that their intensity decreases through time. For the double bridge experiment, this evaporation mechanism is very slow with respect to the time needed by the colony to converge towards the shortest path; it is therefore not necessary to integrate it into the mathematical model.

If using pheromone trails to guide the solution process of a hard combinatorial problem, pheromone evaporation is important in allowing the colony to progressively forget older experiments and converge towards the best areas of the search space.

8.3. Ant system and the traveling salesman problem

The Ant System algorithm proposed by Dorigo et al. [DOR 92, DOR 96] uses artificial ants to solve the traveling salesman problem (TSP). This problem presents an analogy to the shortest path problem solved by real ant colonies. It basically involves finding the shortest tour which visits a given number of cities and comes back to its starting point, as defined in the following.

PROBLEM 8.1.– *An instance of the TSP is defined by a non-directed graph* $G = (V, E)$ *and a function* $d : E \to \mathbb{R}$ *such that:*

– *V is the set of cities to visit;*

– *E is the set of roads connecting pairs of cities; and*

– d_{ij} *is the length of the road connecting city i to city j.*

The goal is to find the shortest Hamiltonian cycle which visits each vertex exactly once.

We shall assume in this section that the graph is complete (so that there exists an edge between every pair of vertices) and that the distance function is symmetric (so that $\forall (i, j) \in E, d(i, j) = d(j, i)$).

In Ant System, each ant builds a Hamiltonian cycle in a greedy way (similarly to approaches introduced in section 6.1). Starting from a randomly chosen initial vertex, the ant iteratively moves to an unvisited vertex until it has visited all vertices. The key point is to appropriately define the transition rule used to choose the next vertex to visit at each step of the greedy construction. This next vertex may be chosen using a *nearest neighbor* heuristic, i.e. the ant may choose to move to the nearest unvisited vertex. This nearest neighbor greedy approach is well known and rather intuitive. It allows us to quickly build a cycle of rather good quality but suboptimal in most cases.

Ant System may be seen as an improvement of such a nearest neighbor greedy approach where the deterministic nearest neighbor transition rule is replaced by a probabilistic transition rule. More precisely, the next vertex to visit is randomly chosen with respect to probabilities which depend on two factors:

– a heuristic factor, the goal of which is to favor the choice of the nearest vertices; and

– a pheromone factor, the goal of which is to bias the choice with respect to the past experience of the colony, thus allowing the colony to progressively build better cycles.

More precisely, Ant System for the TSP is displayed in Algorithm 8.1 and its main features are described in the following sections.

8.3.1. *Pheromone structure*

Pheromone trails are laid on the edges of the graph; τ_{ij} denotes the quantity of pheromone laying on an edge (i, j). At the beginning of the solution process, every trail is initialized to a constant value τ_0.

Intuitively, the amount of pheromone τ_{ij} represents the past experience of the colony with respect to using the edge (i, j) when constructing a cycle. Ant System relies on the assumption that shorter cycles usually share more edges with the optimal cycle than longer cycles. In other words, it assumes that there is a strong correlation between the length of a cycle and the number of edges it shares with the optimal cycle. This correlation, usually called the *fitness–distance correlation*, has been widely studied for the TSP.

Figure 8.3 illustrates this on a very small TSP instance that has 16 vertices (such that we can generate all possible cycles in a reasonable amount of time).

Algorithm 8.1: Ant System for the traveling salesman problem

Input:

a complete non-directed graph $G = (V, E)$

a distance function $d : E \to \mathbb{R}$

a set of numerical parameters $\{\alpha, \beta, \rho, \tau_0, Q, nbAnts\}$

Postrelation: returns a Hamiltonian cycle of G

1 **begin**

2   **for** *each edge* $(i, j) \in E$ **do** $\tau_{ij} \leftarrow \tau_0$

3   **while** *stopping criteria not reached* **do**

4   **for** *each ant* $k \in \{1, \ldots, nbAnts\}$ **do**

5   put ant k on a randomly chosen vertex of V

6   **while** *ant k has not visited all vertices of V* **do**

7   let i be the vertex on which ant k is currently located

8   let *Cand* be the set of unvisited vertices

9   randomly choose $j \in Cand$ with respect to probability

$$p_{ij} = \frac{[\tau_{ij}]^\alpha \cdot [1/d_{ij}]^\beta}{\sum_{l \in Cand}[\tau_{il}]^\alpha \cdot [1/d_{il}]^\beta}$$

10   move ant k to vertex j

11   **for** *each edge* $(i, j) \in E$ **do** $\tau_{ij} \leftarrow \tau_{ij} \cdot (1 - \rho)$

12   **for** *each ant* $k \in \{1, \ldots, nbAnts\}$ **do**

13   let l_k be the length of the cycle built by ant k

14   **for** *each edge* (i, j) *of the cycle built by ant k* **do**

15                  $\tau_{ij} \leftarrow \tau_{ij} + Q/l_k$

16   **return** *the best Hamiltonian cycle built during the search process*

17 **end**

This figure shows us that, for this instance, the more edges a cycle shares with the optimal cycle, the shorter the cycle. For example, the second-best cycle (which is 6 units longer than the optimal cycle) shares 14 edges with it. All 'good' cycles, which are less than 100 units longer than the optimal cycle, share at least 10 edges with it.

Different studies have shown that this correlation is usually observed in instances of the TSP [JON 95, STÜ 00]. Some TSP instances may exhibit low correlations or, even worse, negative correlations such that good cycles

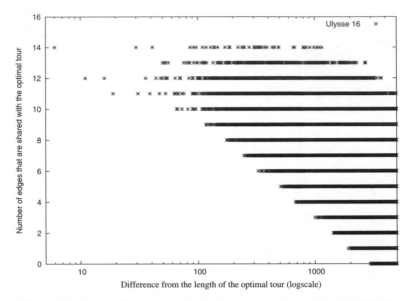

Figure 8.3. *Fitness–distance correlation for instance* `ulysse16` *of the TSPlib: for each Hamiltonian cycle c_i, we plot the point (x_i, y_i) such that x_i is the difference between the length of c_i and the length of the optimal cycle. y_i is the number of edges that c_i shares with the optimal cycle*

share less edges than poorer cycles. For these negatively correlated instances, pheromone trails are misleading and Ant System usually finds poorer cycles than for a pure random search. Note that most heuristic approaches behave poorly for this type of instance as they rely on heuristics that aim at intensifying the search around the best combinations.

8.3.2. *Construction of a Hamiltonian cycle by an ant*

At each iteration (lines 3 to 15), each ant builds a Hamiltonian cycle (lines 5 to 10). First, it randomly chooses an initial vertex with respect to a uniform distribution (line 5). It then iteratively chooses new vertices to visit until it has visited all vertices.

At each iteration, the next vertex to visit is chosen within the set *Cand* of candidate vertices which have not yet been visited by this ant. This choice is made with respect to a probabilistic transition rule (line 9) which depends on a pheromone factor τ_{ij} (which reflects the acquired desire to use edge (i,j)) and a heuristic factor $1/d_{ij}$ (the goal of which is to favor the nearest neighbors). These two factors are weighted by two numerical parameters α and β, which allow us to tune the respective influence of pheromone trails and heuristic information. In particular, when setting the pheromone factor weight α to zero, the probabilistic transition rule only depends on the heuristic factor. The algorithm therefore behaves like a classical greedy randomized algorithm such as those introduced in section 6.1.

Let us clarify exactly what is meant by *choosing a vertex with respect to a probabilistic transition rule*. To choose a vertex, the ant first computes for each candidate vertex $j \in Cand$ its associated transition probability p_{ij}. A floating point number $f \in [0; 1[$ is then randomly generated with respect to a uniform distribution, and the ant selects the candidate vertex using a roulette wheel principle (see section 11.2 for more details).

8.3.3. Pheromone updating step

Once all ants have constructed a Hamiltonian cycle, pheromone trails are updated with respect to this experience. First, pheromone trails are evaporated, i.e. each trail τ_{ij} is multiplied by a factor $1 - \rho$ where $\rho \in [0; 1]$ is the evaporation rate (line 11). This process allows ants to progressively forget older experiences and focus on more recent paths.

Each ant then lays pheromone trails on the edges of the cycle it has constructed (lines 12 to 15). The quantity of pheromone laid depends on the length of the cycle so that edges of shorter cycles receive more pheromone and are therefore more likely to be selected. More precisely, the trail associated with each edge of a cycle is increased by Q/l_k, where Q is a numerical parameter (usually set to a value close to the length of the optimal tour) and l_k is the length of the cycle.

8.3.4. Artificial versus real ants

The artificial ants of Ant System borrow some of their features from real ant colonies. They lay pheromone trails on the path they have followed and randomly choose their path with respect to probabilities that depend on pheromone trails. These pheromone trails progressively decrease by process of evaporation.

However, artificial ants also have extra features. In particular, they have a memory which allows them to be aware of the list of unvisited vertices, thus preventing them from building non-Hamiltonian cycles. They also lay pheromone trails once they have completed a cycle (and not during their progression) and the quantity of pheromone laid depends on the length of the cycle. This feature is very important to allow artificial ants to collectively converge towards shorter cycles. Finally, the probability of an artificial ant choosing an edge not only depends on pheromone trails, but also on a local nearest-neighbor heuristic.

8.4. Generic ACO framework

Ant System has been experimentally evaluated on different instances of the TSP. These experiments have highlighted the interest of biasing a greedy randomized construction with pheromone information which reflects past constructions. However, the results obtained by Ant System are not competitive with state-of-the-art approaches to the TSP (in particular, when considering large instances).

The initial algorithm has therefore been improved, giving rise to different extensions of Ant System such as Ant Colony System [DOR 97], MAX-MIN Ant System [STÜ 00] and Hypercube Framework [BLU 04]. These different extensions have been evaluated for the TSP and also for many other combinatorial optimization problems such as quadratic assignment problems or vehicle routing problems.

The ACO metaheuristic, which has evolved from these different works, is a generic framework for solving combinatorial optimization problems. This framework is described in Algorithm 8.2. Its main steps are detailed in the following sections. More information on ACO and its application to many different combinatorial optimization problems may be found in [DOR 04].

8.4.1. *Pheromone structure and construction graph*

ACO uses stigmergy to guide the search towards the most promising areas of the search space of the problem to be solved. More precisely, combinations are built in a greedy randomized way and pheromone trails are used to bias probabilities. These trails are reinforced with respect to the quality of the constructed combinations. A key point for the success of the approach lies

---

Algorithm 8.2: Generic ACO framework for solving static combinatorial optimization problems

---

1 **begin**
2   Initialize pheromone trails
3   **while** *Stopping criteria not reached* **do**
4   Construct combinations
5   Optional: improve combinations by local search
6   Update pheromone
7 **end**

---

in the choice of the pheromone structure, i.e. the choice of the components on which pheromone trails are laid. Obviously, this choice is related to fitness distance correlation issues, as discussed in the previous section on the TSP. Pheromone trails should be laid on components such that we usually observe a high correlation between the quality of a combination and the number of components it shares with the optimal combination. This pheromone structure depends on the problem to be solved.

When considering ordering problems such that the goal is to find a best order among a set of objects, we may associate a pheromone trail τ_{ij} with every couple of objects so that the quantity of pheromone τ_{ij} represents the learned desire to order object j after object i.

For example, this pheromone structure is used to solve the TSP defined in problem 8.1. A trail τ_{ij} is associated with every pair of vertices and represents the past experience of the colony with respect to visiting vertex j just after vertex i.

Other ordering problems for which this kind of pheromone structure is used include vehicle routing problems, car sequencing problems (see Chapter 12) and job scheduling problems.

When considering subset selection problems such that the goal is to find a best subset among a set of candidate objects, we may associate a pheromone trail τ_i with every object so that the quantity of pheromone τ_i represents the learned desire to select object i in the subset.

This pheromone structure is used, e.g. to solve the MKP defined in problem 3.1. A trail τ_i is associated with every object i and represents the past experience of the colony with respect to adding object i to the knapsack.

Other subset selection problems for which this kind of pheromone structure is used include maximum clique problems, Boolean satisfiability problems or maximum common subgraph problems. More information on solving subset selection problems with ACO is given in Chapter 13.

Many other pheromone structures may be designed, depending on the considered application. In section 14.2, we introduce and compare three pheromone structures for solving the car sequencing problem. In Chapter 13, we introduce and compare two pheromone structures for solving subset selection problems.

By analogy with real ant colonies, ACO algorithms are often introduced within the context of a path-finding problem in a *construction graph*. In this case, vertices of the construction graph usually correspond to combination components whereas edges correspond to successions of component choices during the construction of a combination by an ant. The problem to solve is then formulated as the search for a best path within this graph and pheromone trails are laid on edges and/or vertices of the graph.

At the beginning of an ACO search, all pheromone trails are initialized to a given value τ_0.

8.4.2. *Construction of combinations by ants*

Each ant builds a combination at each cycle of an ACO algorithm, either in parallel or sequentially. The construction of a combination by an ant is carried out in a greedy randomized way. Starting from an empty combination or a combination that contains a first combination component, the ant iteratively adds new combination components until the combination is complete. For many applications, this construction process corresponds to a path in the construction graph.

At each iteration, the next combination component is chosen with respect to a probabilistic transition rule. Given a partial combination S and a set *Cand* of combination components that may be added to S, the ant chooses a component

$i \in Cand$ with the probability:

$$p_S(i) = \frac{[\tau_S(i)]^\alpha \cdot [\eta_S(i)]^\beta}{\sum_{j \in Cand}[\tau_S(j)]^\alpha \cdot [\eta_S(j)]^\beta} \tag{8.1}$$

where $\tau_S(i)$ is the pheromone factor, $\eta_S(i)$ is the heuristic factor and α and β are two parameters.

8.4.2.1. *Pheromone factor*

The pheromone factor $\tau_S(i)$ evaluates the past experience of the colony regarding the selection of the combination component i when the current partial combination is S. The definition of this factor depends upon the chosen pheromone structure.

For the TSP defined in problem 3.1, for example, such that the pheromone structure associates a trail τ_{ij} with every pair of vertices (i, j), the pheromone factor $\tau_S(i)$ is defined by the quantity of pheromone τ_{ki} on the edge connecting the last vertex k added to S and the candidate vertex i.

For the MKP defined in problem 8.1, if the pheromone structure associates a trail τ_i with every object i, then the pheromone factor $\tau_S(i)$ is defined by the quantity of pheromone τ_i associated with the candidate object i.

8.4.2.2. *Heuristic factor*

The heuristic factor $\tau_S(i)$ evaluates the possibility of the combination component i being selected when the current partial combination is S. The definition of this factor depends upon the considered application.

For the TSP defined in problem 3.1, for example, the heuristic factor is inversely proportional to the length of the edge that joins the last vertex added to S to the candidate vertex i, thus decreasing the probability of choosing further vertices.

For the MKP defined in problem 8.1, the heuristic factor usually depends on the profit associated with the candidate object i and on the resources it requires.

8.4.2.3. *Pheromone and heuristic balance*

α and β are two parameters that allow the user to balance the influence of pheromone and heuristic factors in the transition probability.

If $\alpha = 0$ then pheromone is not considered when choosing combination components, i.e. the algorithm behaves as for a pure greedy randomized algorithm. On the contrary, if $\beta = 0$ then transition probabilities are defined with respect to pheromone only, and heuristic factors are not considered.

Note that the absolute values of α and β are important and not just the ratio of them.

Example 8.2. *Let us consider the two following parameter settings:*

$$s_1 = \{\alpha = 1, \beta = 2\} \text{ and } s_2 = \{\alpha = 2, \beta = 4\}.$$

In both settings, β is twice as large as α. However, s_2 more strongly emphasizes differences than s_1. Let us consider the case where ants have to choose between two components a and b with pheromone factors $\tau_S(a) = 1$ and $\tau_S(b) = 2$ and heuristic factors $\eta_S(a) = 2$ and $\eta_S(b) = 3$, respectively. When considering the s_1 setting, choice probabilities are:

$$p(a) = \frac{1^1 \times 2^2}{(1^1 \times 2^2) + (2^1 \times 3^2)} = 0.18$$

$$p(b) = \frac{2^1 \times 3^2}{(1^1 \times 2^2) + (2^1 \times 3^2)} = 0.82.$$

When considering the s_2 setting, however, choice probabilities are

$$p(a) = \frac{1^2 \times 2^4}{(1^2 \times 2^4) + (2^2 \times 3^4)} = 0.05$$

$$p(b) = \frac{2^2 \times 3^4}{(1^2 \times 2^4) + (2^2 \times 3^4)} = 0.95.$$

8.4.3. *Improving combinations with local search*

Once a combination has been constructed by an ant, it may be improved by applying a local search procedure such as those introduced in section 5.2. Different strategies may be considered. In particular, a local search may be applied to every constructed combination or only to the best constructed combinations.

Different neighborhoods and different strategies for choosing the next move to apply within the neighborhood can be considered. The aim is to find the correct balance between the time spent by local search to improve combinations and the quality of these improvements. Typically, a simple greedy local search which improves combinations until reaching a local optima is usually chosen.

Example 8.3. *For the traveling salesman problem a two-opt greedy local search, which considers the neighborhood composed of all cycles obtained by exchanging the endpoints of two edges of the current cycle, may be applied. The search moves towards better neighbors until reaching a locally optimal cycle which cannot be improved by exchanging two edges.*

ACO and LS explore the search space in two complementary ways and their hybridization allows the best of these two approaches to be applied:

– LS is used to improve the combinations that are built by ants; and

– ACO is used to build new starting points from the local optima previously reached by the local search.

ACO approaches which demonstrate the best performances are usually based on such a hybridization. Note that an hybrid ACO/LS approach may be viewed as an instantiation of the GRASP metaheuristic described in section 6.1.

8.4.4. *Pheromone updating step*

Once each ant has constructed a combination (that may have been improved by some local search procedure), pheromone trails are updated.

In a first step, all pheromone trails are decreased by multiplying them by a factor $(1 - \rho)$ where $\rho \in [0; 1]$ is the evaporation rate. This evaporation process allows ants to progressively forget older constructions and to focus on more recent constructions.

In a second step, some combinations are rewarded by laying pheromone trails. The goal is to increase the probability of selecting the components of these combinations during the following constructions. Different strategies of choosing the combinations to be rewarded may be considered. We may reward all the combinations that have been built during the last cycle, as initially proposed in Ant System, or we may consider more elitist strategies such that only the best combinations of the cycle are rewarded.

The search can be further intensified by rewarding the best combination found since the beginning of the search process. These different strategies have a strong influence on the intensification and the diversification of the search, as discussed in Chapter 9.

The pheromone is laid on the trails which are associated with the rewarded combination. These trails depend on the considered application and on the chosen pheromone structure:

– For the TSP defined in problem 3.1, if the pheromone structure associates a trail τ_{ij} with every pair of vertices (i, j) then ants lay pheromone on every trail τ_{ij} such that the vertices i and j have been visited consecutively when building the combination to reward.

– For the MKP defined in problem 8.1, if the pheromone structure associates a trail τ_i with every object i then ants lay pheromone on each trail τ_i such that object i belongs to the combination to reward.

The quantity of pheromone laid is usually proportional to the quality of the rewarded combination. This quantity may be normalized between 0 and 1 by defining it as a ratio between the value of the combination to reward and the optimal value (if it is known) or the best value found since the beginning of the search (including the current cycle). More precisely, if the objective function must be maximized (respectively, minimized) and if the objective value of the combination to be rewarded is x, then the quantity of pheromone laid may be defined by x/x^* (respectively, x^*/x) where x^* is either the optimal value or the best value found since the beginning of the search.

8.4.5. *Parameters of an ACO algorithm*

The main parameters of an ACO algorithm are as follows:

– The number of ants *nbAnts* determines the number of combinations that are built at each cycle before updating the pheromone.

– The pheromone factor weight α determines the influence of pheromone in the probabilistic transition rule.

– The heuristic factor weight β determines the influence of the local heuristic in the probabilistic transition rule.

– The pheromone evaporation rate ρ determines the speed of pheromone trail evaporation.

– The initial setting of pheromone trails is defined by q_0.

The setting of β often changes from one application to another, depending on the reliability of the heuristic factor.

The setting of *nbAnts*, α and ρ are less problem-dependent, but have a strong influence on the quality of the best combination found and the time spent finding it. This point is discussed in more detail in the following chapter.

Chapter 9

Intensification versus Diversification

When exploring a search space in an incomplete and opportunistic way with ACO, as with any other metaheuristic, intensification and diversification have to be balanced in order to find the best combination in the smallest amount of time.

We first state the mechanisms used by ACO to intensify the search towards the best combinations in section 9.1. We introduce those used to diversify the search towards new areas in section 9.2. The balance between intensification and diversification is achieved by tuning parameters, and we show in section 9.3 that the best parameter tuning varies from one instance to another and depends on the correlation between the objective function and the number of shared pheromone components. Finally, in section 9.4 we introduce three measures that may be used to quantify intensification and diversification during the solution process.

9.1. ACO mechanisms for intensifying the search

An ACO search is intensified in an indirect and collective way through pheromone laying. When pheromone is laid on the components of the best combinations found so far, the probability of selecting these components when building new combinations is increased so that the search is intensified around these best combinations.

Intensification is mainly controlled by the two parameters α and ρ:

$- \alpha$ defines the weight of the pheromone factor when choosing components. By increasing the value of α, the probability of choosing the components that have received more pheromone is increased and the search around these components is intensified.

$- \rho$ defines the pheromone evaporation rate. By increasing the value of ρ, the influence of recent pheromone rewards with respect to older rewards is emphasized and the search around the best combinations that have recently been found is intensified.

When intensifying an ACO search by increasing α and/or ρ, ants usually converge quicker towards good combinations. As a counterpart, however, they may converge on suboptimal combinations. This point is more widely discussed in section 9.3.

The intensification of an ACO search can be emphasized by using more elitist transition rules. In particular, in the framework *Ant Colony System* [DOR 97], ants do not always select the next component with respect to the probability defined in equation (8.1). They have a small probability q_0 of greedily selecting the best component according to pheromone and heuristic factors. More precisely, given a partial combination S and a set *Cand* of candidate components that may be added to S, ants select a component $i \in Cand$ with respect to the transition rule:

> **if** $q \leq q_0$ **then** $i = \text{argmax}_{j \in Cand}\{[\tau_S(j)]^{\alpha} \times [\eta_S(j)]^{\beta}\}$
> **else** choose i with respect to probability defined in equation (8.1)

where q is a real number randomly chosen in $[0;1]$ with respect to a uniform distribution and $q_0 \in [0;1]$ is a parameter which allows intensification to be emphasized. In particular, when $q_0 = 1$, ants always choose the best component which maximizes the product of pheromone and heuristic factors. The search is strongly intensified around the components that have received more pheromone. On the contrary, if $q_0 = 0$, then ants always select components with respect to probabilities defined by equation (8.1) so that components that have received less pheromone still have a chance of being selected.

Intensification may also be emphasized by considering elitist strategies when laying pheromone trails:

– In *Elitist Ant System* [DOR 92], in addition to the reward of all the combinations that have been constructed during the last cycle, we also reward the best combination that has been constructed since the start of the search.

– In *Rank-based Ant System* [BUL 99], the different combinations that are constructed during a cycle are ranked by decreasing quality. The quantity of pheromone laid by each ant is weighted by the rank of the combination it has built. Only the best w combinations are rewarded, and the quantity of pheromone laid on the components of the kth combination is weighted by $(w + 1 - k)$. The best combination built from the beginning of the search process may also be rewarded.

– In both *Ant Colony System* [DOR 97] and *MAX-MIN Ant System* [STÜ 00] only the best combination of the cycle or the best combination built since the beginning of the search process is rewarded.

9.2. ACO mechanisms for diversifying the search

Intensification may be overemphasized if the components of the best combinations found so far are over-rewarded, if the pheromone factor is over-weighted in the transition rule used to select components and/or if pheromone trails are over-evaporated so that the choice of components is mainly guided by the last constructions. In this case, we may observe an early stagnation phenomenon such that ants converge towards a suboptimal combination and are no longer able to discover new combinations. In order to avoid such early stagnation phenomenon, intensification must be counter-balanced by some diversification mechanisms.

In an ACO algorithm, search diversification is ensured by the probabilistic transition rule. More precisely, the probability of selecting a component depends on pheromone and heuristic factors. We must therefore check that these factors never become null. To this aim, a lower bound $\tau_{\min} > 0$ on pheromone trails is usually set.

When ensuring that the probability of selecting a component can never become null in this way, the *convergence* of ACO algorithms can be proven as proposed by Stützle and Dorigo in [STÜ 02]. This convergence proof ensures that the algorithm will always find the optimal combination provided that the number of cycles is not bounded. If this is a desirable property for any heuristic algorithm, the proof does not reveal any information about the number of cycles that are needed to find the optimal combination; this number may be very large.

In order to ensure a good diversification of an ACO search and, more particularly, at the begining of the search process, Stützle and Hoos have introduced two very important features in the MAX-MIN Ant System [STÜ 00]:

– First, pheromone trails are bound between two parameters τ_{min} and τ_{max} such that $0 < \tau_{min} < \tau_{max}$. The goal is not only to ensure that the pheromone factor associated with a component never becomes null, but also to ensure that the relative difference between two pheromone factors cannot become too large. This prevents the formation of pheromone highways that would over-attract the search.

– Second, pheromone trails are initialized at the upper bound τ_{max} at the beginning of the search process. This point allows diversification at the beginning of the search process to be emphasized, thus preventing early stagnation. Indeed, after k cycles, the lowest pheromone trails (those that have never been rewarded but instead evaporated at each cycle) are greater or equal to $\tau_{max}(1 - \rho)^k$, whereas the highest pheromone trails are smaller or equal to τ_{max}. As a consequence, the difference between two pheromone trails is bound by the ratio $(1 - \rho)^k$ where the pheromone evaporation rate ρ is usually very small.

9.3. Balancing intensification and diversification

As explained in the previous sections, the balance between intensification and diversification is mainly achieved by tuning parameters. The goal is to find the best balance, i.e. one which allows the search to find the best solution within the smallest CPU time. Unfortunately, this best balance varies from one problem to another and also from one instance to another. In particular, it depends on the shape of the search landscape associated with the instance.

Let us first define a search landscape in the context of an ACO search. The search landscape was introduced in section 2.3.2 with respect to a neighborhood relationship. This neighborhood depends on the approach considered for solving the problem and induces a distance metric among combinations (corresponding to the length of the shortest path in the neighborhood graph). When considering a perturbative heuristic approach (e.g. local search), the distance between combinations in the search landscape corresponds to the smallest number of search steps (such as moves for local search) needed to transform one combination into another. In this case, the *fitness–distance correlation* may be used as an indicator of the shape of the search landscape, thus allowing a good balance between intensification and diversification to be chosen:

– A very high correlation between the quality of a combination and its distance to the closest optimal combination indicates that the search landscape has a *Massif Central* shape, i.e. the search should be intensified around the best local optima.

– A lower correlation indicates that the search landscape is rougher, i.e. a mild amount of diversification should be introduced.

– A negative correlation indicates that the search landscape has a misleading shape, i.e. it is best to highly diversify the search.

When considering an ACO approach, it is meaningless to define the distance between two combinations with respect to a number of search steps. This is because ACO does not build new combinations by perturbating existing combinations, but iteratively builds new combinations from scratch. However, we may define a similarity measure based on the pheromone structure, i.e. the set of components on which pheromone is laid. Indeed, each time a combination is rewarded by laying some pheromone on its components, the probability of selecting these components during the next constructions is increased. The similarity of two combinations may therefore be defined by the number of pheromone components they share: the higher the similarity, the more the reward of one of these two combinations increases the probability of constructing the other combination.

Example 9.1. *For the TSP the pheromone components associated with a tour are the edges of this tour; the similarity between two tours should therefore be defined by the number of edges they share.*

The correlation between the quality of a combination and its similarity to the optimal combination gives a very good indication of the levels of intensification and diversification that should be achieved to reach the best performance.

Let us illustrate this on the clique example defined in problem 2.2. The basic ACO algorithm for solving this problem is briefly described in Chapter 13 [SOL 06]. We consider here a pheromone structure which associates a pheromone component τ_i with every vertex i. Intuitively, this pheromone component represents the learnt desirability of selecting vertex i in a clique. Interestingly, the ACO algorithm does not use any heuristic information in the probabilistic transition rule so that the solving process is only guided by pheromone trails: the next vertex i to be added to a partial clique is chosen with respect to the probability

$$p_i = \frac{\tau_i^\alpha}{\sum_{j \in Cand} \tau_j^\alpha}.$$

This probabilistic transition rule intensifies the search towards cliques that share many vertices with the best cliques found so far. Intensification should therefore be emphasized when solving instances that exhibit a strong correlation between the size of a clique and the number of vertices it shares with the optimum clique. Diversification should always be emphasized when solving instances with lower correlations.

Let us consider, for example, the following classes of instances of the maximum clique problem (http://dimacs.rutgers.edu/):

– The Cn.p graphs are randomly generated graphs with n vertices and a density of 0.p, i.e. an edge is created between any pair of vertices with probability 0.p.

– The brock$n$_m graphs have n vertices and a density between 0.496 and 0.74. These graphs contain large cliques hidden among a connected population of significantly smaller cliques.

– The gen$n$_p0.p_m graphs have n vertices, a density of 0.p and a maximum clique of known size m.

Each class contains different instances of different sizes. For each of these classes, we first consider the smallest instance, i.e. gen200_p0.9_55 (whose maximum clique has 55 vertices), C125.9 (whose maximum clique has 34 vertices) and brock200_4 (whose maximum clique has 17 vertices). We have chosen small instances as we want to compute a representative sampling of the search space in order to measure the fitness-similarity correlation. To this aim, we have randomly generated 10 million maximal cliques (which are not strictly included in another clique) for each instance.

For each instance, Figures 9.1a, 9.2a and 9.3a plot the size and the similarity to the maximum clique of these 10 million cliques.

– The plot for instance gen200_p0.9_55 shows a very strong correlation between the quality of the combination and the number of vertices it shares with the optimal solution.

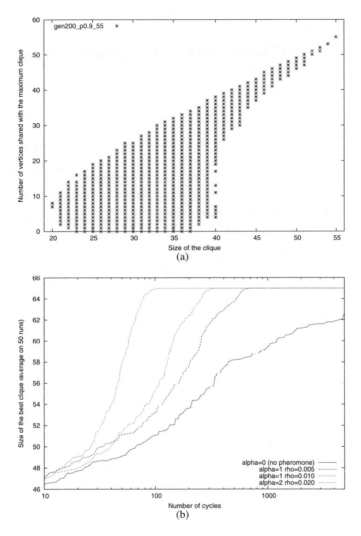

Figure 9.1. *(a) Fitness-similarity plot for* gen200_p0.9_55 *and (b) influence of α and ρ on the solving process for* gen400_p0.9_65. *Each point* (x, y) *in (a) corresponds to a maximal clique such that* x *is the size of the clique and* y *is the number of vertices it shares with the optimal solution. Each curve in (b) plots the evolution of the size of the best clique found so far with respect to the number of cycles for a different setting of α and ρ*

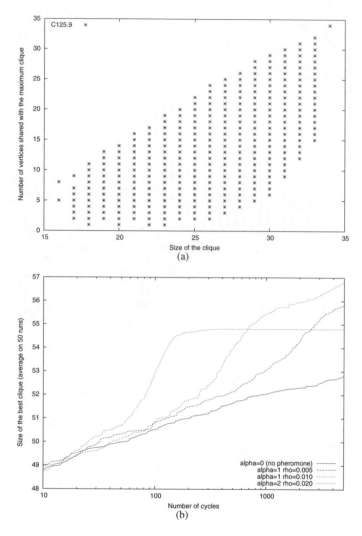

Figure 9.2. *(a) Fitness-similarity plot for* C125.9 *and (b) influence of* α *and* ρ
on the solving process for C500.9. *Each point* (x, y) *in (a) and each curve in*
(b) as for Figure 9.1

– The plot for instance C125.9 also shows a correlation, but it is weaker
as some good cliques (e.g. that have 33 vertices) only share approximately
one-third of their vertices with the optimal clique.

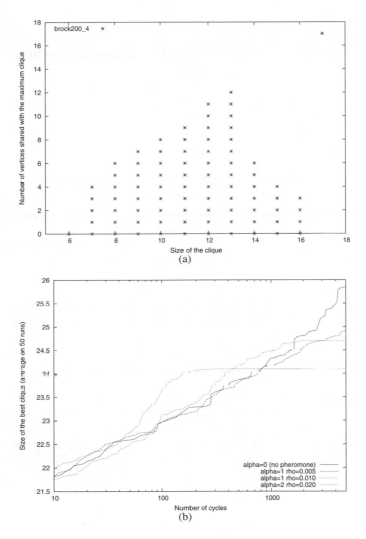

Figure 9.3. *(a) Fitness-similarity plot for* brock200_4; *(b) influence of* α *and* ρ *on the solving process for* brock400_4. *Each point* (x, y) *in (a) and each curve in (b) as for Figure 9.1*

– The plot for instance brock200_4 shows a negative correlation as good cliques (that have 16 vertices) share much less vertices with the optimal solution than smaller cliques (that have 12 or 13 vertices).

Let us return to the mechanisms used by ACO to progressively intensify the search towards some subareas. At each cycle, some pheromone is added to the vertices of the best clique of the cycle and the probability of selecting these vertices when building new cliques is therefore increased. (Recall that for this maximum clique problem, the probability of selecting a vertex only depends on pheromone trails as no heuristic information is used). The influence of pheromone should therefore be emphasized when solving instances that exhibit a high fitness-similarity correlation, whereas it should be decreased when solving instances that exhibit lower fitness-similarity correlation.

For the gen200_p0.9_55 instance, when ants reward a good clique (e.g. with 50 or more vertices) they increase the probability of building the maximum clique (which shares more than 45 vertices with any clique that has more than 50 vertices). For this instance, pheromone is a very good guide and a parameter setting which strongly intensifies the influence of pheromone should be selected in order to speed up the convergence of the colony towards the optimal solution.

On the contrary, for the instance brock200_4 some very good cliques (with 14 to 16 vertices) do not share any vertex with the maximum clique. The probability of building the maximum clique is decreased when rewarding these good cliques. For this instance, pheromone is misleading so that a parameter setting which strongly diversifies the search should be selected.

To illustrate this, we have run ACO with different parameter settings ranging between $\alpha = 0$ (so that pheromone is not used and the search is highly diversified) to $\alpha = 2$ and $\rho = 2\%$ (so that pheromone has a strong influence and the search is highly intensified). For these experiments we have considered larger instances taken in the three classes, i.e. gen400_p0.9_65 (whose maximum clique has 65 vertices), C500.9 (whose maximum clique has 57 vertices) and brock400_4 (whose maximum clique has 33 vertices).

We have chosen larger instances than those used to study fitness-similarity correlations since the optimal solution is usually found rather quickly on small instances (whatever the parameter setting). However, all instances within a same class have been generated according to similar rules. It is therefore most probable that these instances exhibit similar fitness-similarity correlations and similar behavior with respect to parameter settings.

For each instance, Figures 9.1b, 9.2b and 9.3b plot the evolution of the size of the best clique found so far during the solution process for different parameter settings.

– For instance gen400_p0.9_65, we observe that when intensifying the search (by increasing α and/or ρ) ants converge quicker towards the optimal solution. It is still not found after 5000 cycles when $\alpha = 0$, but is found around cycle 600 when $\alpha = 1$ and $\rho = 0.5\%$, around cycle 300 when $\alpha = 1$ and $\rho = 1\%$ and around cycle 100 when $\alpha = 2$ and $\rho = 2\%$.

– For instance C500.9, we observe that the quality of the final solution is better when balancing intensification with diversification but the time needed to converge on this value is also higher. Hence, when $\alpha = 2$ and $\rho = 2\%$, ants find better solutions during the first cycles. After 100 or so cycles, ants have converged towards a suboptimal clique (with 54 or 55 vertices) and are not able to diversify their search to find the optimal solution. The best balance between intensification and diversification is achieved when $\alpha = 1$ and $\rho = 1\%$. With this setting, ants converge towards the optimal solution (for nearly all runs) after 4000 or so cycles.

– For instance brock400_4, we observe that pheromone misleads the search towards suboptimal cliques. When $\alpha = 2$ and $\rho = 2\%$, ants converge towards a clique that has 24 or so vertices in $\sim$200 cycles; when $\alpha = 1$ and $\rho = 1\%$, they converge towards slightly better cliques in $\sim$1000 cycles. All brock instances have been built in such a way that the optimal solution is hidden so that they have negative fitness-similarity correlations. As a consequence, for all instances of this class, pheromone is misleading and the best results are obtained when α is set to 0 so that cliques are randomly built. Note that most metaheuristics fail to find optimal solutions to these instances.

We conclude this study by noting that the problem of finding the best balance between intensification and diversification is clearly a multi-objective optimization problem. Better combinations are usually obtained by giving the solution process more time.

For example, let us consider instance brock400_4. The three settings $s_1 = (\alpha = 2, \rho = 2\%)$, $s_2 = (\alpha = 1, \rho = 1\%)$ and $s_3 = (\alpha = 0)$ are all pareto-optimal with respect to the two objective functions time and quality: the best setting is s_1 for short CPU time limits, s_2 for intermediate CPU time limits and s_3 for long CPU time limits.

9.4. Measures of diversification/intensification

In order to tune an ACO algorithm and set the parameters to values which allow an efficient search, it is helpful to have numerical measures that allow intensification and diversification to be quantified during the search process. In particular, such measures allow the programmer to dynamically detect situations of over-intensification (such that ants are no longer able to discover new combinations) or of over-exploration (such that pheromone does not influence the search process at all) during the search process.

We now describe three measures: the λ-branching factor, the resampling ratio and the similarity rate.

9.4.1. *The λ-branching factor*

To quantify the evolution of intensification during the search process, we can measure the distribution of pheromones on the pheromone structure. If most candidate components have a very low pheromone factor and only a few components have a high pheromone factor, then ants will nearly always choose the same highly marked components. This will be reinforced in an autocatalytic process so that the search will be over-intensified around these components.

More precisely, Dorigo and Gambardella introduced the λ-branching factor in [DOR 97]. This factor has been introduced for the traveling salesman problem, and we generalize it to any combinatorial optimization problem. Given a set *Cand* of candidate components, this factor is defined by the number of components $i \in Cand$ such that:

$$\tau_S(i) \geq \tau_m + \lambda(\tau_M - \tau_m)$$

where $\tau_S(i)$ is the pheromone factor of the component i; τ_m (respectively, τ_M) is the pheromone factor of the component $j \in Cand$ that has the smallest (respectively, largest) pheromone factor and λ is a parameter that belongs to $[0; 1]$.

The average λ-branching factor for a cycle is defined as the average of all λ-branching factors for every construction step. It corresponds to the average number of components that have a high pheromone factor with respect to other components, where the parameter λ defines the threshold above which a pheromone factor is considered as high.

9.4.2. *Resampling ratio*

This measure has been used in [VAN 02, VAN 04] in order to evaluate the ability of a heuristic algorithm to sample a search space. Let us denote the number of different combinations that have been constructed by an algorithm during a whole run by *#Diff* and the total number of combinations that have been constructed by *#Tot*. The resampling ratio is defined:

$$\frac{\#Tot - \#Diff}{\#Tot}.$$

A ratio close to zero indicates an efficient sampling, in the sense that the algorithm rarely computes the same combination more than once. A ratio close to 1 indicates a stagnation of the search process around a small set of combinations that are very often recomputed.

Table 9.1 provides an insight into the performance of an ACO algorithm for the maximum clique problem by means of this resampling ratio. The table shows that this ACO algorithm never recomputes the same combination twice when the parameter setting limits the influence of the pheromone on the solution process, i.e. when setting α to 1 and ρ to 0.005 or 0.01. However, when increasing the influence of pheromone by increasing α or ρ, the resampling rate increases by 10% after $\sim$1000 cycles when $\alpha = 2$ and $\rho = 0.02$.

Number of cycles:	500	1000	1500	2000	2500
$\alpha = 1, \rho = 0.005$	0.00	0.00	0.00	0.00	0.00
$\alpha = 1, \rho = 0.01$	0.00	0.00	0.00	0.00	0.00
$\alpha = 2, \rho = 0.01$	0.00	0.04	0.06	0.07	0.07
$\alpha = 2, \rho = 0.02$	0.06	0.10	0.12	0.13	0.13

Table 9.1. *Evolution of the resampling ratio for the problem of finding a maximum clique in the graph* C500.9. *Each line gives the settings of α and ρ and the resampling ratios after 500, 1000, 1500, 2000 and 2500 cycles (averaged over 50 runs)*

9.4.3. *Similarity ratio*

The resampling ratio allows the size of the sampled space to be quantified and shows that ACO has a higher search ability when $\alpha = 1$ and $\rho = 0.01$ than when $\alpha - 2$ and $\rho = 0.02$ (for the considered C500.9 instance). However, the resampling ratio gives no information about the distribution of the computed combinations within the whole search space. A pure random search almost never resamples the same combination twice but, as it does not intensify the search around promising combinations, it is usually not able to find good combinations. To provide a complementary insight into the performance of

ACOs, a similarity ratio may be computed which indicates the similarity in the computed combinations, i.e. by how much the search is intensified. This similarity ratio corresponds to the pairwise population diversity measure introduced for genetic approaches, e.g. in [MOR 01, SID 01].

Generally speaking, the similarity ratio of a collection S of combinations is defined by the ratio between the average size of the intersection of every pair of combinations in S with respect to the average size of the combinations of S. A similarity ratio equal to 1 indicates that all the combinations in S are identical. A similarity ratio equal to 0 indicates that all pairs of combinations in S have an empty intersection (they never share components).

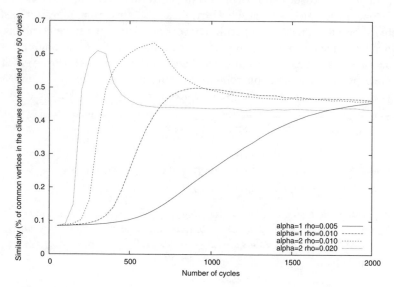

Figure 9.4. *Evolution of the similarity ratio for the problem of finding a maximum clique in the graph* C500.9 *for different settings of α and ρ*

For subset selection problems (such as the maximum clique problem), combinations are sets of objects and the intersection of two combinations is well defined. For problems that involve the search of a best Hamiltonian path in a graph (such as the traveling salesman problem or the car sequencing problem), combinations are paths in the graph. The intersection of two combinations may be defined by the set of edges that are common to the two paths.

Figure 9.4 plots the evolution of the similarity ratio of the cliques computed during a cycle of an ACO algorithm for the maximum clique problem. This yields information about the distribution of the computed cliques within the space of all possible cliques.

Let us consider the curve plotting the evolution of the similarity ratio when α is set to 1 and ρ to 0.01. The similarity increases from less than 10% at the beginning of the solution process to 45% after $\sim$1000 cycles. This shows that ants progressively focus on a subarea of the search space, so that two cliques constructed after cycle 1000 share on average nearly one-half of their vertices.

When considering this together with the fact that the resampling ratio is null, it can be concluded that in this case ACO reaches a good compromise between diversification (as it never computes the same combination twice) and intensification (as the similarity of the computed combinations is increased).

Figure 9.4 also shows that when α and/or ρ increase, the similarity ratio increases sooner and faster. However, the similarity ratio of all runs converges towards the same value, whatever the setting of α and ρ. After $\sim$2000 cycles, the cliques computed during every cycle share nearly 45% of their vertices.

Chapter 10

Beyond Static Combinatorial Problems

ACO explores the search space of combinatorial optimization problems by building combinations in a greedy randomized way. It uses a pheromone-based learning mechanism in order to progressively bias transition probabilities that are used to build combinations.

This basic principle has been extended to deal with other classes of problems. In section 10.1 we show how to use ACO to solve multi-objective optimization problems, which have several objective functions to optimize. In section 10.2, we show how ACO may be used to solve dynamic problems such that the data of the instance to solve dynamically changes during the solution process. We describe an extension of ACO to solve continuous optimization problems, such that the domains of the variables are continuous intervals instead of finite sets of values, in section 10.3.

10.1. Multi-objective problems

10.1.1. *Definition of multi-objective problems*

In many real-life optimization problems there are several objectives to optimize. More formally, a multi-objective optimization problem (MOP) is defined by a tuple (X, D, C, F) such that: X is a finite set of variables; for every variable $x_i \in X$, $D(x_i)$ is a finite set of values defining the domain of x_i; C is a set of constraints; and F is a set of $m \geq 2$ objective functions.

A MOP may be transformed into a single-objective optimization problem by aggregating the different objective functions into a single function (for example, a weighted sum). A MOP may also be transformed into a sequence of single-objective problems by defining an order over the different objectives. In a first step, the most important objective function is optimized. In a second step, the second objective function is used to break ties among the set of optimal solutions with respect to the first objective. The third objective function is then used to break further ties, and so on.

However, in many cases, the different objectives of a MOP cannot be ranked or weighted in an *a priori* way; it is therefore most desirable to propose a set of solutions to the decision maker. This set is called the Pareto set or non-dominated solution set.

Example 10.1. *When planning trips, we usually want to minimize both traveling times and costs: a journey t with cost c and duration d is preferred to a journey t' with cost c' > c and duration d' > d, but it is not comparable with a journey t'' with cost c'' < c and duration d'' > d (or conversely, with cost c'' > c and duration d'' < d). The two journeys t and t'' are both optimal with respect to different criteria so they should both be proposed to the user.*

More formally, the space of feasible solutions of a MOP (X, D, C, F) is the set of complete assignments which satisfy all the constraints of C, i.e. the set of solutions of the CSP (X, D, C). We define a partial order relation on this set: a feasible solution s *dominates* another feasible solution s' if and only if s is at least as good as s' for each of the m objectives to optimize and strictly better than s' for at least one of these objectives. The goal of a MOP (X, D, C, F) is to find the Pareto set of all non-dominated solutions.

Example 10.2. *Figure 10.1 displays an example of Pareto set. The best solution with respect to the first objective function is a and the best solution with respect to the second objective function is k. Other solutions (from b to j) are Pareto optimal solutions which correspond to different compromises between the two objectives.*

In most cases, the Pareto set cannot be computed exactly and it is approximated by a set of feasible solutions S such that (1) no solution of S is dominated by another solution of S; (2) solutions of S are as close as possible to the Pareto set; and (3) solutions of S are as evenly distributed as possible in order to propose a representative sampling of compromise solutions.

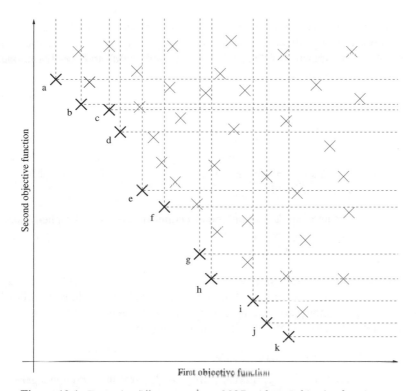

Figure 10.1. *Example of Pareto set for a MOP with two objective functions to minimize: each cross corresponds to a feasible solution. Feasible solutions that belong to the Pareto set are in bold. For each Pareto-optimal feasible solution, dashed lines delimit the set of solutions that are dominated (right-upper sides of dashed lines)*

10.1.2. *Solving multi-objective problems with ACO*

Many different ACO algorithms have been proposed for solving MOPs, and these algorithms are often referred to as MOACO algorithms (see [ANG 09] for a recent survey).

MOACO algorithms basically follow the generic ACO framework described in algorithm 8.2: they sample the search space by iteratively building feasible solutions in a greedy randomized way, and pheromone trails are used to progressively bias probabilities in order to intensify the search around the best feasible solutions.

However, this basic principle has to be adapted for the fact that there are several objective functions to optimize. In particular, the pheromone structure, the probabilistic transition rule used to build combinations and the pheromone updating step have to be adapted.

10.1.2.1. *Pheromone structure*

The pheromone trail associated with a component is an indication of the past experience of the colony with respect to choosing this component. When there is only one objective function, this past experience is defined with respect to this objective. However, when there are several objectives, different strategies may be considered.

We may define a single pheromone structure. In this case, the pheromone trail associated with a component reflects the interest of this component with respect to the different objectives.

We may also define several pheromone structures. In particular, we may associate a different pheromone structure with each objective function. In this case, each pheromone structure reflects the past experience of the colony with respect to each different objective function separately.

10.1.2.2. *Probabilistic transition rule*

As for classical ACO algorithms, combinations are constructed in a greedy randomized way: at each step of the construction, a combination component is chosen with respect to a transition probability which depends on a pheromone factor and a heuristic factor. When there is only one objective function, all ants consider the same probabilistic transition rule. Pheromone and heuristic factors both evaluate the desirability of choosing the candidate component with respect to this single objective. However, when there are several objectives, different strategies may be considered.

The heuristic factor may be defined by an aggregation (such as a weighted sum) of the different heuristic information associated with the different objectives. In this case, it is possible to dynamically change the weights during the construction of a combination or from one construction to another. By changing the respective influence of the different objectives, we ensure a better covering of the Pareto set. Another possibility is to associate different types of heuristic information with each objective and to use these different types of heuristic information separately. In this case, the set of ants is usually partitioned into different colonies such that each colony considers different heuristic information in order to optimize a different objective.

The definition of the pheromone factor depends on the definition of the pheromone structure. If there is only one pheromone structure for all objectives, then the pheromone factor is defined in a straightforward way with respect to this pheromone structure. However, if there are several pheromone structures, the pheromone factor may either be defined by an aggregation of these different pheromone structures or ants may be partitioned into different colonies which exploit the different pheromone structures separately (as for heuristic factors).

10.1.2.3. *Pheromone updating step*

As for classical ACO algorithms, pheromone trails are evaporated at the end of each cycle. The pheromone trails associated with the best combinations are then increased. Once again, we may consider different strategies when choosing the combinations to be rewarded. A first possibility is to reward the best combinations with respect to each objective separately. A second possibility is to reward every non-dominated combination. In this case, we may either reward all the combinations in the Pareto set or only the new non-dominated combinations.

10.2. Dynamic optimization problems

10.2.1. *Definition of dynamic optimization problems*

Many real-world optimization problems evolve in an environment which is dynamically changing; solutions must therefore be adapted to changes. For instance, in online scheduling systems, the set of jobs to schedule is not necessarily known in advance or some machines may break down. When a new set of jobs arrives, or when a machine breaks down, the schedule must be updated and a new optimal solution must be found.

More formally, a dynamic combinatorial optimization problem (DCOP) is defined by a sequence $< P^1, P^2, \ldots, P^m >$ such that for all $t \in 1, \ldots, m$, $P^t = (X^t, D^t, C^t, f^t)$ defines the COP to solve at time t. Changes that occur at each time step may affect the decision variables (which may be added or removed), the domains (values may be added or removed), the constraints (which may be added, removed or updated) or the objective function (which may be updated).

Note that the sequence of problems to solve is not known *a priori*: changes occur in an unpredictable way and no information about them is available ahead of time. For example, the time-dependent TSP is not a DCOP even though travel time between cities changes with respect to the traffic load. Indeed, the traffic load is known in advance so that changes are known before starting the solution process.

In DCOPs, the changes that occur at each time step cannot be predicted so each new solution must be computed as and when changes occur. A first possibility is to restart the solution process from scratch. However, the changes are usually rather small and, even though a small change may have a large influence on the optimal solution, the new optimal solution is rather close to the old one in most cases. It is therefore more interesting to transfer knowledge from one problem to the next in order to solve it quicker.

10.2.2. *Solving dynamic optimization problems with ACO*

ACO algorithms gather knowledge of the problem to be solved by means of a pheromone structure. The pheromone trail associated with a component represents the learnt experience of the colony with respect to selecting this component in a solution. When changes occur, we may use this pheromone structure to solve the new problem. Of course, this pheromone structure must be updated by removing (respectively, adding) pheromone trails corresponding to components that have been deleted (respectively, added) and by initializing new pheromone trails to some given initial value.

However, if the pheromone structure is reused for solving the new problem without any adaptation, the search may be over-intensified around the best solutions of the last problem (the components of which have large pheromone trails). In this case, the algorithm is not able to explore the search space of the new problem and becomes stuck in old local optima. Once again, we have to balance intensification with diversification. This may be achieved by using smoothing techniques. Each time a change occurs, pheromone trails are smoothed in order to reduce relative differences between them (thus increasing diversification). For example, we may increase $\tau_{\min}$ and/or decrease $\tau_{\max}$ (when using the MAX-MIN Ant System), or we may set each pheromone trail to the average of the previous pheromone quantity and a default pheromone quantity [GUN 01].

Another popular approach for solving DCOP with ACO is to use the population-based ACO (P-ACO) framework introduced by Guntsch and Middendorf [GUN 02]. As for classical ACO algorithms, P-ACO algorithms solve COPs by iteratively building combinations in a greedy randomized way. The probabilistic transition rule used by ants to choose components is the same, i.e. it is defined proportional to pheromone and heuristic factors weighted by two parameters α and β. The pheromone structure is also the same. However, it is updated differently:

– In ACO, the pheromone structure is updated in two steps by evaporating all trails and then laying some pheromone on the components of the best combinations.

– In P-ACO, the pheromone structure is updated with respect to a population of combinations. Each time a combination enters (respectively, leaves) the population, the pheromone trails associated with its components are increased (respectively, decreased).

There exist different strategies for managing the population, i.e. for deciding which combinations enter or leave the population. For example, in the *age* strategy, the best combination of the cycle always enters the population. Once the population has reached a given size, the oldest combination of the population leaves it.

P-ACO may be used to solve static COPs. It is also very well suited for solving DCOPs. Indeed, the pheromone structure may be easily recomputed from the population. The quantity of pheromone laying on a component c is equal to the sum, for each combination s of the population which contains c, of the pheromone increase due to s (which is usually proportional to $f(s)$). Each time a change occurs, the combinations of the population are therefore repaired with respect to the changes and then used to compute new pheromone trails. The procedure used to repair combinations is problem dependent.

Example 10.3. *For the TSP, when a city is removed each tour is updated by simply removing this city so that its successor and predecessor become neighbors in the tour. When a city is added, each combination is updated by inserting this city into the tour at the place of smallest length increase.*

10.3. Optimization problems over continuous domains

10.3.1. *Definition of continuous optimization problems*

Continuous Optimization Problems (CnOPs) are defined such that the domains of the variables are continuous intervals in $\mathbb{R}$. Typically, applications dealing with geometrical objects often involve CnOPs as variables which represent coordinates or distances usually defined over continuous domains. CnOPs are not combinatorial problems and solving them cannot be reduced to the review of a finite set of combinations.

More formally, a CnOP may be defined by a quadruple (X, D, C, f) such that X is a finite set of variables. For every variable $x_i \in X$, $D(x_i) \subseteq \mathbb{R}$ is the domain of x_i, C is a set of numerical constraints and $f : X \to \mathbb{R}$ is an objective function. The goal is to find an assignment of values to the variables of X that satisfies all constraints of C and minimizes f.

Some CnOPs may be solved by dedicated algorithms. Linear programs are particular cases of CnOPs such that the objective function f and the constraints C are linear. These linear programs are solved very efficiently by combining Simplex and Gauss algorithms. CnOPs may generally be solved by using interval methods which extend classical arithmetic operators to continuous intervals and constraint propagation methods to interval propagation such as Numerica [VAN 97].

Some metaheuristics introduced in Chapter 5 such as GA or PSO may be used in a very straightforward way to solve CnOPs. The construction of new combinations (by crossover and mutation for GAs and by combining a velocity with a current position for PSO) is even simpler when domains are defined over the reals as there is no need to ensure that the constructed combination has integer values.

10.3.2. *Solving continuous optimization problems with ACO*

The extension of ACO to solve CnOPs is not straightforward. Indeed, the pheromone structure which is used to progressively bias transition probabilities contains a finite set of components. To solve CnOPs with ACO, we may discretize continuous domains, i.e. split each continuous interval into a finite set of smaller intervals.

Example 10.4. *Let us consider the continuous interval* $[4.3; 4.7]$*. This interval may be split into smaller intervals:*

$$[4.3; 4.7] = [4.3; 4.4[\cup [4.4; 4.5[\cup [4.5; 4.6[\cup [4.6; 4.7].$$

A symbolic value l_I *may be associated with each interval* I *so that the continuous interval* $[4.3; 4.7]$ *may be modeled by the set* $\{l_{[4.3,4.4[}, l_{[4.4;4.5[}, l_{[4.5;4.6[}, l_{[4.6;4.7]}\}$.

However, depending on the size of the initial intervals and the required precision, such a discretization may lead to huge domains and ACO may therefore perform poorly.

We now describe an extension of ACO called $ACO_\mathbb{R}$, introduced by Socha and Dorigo to solve CnOPs (see [SOC 08] for more details). As for ACO, $ACO_\mathbb{R}$ builds candidate solutions (i.e. assignments) in a greedy randomized way and probabilistic choices are progressively biased with respect to past constructions. However, the finite pheromone structure used to bias probabilities in ACO is replaced by an archive T which contains the k best assignments built since the beginning of the search. This archive is initialized by k assignments, randomly constructed according to a uniform distribution.

At each cycle of $ACO_\mathbb{R}$, each ant builds an assignment in a greedy randomized way. Starting from an empty assignment, it iteratively chooses a value for a non-assigned variable until all variables have been assigned. Given a non-assigned variable x_i, the value to be assigned to x_i is chosen in two steps.

– In a first step, the ant randomly chooses an assignment $\mathcal{A}_l \in T$ with respect to a probability p_l which is proportional to its weight ω_l, i.e.

$$p_l = \frac{\omega_l}{\sum_{\mathcal{A}_r \in T} \omega_r}$$

where the weight ω_l of an assignment $\mathcal{A}_l \in T$ depends on its quality $f(\mathcal{A}_l)$. Let $x \in \{1, \ldots, k\}$ be the rank of $\mathcal{A}_l$ in T (i.e. $\mathcal{A}_l$ is the xth best assignment of the archive) and the weight of $\mathcal{A}_l$ is

$$\omega_l = \frac{\exp(-\frac{x-1)^2}{2q^2k^2})}{qk\sqrt{2\pi}}$$

where q is a parameter such that the lower its value, the more the better-ranked assignments are preferred.

– In a second step, the ant randomly chooses a value $v_i \in D(x_i)$ with respect to a Gaussian distribution. The mean μ_i of this Gaussian distribution is defined by the value of x_i in $\mathcal{A}_l$ (denoted x_i^l). The standard deviation σ_i of the Gaussian distribution is defined with respect to the average distance between the value of x_i in $\mathcal{A}_l$ and the values of x_i in the other assignments in the archive:

$$\sigma_i = \xi \frac{\sum_{\mathcal{A}_r \in T} |x_i^l - x_i^r|}{Card(T)}$$

where $\xi > 0$ is a parameter which is used to tune the convergence speed. When the value of ξ is increased, the standard deviation is increased so that the probability of choosing a value significantly different from $\mu_i = x_i^l$ is increased. Hence, the higher the value of ξ, the lower the convergence speed.

Once every ant has built an assignment, the archive T is updated so that it contains the k best assignments constructed since the beginning of the search.

Socha and Dorigo have conducted experiments to compare $\text{ACO}_{\mathbb{R}}$ to other existing metaheuristics for solving CnOPs such as GAs and PSO. Experimental results have shown that $\text{ACO}_{\mathbb{R}}$ obtains competitive results (see [SOC 08] for more details).

Chapter 11

Implementation Issues

An ACO algorithm basically iterates on cycles that alternate greedy randomized constructions with pheromone updating steps. The core of the implementation is the procedure that greedily builds a combination. A first key point for an efficient implementation of this procedure is to design incremental data structures to efficiently evaluate the pheromone and heuristic factors. This point is discussed in section 11.1. A second key point is the implementation of the procedure that randomly chooses a component with respect to probabilities, discussed in section 11.2. In section 11.3, we discuss some issues related to the hybridization of ACO with a local search procedure that improves the combinations constructed by ants. Finally, in section 11.4, we show how to efficiently compute the resampling and similarity ratios that were introduced in section 9.4.

11.1. Data structures

There are three sets of data structures that must be maintained during an ACO run: data structures associated with pheromone factors, with heuristic factors and with ants.

11.1.1. *Data structures associated with pheromone factors*

During an ACO run, a data structure which gives its pheromone factor for each combination component has to be maintained. In many cases, the pheromone structure is an n-dimensional array which associates a quantity of pheromone to a tuple corresponding to a component. The pheromone factor is obtained by simple access to an element of this array.

Example 11.1. *For the traveling salesman problem, quadratic assignment problem or the car sequencing problem, the pheromone structure is maintained in a 2D array that gives the quantity of pheromone laying on a binary component: a couple of cities for the traveling salesman problem, a couple of facilities/locations for the quadratic assignment problem or a couple of cars for the car sequencing problem.*

In some cases, it may occur that the pheromone factor associated with a component is not statically defined by the quantity of pheromone laying on this component. It may be defined by an aggregation of pheromone trails that depends on the partial combination under construction, so that the pheromone factor dynamically changes during the construction of a combination by an ant. In this case, we may introduce an additional data structure which is associated with every ant and which is used to incrementally update pheromone factors during the construction of a combination.

Example 11.2. *For the MKP defined in problem 3.1, we may define the pheromone factor associated with a candidate object i as the sum of all pheromone trails laid between i and every object that has already been selected by the ant in the partial combination S. This pheromone factor represents the learnt desirability of selecting object i when the objects of S have already been selected (see Chapter 13 for more details).*

In this case, we have to maintain a first data structure (a 2D array) which gives the quantity of pheromone laying on each pair of objects. We also have to maintain a second data structure for each ant (a 1D array) which gives the pheromone factor associated with each candidate object i: this array is initialized to zero. Each time an object j is selected, it is updated by adding the quantity of pheromone laying on the pair (i, j). This allows the pheromone factor to be calculated in $\mathcal{O}(1)$ instead of $\mathcal{O}(card(S))$.

In all cases, the array that contains the pheromone structure is updated at the end of each cycle once every ant has constructed a combination regarding the evaporation and pheromone-laying steps.

11.1.2. *Data structures associated with heuristic factors*

The data structures associated with heuristic factors depend on the problem to be solved. For some problems, the heuristic factor is *static*, i.e. the heuristic factor associated with a component does not change during the construction of a combination.

Example 11.3. *For the TSP defined in problem 8.1, the heuristic factor associated with the edge (i, j) is proportionally inverse to the distance d_{ij}. This implies that η_{ij} is always equal to $1/d_{ij}$ during the whole ACO run.*

For the MKP defined in problem 3.1, the heuristic factor associated with an object i may be defined by a ratio between its profit p_i and its dimensions d_{ik}. This implies that η_i is always equal to $p_i / \sum_{j \in \{1,...,k\}} d_{ij}$ during the whole ACO run.

When the heuristic factor is static, it may be computed once and stored in an array at the beginning of the search process. Note that, in this case, it is best to compute and store the heuristic factor weighted by the parameter β, thus avoiding having to recompute η^{β} for each transition step.

The heuristic factor is *dynamic* for other problems, i.e. the heuristic factor associated with a component depends on the partial combination under construction.

Example 11.4. *For the multidimensional knapsack problem, the heuristic factor associated with an object i may be defined by a ratio between its profit p_i and its relative dimensions d_{ik} with respect to the space left in the knapsack. More precisely, let S be the set of objects that have already been selected in the current combination under construction, and let x_j be the space left in dimension j when all objects of S have been stored in the knapsack (i.e. $x_j = c_j - \sum_{k \in S} d_{kj}$). We define the dynamic heuristic factor associated with an object i by $\eta_i = p_i / (x_i - d_i)$ (provided that $x_i \leq d_i$).*

For constraint satisfaction problems, the heuristic factor associated with the assignment of a variable to a value is usually defined with respect to the number of new constraint violations due to this assignment. This number clearly depends on the previous assignments made so that it dynamically changes after each variable assignment (see Chapter 13 for more details).

When the heuristic factor is dynamic, it is best to maintain a data structure that is incrementally updated each time a component is added to the combination under construction, thus allowing the heuristic factor to be computed efficiently.

11.1.3. *Data structures associated with ants*

For each ant, three data structures must be maintained:

– The first data structure contains the current combination built by the ant. This data structure is usually a 1D array which is updated, at each step of the combination construction by an ant, by simply adding the selected component.

– The second data structure contains the value of the objective function associated with the current combination built by the ant. This data structure is usually incrementally updated at each step of the combination construction by an ant, with respect to the selected component.

Example 11.5. *For the traveling salesman problem, the objective value is increased by the distance between the most recently visited city and the newly selected city. For the multidimensional knapsack, the objective value is increased by the profit of the newly selected object.*

– The third data structure contains the set of candidate components that may be added to the current combination built by the ant. In some cases, such as the traveling salesman problem, this data structure is updated at each step of the combination construction by an ant by simply removing the last selected component. In other cases, such as the multidimensional knapsack problem, components which violate the problem-dependent constraints with respect to the last selected component must be removed.

11.2. Selection of a component with respect to probabilities

During greedy randomized constructions, the selection of components with respect to probabilities should be implemented carefully as this step is at the core of the algorithm. Indeed, at each iteration of a greedy construction, a candidate component $i \in Cand$ is chosen with respect to the probability $p_S(i)$ defined by equation (8.1). From a practical point of view, this choice is implemented in two steps.

The first step involves the computation, for each candidate $i \in Cand$, of its attractivity $\mathcal{A}(i)$ which corresponds to the numerator of equation (8.1), i.e.

$$\mathcal{A}(i) = [\tau_S(i)]^\alpha \cdot [\eta_S(i)]^\beta.$$

Note that if parameters α and β have integer values, library exponentiation functions which have been designed for floating point powers (such as the function *pow* of the library *math.h* of the C language) should not be used: these functions are much more time consuming than those that raise a value to an integer power.

The second step involves the choice of a candidate $i \in Cand$ with respect to a probability proportional to its attractivity $\mathcal{A}(i)$. This choice is made similarly to a roulette wheel in a casino: for each candidate, the proportion of the wheel associated with this candidate is defined by its attractivity $\mathcal{A}(i)$. The rotation of the wheel is simulated by randomly generating a floating point number within $[0; 1[$ according to a uniform distribution law, and by selecting the candidate whose proportion corresponds to f.

Example 11.6. *Let us consider the case of four candidates* c_1, c_2, c_3 *and* c_4 *such that:*

$$\mathcal{A}(c_1) = 2, \ \mathcal{A}(c_2) = 1, \ \mathcal{A}(c_3) = 1 \ and \ \mathcal{A}(c_4) = 4$$

so that choice probabilities are:

$$p(c_1) = 1/4, \ p(c_2) = 1/8, \ p(c_3) = 1/8 \ and \ p(c_4) = 1/2.$$

The corresponding roulette wheel is depicted in Figure 11.1.

In this case,
– c_1 is selected if $0 \leq f < 1/4$;
– c_2 is selected if $1/4 \leq f < 3/8$;
– c_3 is selected if $3/8 \leq f < 1/2$; and
– c_4 is selected if $f \geq 1/2$.

This roulette wheel selection is repeated often, i.e. at each step of each combination construction. It must therefore be implemented carefully. To this aim, we use an array *sum* indexed on the set of candidates $\{1, \ldots, nbCand\}$: for each candidate $i \in \{1, \ldots, nbCand\}$, $sum[i]$ contains the sum of the attractivities of all candidates that precede i, including i. A floating point number $f \in [0; 1[$ is then randomly generated with respect to a uniform distribution law and the corresponding index is searched in the array: this index is the smallest $i \in \{1, \ldots, nbCand\}$ such that $f < sum[i]/total$ where *total* is the sum of all attractivities, i.e. $total = sum[nbCand]$.

Algorithm 11.1: dichotomicSearch($nbCand, sum, f$)

Input:
    an integer $nbCand$
    an array sum indexed from 1 to $nbCand$
    a floating point value $f \in [0; 1[$

Precondition:
    $\forall i \in 1, \ldots, nbCand, \; sum[i] = \sum_{j=1}^{i} \mathcal{A}(j)$

Postrelation:
    returns the smallest integer $i \in [1; nbCand]$ such that
    $f < \frac{sum[i]}{sum[nbCand]}$

1 **begin**
2 | $total \leftarrow sum[nbCand]$
3 | $left \leftarrow 1$
4 | $right \leftarrow nbCand$
5 | **while** $left < right$ **do**
       | /* Invariant property: ($left = 1$ and
       | $f < sum[right]/total$) or
       | ($sum[left - 1]/total \leq f < sum[right]/total$)   */
6 | $middle \leftarrow (left + right + 1)/2$
7 | **if** $f < sum[middle - 1]/total$ **then**
8 | | $right \leftarrow middle - 1$
9 | **else if** $f \geq sum[middle]/total$ **then**
10 | | $left \leftarrow middle + 1$
11 | **else**
       | /* $sum[middle - 1] \leq f < sum[middle]$ */
12 | | **return** $middle$
13 | **return** $left$
14 **end**

In the previous example, we compute the array:

sum : | 2 | 3 | 4 | 8 |
      c_1 c_2 c_3 c_4

such that c_1 is selected if $0 \leq f < 2/8$; c_2 is selected if $2/8 \leq f < 3/8$; etc.

If the number of candidates is small enough, a candidate may be selected by sequentially scanning the array *sum*. However, if the number of candidates

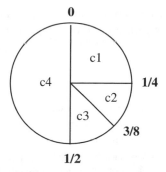

Figure 11.1. *Roulette wheel associated with probabilities* $p(c_1) = 1/4$,
$p(c_2) = p(c_3) = 1/8$ *and* $p(c_4) = 1/2$

is large, it is preferable to select candidates by performing a dichotomic search as described in algorithm 11.1. The complexity of selecting a candidate in this case is $\mathcal{O}(\log_2(nbCand))$ instead of $\mathcal{O}(nbCand)$ (however, the computation of the array *sum* is still $\mathcal{O}(nbCand)$).

11.3. Implementation of a local search procedure

Once a combination has been constructed by an ant, it may be improved by applying some local search procedures (such as those described in section 5.2). A key point for efficient implementation of a local search procedure relies on the use of incremental data structures. These allow us to efficiently evaluate the impact of a move on the objective function.

We shall not develop these techniques in this book. The interested reader may refer to [VAN 05] and [STÜ 04] for more details, however.

11.4. Computation of diversification/intensification measures

The resampling and similarity ratios are both useful for tuning an ACO algorithm. The evolution of these ratios during the solution process allows over-diversification or over-intensification phenomenon to be dynamically detected. In particular, when the resampling ratio increases, the search is over-intensified and it should be more diversified in order to avoid stagnation. On the contrary, when the similarity ratio does not increase, the search is over-diversified, implying that it behaves as for a pure random search.

These two ratios may be incrementally computed during the construction of combinations without significantly increasing CPU times.

11.4.1. *Resampling ratio*

The resampling ratio may be approximated very quickly by using a hash table. Each time a combination is constructed, two different hash keys are computed (this may be done in an incremental way during the construction of the combination). The first key yields the entry index in the table. The second key is stored in the table (instead of storing the whole combination, as this would be too expensive both with respect to memory consumption and the CPU time needed to compare combinations).

This technique allows resamplings to be detected with a very small error rate which corresponds to the probability that two different combinations have exactly the same two hash keys. Indeed, if a combination is resampled, then it has the same couple of hash keys as a previously computed combination and a collision occurs in the table, thus indicating a resampling.

However, there is a small probability that two different combinations have the same hash key couples. This probability may be set as small as necessary by increasing the size of the hash table and choosing appropriate hashing functions that ensure a uniform distribution of hash keys (see [COR 90] for more details on hash tables). Note also that this error rate is pessimistic, i.e. the approximated resampling rate gives an upper bound for the real resampling rate.

11.4.2. *Similarity ratio*

The similarity ratio of a set of n combinations, where each combination is composed of m components, may be measured by computing the intersection of each pair of combinations. The resulting algorithm has a time complexity of $\mathcal{O}(n^2m)$. A much more efficient method of measuring this similarity ratio consists of maintaining an array freq such that, for each combination component i, freq[i] is equal to the number of combinations that contain the component i. In this case, the similarity ratio of a set S of combinations is given by:

$$\frac{\sum_{i \in comp}(\texttt{freq[i]} \times (\texttt{freq[i]} - 1))}{(card(S) - 1) \times \sum_{s_k \in S} card(s_k)}$$

where *comp* is the set of combination components of S, i.e.

$$comp = \{i \mid \exists s_k \in S, i \text{ is a component of } S_k\}.$$

This computation may be carried out incrementally during the construction of the combinations; see [MOR 01] for more details.

PART III

CP with ACO

Introduction to Part III

The first ant-based algorithm proposed by Dorigo in 1992 was applied to the traveling salesman problem. Since this pioneering work, ACO has been applied to a large number of combinatorial optimization problems and has shown to be very competitive for many challenging problems.

However, solving a new combinatorial optimization problem with ACO usually implies a fastidious work of modeling and implementation. First, an appropriate pheromone structure has to be designed which is able to guide the search towards the best combinations. The resulting ACO algorithm then has to be efficiently implemented. If procedures that manage and exploit pheromone structures may be partly reused from one ACO algorithm to another, the programmer often has to design and implement problem-dependent data structures which allow an efficient and incremental evaluation of the heuristic factors associated with candidate components and the objective function.

An appealing solution which can ease the use of ACO for solving new combinatorial problems is to integrate ACO within a constraint programming language. The user states their problem in a high-level declarative language by means of constraints; this problem is then automatically solved by an embedded ACO solver.

In Part III, we study the feasibility of such an ACO CP approach. We first show in the following two chapters that the ACO metaheuristic may be used to efficiently solve constraint satisfaction problems. In Chapter 12, we consider a particular CSP, i.e. the car sequencing problem introduced in section 3.7. This problem is emblematic and has already been tackled by a large number of different approaches. It is therefore interesting to evaluate the capabilities of ant colonies in this problem.

In Chapter 13, we expand the study to any kind of constraint satisfaction problem without *a priori* knowledge of the constraints used, provided that all domains are finite sets of values. In this case, solving a constraint satisfaction problem may be viewed as a subset selection problem. Given a set of variable/value couples (representing all possible variable assignments), the goal is to find a subset of couples corresponding to a complete assignment and satisfying as many constraints as possible. We show how to solve such subset selection problems with the ant colony optimization metaheuristics. We evaluate the performance of this approach on randomly generated binary instances such as those introduced in section 3.6 and on instances used for a constraint solver competition which took place in 2006.

In Chapter 14, we describe a framework for integrating ACO into a constraint programming library. This integration allows us to apply all the modeling work that has been carried out in the constraint programming community since the 1980s. More importantly, it enables us to reuse the many procedures that have been implemented for defining, checking and propagating constraints.

Finally, we conclude this book with Chapter 15 which provides general hints on the design of a real constraint programming language based on ant colony optimization.

Chapter 12

Sequencing Cars with ACO

We now illustrate the abilities of the ACO metaheuristic when applied to the car sequencing problem introduced in section 3.7. This is a rather straightforward application of ACO as it may be modeled as a best path-finding problem in a very natural way. An interesting feature of this problem, however, is that two complementary pheromone structures can be combined: the first is used to learn good subsequences of cars whereas the second is used to identify critical cars. Combining these two structures allows ACO to obtain very competitive results.

We first introduce some notation used in this chapter in section 12.1. We then describe in sections 12.2, 12.3 and 12.4 three ACO algorithms for the car sequencing problem. The first ACO algorithm uses pheromone to learn of good subsequences of cars. The second ACO algorithm uses pheromone to identify the most critical cars and the third ACO algorithm combines the pheromone structures of the first two. We experimentally compare these three ACO algorithms in section 12.5. Finally, we compare the best ACO algorithm with state-of-the art approaches for this problem in section 12.6.

12.1. Notation

The car sequencing problem has been described in section 3.7. Given an instance (C, O, p, q, r), we use the following notation to denote and manipulate sequences:

– a *sequence*, denoted $\pi = <c_{i_1}, c_{i_2}, \ldots, c_{i_k}>$, is a succession of cars;

– the set of all sequences that may be built with a set of cars C is denoted Π_C;

– the *length* of a sequence π, denoted $|\pi|$, is the number of cars that it contains;

– the *concatenation* of two sequences π_1 and π_2, denoted $\pi_1 \cdot \pi_2$, is the sequence composed of the cars of π_1 followed by the cars of π_2;

– a sequence π_s is a *subsequence* of another sequence π, denoted $\pi_s \subseteq \pi$, if there exist two (possibly empty) sequences π_i and π_j such that $\pi = \pi_i \cdot \pi_s \cdot \pi_j$;

– the number of cars requiring an option o_i in a sequence π (respectively, in a set S) of cars is denoted $r(\pi, o_i)$ (respectively, $r(S, o_i)$) and is defined $r(\pi, o_i) = \sum_{<c_l> \sqsubseteq \pi} r(c_l, o_i)$ (respectively, $r(S, o_i) = \sum_{c_l \in S} r(c_l, o_i)$);

– the *cost* of a sequence π is the number of violated capacity constraints, i.e.

$$cost(\pi) \quad = \quad \sum_{o_i \in O} \quad \sum_{\substack{\pi_k \sqsubseteq \pi \text{ such that} \\ |\pi_k| = q(o_i)}} violation(\pi_k, o_i)$$

$$\text{where } violation(\pi_k, o_i) \quad = \quad \begin{cases} 0 & \text{if } r(\pi_k, o_i) \leq p(o_i); \\ 1 & \text{otherwise.} \end{cases}$$

– the class of a car is defined by the set of options that must be installed in this car, i.e.

$$\forall c_i \in C, class(c_i) = \{o_k \in O \mid r(c_i, o_k) = 1\}.$$

12.2. A first pheromone structure for identifying good car sequences

Solving an instance (C, O, p, q, r) of the car sequencing problem involves finding a permutation of the set of cars C that satisfies the capacity constraints defined by p and q. This problem can easily be modeled as the search for a best Hamiltonian path in a graph that associates a vertex with each car. Such Hamiltonian path-finding problems are classical applications for the ACO metaheuristic. For these problems, ants lay pheromone on the graph edges in order to learn of promising sequences of vertices. We describe a first ACO algorithm based on this principle in this section.

Basically, the algorithm follows the MAX-MIN Ant System scheme [STÜ 00] which is described in algorithm 12.1. In order to better control the balance between intensification and diversification, the MAX-MIN Ant System introduces the following features:

– pheromone trails are bound between $\tau_{\min}$ and $\tau_{\max}$ such that $0 < \tau_{\min} < \tau_{\max}$ in order to limit the relative differences between pheromone trails, thus ensuring a good diversification;

– pheromone trails are initialized to the maximal bound $\tau_{\max}$ in order to improve diversification at the beginning of the search process; and

– only the best combinations are rewarded at the end of each cycle, in order to intensify the search around these best combinations.

Algorithm 12.1: MAX-MIN Ant System

---

1 **begin**
2 | Initialize pheromone trails to $\tau_{\max}$
3 | **repeat**
4 | | Each ant builds a combination
5 | | Evaporate pheromone trails by multiplying them by $1 - \rho$
6 | | Lay pheromone trails with respect to the best combinations
7 | | **if** *a pheromone trail is smaller than* $\tau_{\min}$ **then** set it to $\tau_{\min}$
8 | | **if** *a pheromone trail is greater than* $\tau_{\max}$ **then** set it to $\tau_{\max}$
9 | **until** *maximum number of cycles reached* **or** *optimal solution found* ;
10 **end**

We describe the pheromone structure, the procedure used by ants to build car sequences and the pheromone laying step in the following sections.

12.2.1. *Pheromone structure*

The construction graph associated with an instance (C, O, p, q, r) is the complete directed graph which associates a vertex with each car $c_i \in C$. Ants communicate by laying pheromone trails on the edges of this graph. The quantity of pheromone laying on an edge $(c_i, c_j) \in C \times C$ is denoted $\tau_1(c_i, c_j)$. Intuitively, this pheromone trail represents the learnt desirability of scheduling car c_j just after car c_i.

Let us first note that, contrary to the traveling salesman problem, the construction graph is directed. As a consequence, $\tau_1(c_i, c_j)$ and $\tau_1(c_j, c_i)$ may have different values.

Let us also note that the construction graph associates one vertex with each car and not each car class (which groups all cars requiring the same sets of options into the same class). Indeed, the goal here is to determine a good sequence of cars.

If car classes do not contain the same number of cars, then we should be able to determine that the first car of class cl_1 should be just before a car of the class cl_2, whereas the second car of the class cl_1 should be followed by a car of the class cl_3.

12.2.2. *Construction of a sequence by an ant*

Algorithm 12.2 describes the greedy randomized procedure used by ants to build sequences: starting from an empty sequence cars are iteratively added at the end of the sequence until all cars have been sequenced. The sequence π could be initialized to a non-empty sequence in order to take into account the last cars sequenced on the line the previous day, as is the case in the problem proposed by Renault for the ROADEF challenge.

At each step, the set of candidate cars (*cand*) is restricted to the set of cars that introduce the smallest number of new constraint violations (line 5).

Note that this elitist strategy, which discards cars introducing more constraint violations, may not be optimal for solving overconstrained instances. To solve these, it may be preferable not to discard cars introducing more constraint violations but to decrease the probability of selecting them, as proposed in [GRA 04, SOL 00].

To break symmetries, we also restrict the set of candidate cars to those which require different options. This is done by keeping, for each car class, the non-sequenced car that has the smallest number (line 6). Given this set of candidate cars, the next car is chosen with respect to a transition probability function *proba* which is a parameter of the function *buildSequence*.

For this first ACO algorithm, this transition probability function is defined as follows:

Algorithm 12.2: buildSequence

Input:

an instance (C, O, p, q, r) of the car sequencing problem

a transition probability function $proba : C \times \mathcal{P}(C) \times \Pi_C \rightarrow]0; 1]$

Postrelation:

returns a sequence π which is a permutation of C

1 **begin**

2    $\pi \leftarrow <>$

3    $Cand \leftarrow C$

4   **while** $Cand \neq \emptyset$ **do**

5        $Cand' \leftarrow \{c_k \in Cand \mid \forall c_j \in Cand, cost(\pi . <c_k>) \leq cost(\pi . <c_j>)\}$

6        $Cand'' \leftarrow \{c_k \in Cand' \mid \forall c_j \in Cand', class(c_k) = class(c_j) \Rightarrow k \leq j\}$

7   choose $c_i \in Cand''$ with respect to probability $proba(c_i, Cand'', \pi)$

8        $\pi \leftarrow \pi \cdot <c_i>$

9   remove c_i from $Cand$

10   **return** π

11 **end**

---

if $\pi - <>$ **then**

$$proba(c_i, Cand'', \pi) = \frac{[\eta(c_i, \pi)]^\beta}{\sum_{c_k \in Cand''} [\eta(c_k, \pi)]^\beta}$$

else

let c_j be the last car of π so that $\pi = \pi' . <c_j>$

$$proba(c_i, Cand'', \pi) = \frac{[\tau_1(c_j, c_i)]^{\alpha_1} \cdot [\eta(c_i, \pi)]^\beta}{\sum_{c_k \in Cand''} [\tau_1(c_j, c_k)]^{\alpha_1} \cdot [\eta(c_k, \pi)]^\beta}$$

where

– $\eta(c_i, \pi)$ is a heuristic factor defined below;

– $\tau_1(c_j, c_i)$ is the pheromone factor which represents the past experience of the colony with respect to sequencing car c_i just after the last car c_j sequenced in π (this pheromone factor is ignored when choosing the first car of the sequence); and

– α_1 and β are two parameters that allow these two factors to be balanced.

We have introduced and compared in [GOT 03] five different definitions for the heuristic function η for the car sequencing problem. These definitions are based on utilization rates of required options and favor the choice of cars requiring options with high demands with respect to capacities. The heuristic function which obtained the best average results is defined as:

$$\eta(c_i, \pi) = \sum_{o_j \in O} r(c_i, o_j) \cdot \frac{\text{reqSlots}(o_j, n_j)}{card(Cand)}$$

where n_j is the number of cars that require option o_j and have not yet been sequenced in π (i.e. $n_j = r(Cand, o_j)$) and $\text{reqSlots}(o_j, n_j)$ is the smallest number of slots that allows n_j cars requiring option o_j to be sequenced without violating the capacity constraint associated with o_j. For the definition of $\text{reqSlots}(o_j, n_j)$, we consider the formula introduced in [BOY 07]. The latter is more accurate than that used in [GOT 03] because it takes into account the fact that n_j may not be a multiple of q_j, i.e.

if $n_j \% p_j = 0$ **then**

$$\text{reqSlots}(o_j, n_j) = q_j \cdot \frac{n_j}{p_j} - q_j + p_j$$

else

$$\text{reqSlots}(o_j, n_j) = q_j \cdot \frac{n_j - n_j \% p_j}{p_j} + n_j \% p_j$$

where $\%$ is the modulo operator which returns the rest of the integer division.

12.2.3. *Pheromone laying step*

Once every ant has constructed a sequence, pheromone trails are updated. First, all pheromone trails are decreased in order to simulate evaporation. Pheromone trails are then laid in order to further attract ants towards the corresponding areas of the search space.

We consider an elitist strategy, where only the best ants of the cycle (those which have constructed a minimum cost sequence) lay pheromone. These best ants lay pheromone on edges corresponding to couples of consecutively visited cars, and the quantity of pheromone laid is inversely proportional to the number of violated constraints.

More precisely, let S_π be the set of sequences constructed during the last cycle. The pheromone laying step is defined as:

for each sequence $\pi_i \in S_\pi$ **do**
  if $\forall \pi_k \in S_\pi, cost(\pi_k) \geq cost(\pi_i)$ **then**
    for each couple of consecutive cars $< c_j, c_l > \sqsubseteq \pi_i$ **do**

$$\tau_1(c_j, c_l) \leftarrow \tau_1(c_j, c_l) + \frac{1}{cost(\pi_i)}.$$

12.3. A second pheromone structure for identifying critical cars

The heuristic function η combined with the first pheromone structure in the transition probability function defined in section 12.2 favors the choice of critical cars, i.e. cars that require options with high utilization rates so that they cannot be scheduled without violating capacity constraints. We now introduce a new pheromone structure for identifying these critical cars with respect to past experiences of the colony.

12.3.1. *Pheromone structure*

Pheromone trails are laid on car classes, which group all the cars requiring the same subset of options. Given a set C of cars, the set of all car classes is defined by

$$classes(C) = \{class(c_i) \mid c_i \in C\}$$

Given a car class $cc \in classes(C)$, we denote the quantity of pheromone laying on it as $\tau_2(cc)$. Intuitively, this quantity represents the past experience of the colony concerning the difficulty of sequencing cars of this class without violating capacity constraints.

Contrary to the first pheromone structure introduced in section 12.2, the second pheromone structure introduced here is not managed according to the MAX-MIN Ant System of [STÜ 00]. Indeed, imposing lower and upper bounds on pheromone trails and initializing them to the upper bound favor a larger exploration of the search space at the beginning of the search. However, as a counterpart, the time spent before converging towards good solutions is increased.

First experiments showed us that it is necessary to quickly identify critical cars to build good solutions: without such identification (for example, when running algorithm 12.2 with the β parameter set to zero), the constructed sequences violate hundreds of capacity constraints. Hence, to favor a quicker feedback on the critical cars we only introduce a lower bound τ_{min_2} (ensuring that the probability of choosing a car cannot become null), and pheromone trails are initialized to the lower bound τ_{min_2} at the beginning of the search.

12.3.2. *Construction of a sequence by an ant*

Ants incrementally build sequences following algorithm 12.2 which was introduced in section 12.2. To choose the next car c_i to be added at the end of the current sequence π, the transition probability function only depends on a pheromone factor which evaluates the learnt hardness of the class of c_i, i.e.

$$proba(c_i, Cand'', \pi) = \frac{[\tau_2(class(c_i))]^{\alpha_2}}{\sum_{c_k \in Cand''}[\tau_2(class(c_k))]^{\alpha_2}}$$

where α_2 is a numerical parameter which allows the weight of the pheromone factor to be tuned.

12.3.3. *Pheromone updating step*

Ants lay pheromone on car classes during the construction of sequences: each time a car cannot be scheduled without introducing new constraint violations, some pheromone is added to the classes of cars that still have to be scheduled (thus indicating that the cars of these classes should have been scheduled earlier). The quantity of pheromone added is equal to the number of new constraint violations introduced by the cars of this class. More precisely, we modify algorithm 12.2 by inserting the following lines between lines 4 and 5:

> **if** $\forall c_i \in cand,\ cost(\pi.<c_i>) - cost(\pi) > 0$ **then**
>   **for** each car class $cc \in classes(Cand)$ **do**
> $\tau_2(cc) \leftarrow \tau_2(cc) + cost(\pi.<cc>) - cost(\pi)$

Note that this pheromone laying procedure occurs during the construction step and not after all ants have completed their construction step, which is the case for most ACO algorithms. Indeed, the quantity of pheromone laid does not depend on the global quality of the sequence but on the local evaluation of the car class with respect to the partial sequence that is currently built. Note also that every ant adds pheromone.

Finally, pheromone is evaporated after every sequence construction. This is completed by multiplying the quantity of pheromone $\tau_2(cc)$ laying on each car class $cc \in classes(C)$ by a factor $(1 - \rho_2)$ where ρ_2 is the evaporation rate such that $0 \leq \rho_2 \leq 1$.

12.4. Combining the two pheromone structures

The two proposed pheromone structures achieve two complementary goals: the first identifies promising subsequences of cars and the second identifies critical car classes. These two complementary pheromone structures can therefore be combined in a single ACO algorithm.

12.4.1. *First pheromone structure*

Ants lay pheromone on couples of cars $(c_i, c_j) \in C \times C$ and the quantity of pheromone $\tau_1(c_i, c_j)$ represents the past experience of the colony with respect to sequencing car c_j just after car c_i.

For this first pheromone structure, pheromone trails are bound within the interval $[\tau_{\min_1}; \tau_{\max_1}]$ and are initialized to the upper bound $\tau_{\max_1}$. Pheromone trails are updated at the end of each cycle once every ant of the colony has computed a complete sequence, only the best ants of the cycle lay pheromone.

12.4.2. *Second pheromone structure*

Ants also lay pheromone on car classes $cc \in classes(C)$ and the quantity of pheromone $\tau_2(cc)$ represents the past experience of the colony with respect to the difficulty of sequencing cars of the class cc without violating constraints.

For this second pheromone structure, a lower bound $\tau_{\min_2}$ is imposed and pheromone trails are initialized to this lower bound. Pheromone is laid by every ant while it constructs a sequence, and the evaporation step occurs at the end of every sequence construction by an ant.

12.4.3. *Construction of a sequence by an ant*

Ants use the procedure described in algorithm 12.2 to build their sequences. However, they consider a new definition of the transition probability function.

This probability now depends on two different pheromone factors: the first evaluates the interest of sequencing the candidate car just after the previously sequenced car and the second evaluates the hardness of sequencing the candidate car. These two factors are weighted by the parameters α_1 and α_2, respectively, that allow them to be balanced. More precisely, the probability is defined as:

if $\pi =<>$ **then**

$$proba(c_i, Cand'', \pi) = \frac{[\tau_2(class(c_i))]^{\alpha_2}}{\sum_{c_k \in Cand''}[\tau_2(class(c_k))]^{\alpha_2}}$$

else

let c_j be the last car sequenced in π so that $\pi = \pi'. < c_j >$

$$proba(c_i, Cand'', \pi) = \frac{[\tau_1(c_j, c_i)]^{\alpha_1} \cdot [\tau_2(class(c_i))]^{\alpha_2}}{\sum_{c_k \in Cand''}[\tau_1(c_j, c_k)]^{\alpha_1} \cdot [\tau_2(class(c_k))]^{\alpha_2}}$$

12.5. Comparison of the different ACO algorithms

12.5.1. *Considered algorithms*

To compare the pheromone structures τ_1 and τ_2 and the greedy heuristic function η, we consider four different instantiations of algorithm 12.2 based on four different definitions of the transition probability function *proba*:

1) In Greedy(η), the transition probability function *proba* is defined as in section 12.2 but the pheromone factor is ignored by setting the weight of this factor, α_1, to zero. Hence, this algorithm only uses the heuristic function η to choose cars. As the pheromone factor is ignored, the procedures of pheromone laying and evaporation are not performed.

2) In ACO(τ_1, η), the transition probability function *proba* is based on a combination of the first pheromone structure τ_1 and the greedy heuristic function η as described in section 12.2.

3) In ACO(τ_2), the transition probability function *proba* is based on the second pheromone structure τ_2 as described in section 12.3.

4) In ACO(τ_1, τ_2), the transition probability function *proba* is based on a combination of the two pheromone structures τ_1 and τ_2 as described in section 12.4.

All algorithms have been implemented in C and run on a 2 GHz Pentium 4.

12.5.2. Test suite

Many algorithms for the car sequencing problem, and more particularly those embedded in constraint programming languages, are evaluated on a benchmark initially introduced by Lee in [LEE 98]. This benchmark is available in the CSPlib benchmarking library [GEN 99] and contains 70 feasible instances. Each instance has 200 cars and 5 options.

These instances are trivially solved by the four different instantiations of algorithm 12.2. In particular, Greedy(η) is able to solve every instance of the benchmark in 17 constructions on average (106 constructions for the hardest instance of the benchmark and 1 construction for the easiest ones). The CPU time required to solve each instance is lower than 0.01 sec.

In order to evaluate ACO algorithms and compare the different pheromone structures, we therefore consider a harder benchmark which was introduced by Perron and Shaw [PER 04]. In this test suite, all instances have $|O| = 8$ options and $|classes(C)| = 20$ different car classes; capacity constraints are randomly generated while ensuring that $\forall o_i \in O, 1 \le p_i \le 3$ and $p_i < q_i \le p_i + 2$. The number of cars $|C|$ to be sequenced varies between 100 and 500: 32 (respectively, 21 and 29) instances have 100 (respectively, 300 and 500) cars. All instances are feasible and have at least one solution that satisfies all capacity constraints.

12.5.3. Parameter settings

Each run of each considered algorithm is limited to 150,000 constructions of sequences: for ACO(τ_1, η) and ACO(τ_1, τ_2) we have fixed the maximum number of cycles to 5000 and the number of ants to 30; for Greedy(η) and ACO(τ_2) we have fixed the maximum number of cycles to 150,000 as a single sequence is built at each cycle. Note that the construction of 150,000 sequences roughly corresponds to 20 (respectively, 50 and 100) seconds of CPU time on a 2 GHz Pentium 4 for instances with 100 (respectively, 300 and 500) cars. The setting of the other parameters is summarized in Table 12.1.

To tune parameters, we have run algorithms on a subset of the test suite instances that contains 32 instances (9 instances with 100 cars, 7 instances with 300 cars and 16 instances with 500 cars). These 32 instances have been selected for tuning parameters because they appeared to be the most difficult for the greedy algorithm (other instances are trivially solved whatever the parameter setting).

Heuristic η	1st pheromone structure				2nd pheromone structure		
β	α_1	ρ_1	τ_{min_1}	τ_{max_1}	α_2	ρ_2	τ_{min_2}
Greedy(η) 6	0	–	–	–	–	–	–
ACO(τ_1, η) 6	2	1%	0.01	4	–	–	–
ACO(τ_2) –	–	–	–	–	6	3%	1
ACO(τ_1, τ_2) –	2	1%	0.01	4	6	3%	1

Table 12.1. *Parameter settings of the different compared algorithms*

Both Greedy(η) and ACO(τ_1, η) use the greedy heuristic η in their probability transition function and have to set the parameter β that determines the weight of this heuristic. Experiments have been carried out with different values for β ranging between 1 and 10. The best average results were obtained when β is fixed to 6 (even although equivalent results are obtained when $\beta \in [4; 8]$).

The three ACO variants use the pheromone structures τ_1 and/or τ_2 in their probability transition functions and have to set the pheromone factor weight α, the pheromone evaporation rate ρ and the bounds τ_{min} and τ_{max} associated with these pheromone structures. As already discussed in section 9, setting these parameters makes it possible to balance between two dual goals when exploring the search space, i.e. intensify the search around the most promising areas of the search space while also diversifying the search towards new undiscovered areas.

Diversification may be emphasized by decreasing α and/or ρ and/or by decreasing the difference between τ_{min} and τ_{max}. When increasing the exploratory ability of ants in this way, better solutions are usually found but it takes longer to find them.

We have chosen two different parameter settings for the two pheromone structures τ_1 and τ_2. Indeed, as pointed out in section 12.3, the identification of critical cars appears to be essential for building good solutions. α_2 and ρ_2 have to be set to values that favor intensification in order to obtain quick feedback, i.e. $\alpha_2 = 6$ and $\rho_2 = 0.03$. On the contrary, we have chosen a setting that ensures a good diversification of the search for the first pheromone structure, i.e. $\alpha_1 = 2$ and $\rho_1 = 0.01$.

Note that the performances of the three ACO variants are rather stable with respect to these pheromone parameter settings. For example, when running ACO(τ_1, τ_2) with different values for α and ρ (with $\alpha_1 \in \{1, 2, 3, 4\}$, $\rho_1 \in$

$\{0.5\%, 1\%, 2\%, 3\%\}$, $\alpha_2 \in \{4, 6, 8, 10\}$ and $\rho_2 \in \{1\%, 2\%, 3\%, 5\%\}$), the final success rates (over 50 runs on each of the 82 instances) vary between 85.3% for the worst configuration and 94.7% for the best, with an average of 91.3%.

12.5.4. *Experimental results*

Figure 12.1 displays the evolution of the percentage of successful runs (that have found a solution) of the four considered algorithms with respect to CPU time.

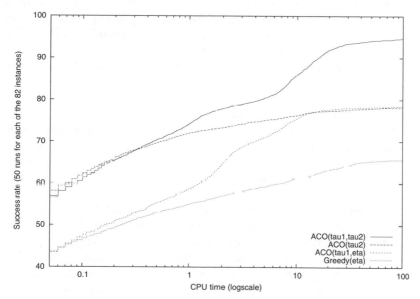

Figure 12.1. *Comparison of Greedy(η), ACO(τ_1, η), ACO(τ_2) and ACO(τ_1, τ_2). Each curve plots the evolution of the percentage of successful runs (over 50 runs on each of the 82 instances) with respect to CPU time (in logscale)*

Let us first compare Greedy(η) with ACO(τ_2) since both algorithms build sequences with respect to a greedy heuristic that evaluates the hardness of car classes, but differ in the way this estimation is done. Greedy(η) considers the sum of the utilization rates of the required options, whereas ACO(τ_2) learns this with respect to past experiences of the colony. Figure 12.1 shows that the success rate of $ACO(\tau_2)$ is always more than 10% and as high as the success rate of Greedy(η). After 0.05 sec of CPU time, Greedy(η) and $ACO(\tau_2)$ have solved 42.5% and 55.8% of the runs, respectively. After 100 sec of CPU time, they have solved 65.6% and 77.6% of the runs, respectively.

Let us then compare Greedy(η) with $ACO(\tau_1, \eta)$ (respectively, $ACO(\tau_2)$ with $ACO(\tau_1, \tau_2)$) to evaluate the benefit of integrating the first pheromone structure τ_1 within the transition probability function.

Figure 12.1 shows that at the beginning of the solution process, the success rates of Greedy(η) and $ACO(\tau_1, \eta)$ (respectively, $ACO(\tau_2)$ and $ACO(\tau_1, \tau_2)$) are very close. Indeed, the setting of the parameters for managing τ_1 has been chosen in order to favor exploration, so that during the first cycles τ_1 does not significantly influence transition probabilities. At the beginning of the search process, pheromone trails are initialized to the upper bound τ_{max_1} so that after k cycles, the quantity of pheromone is bound between $\tau_{max_1}(1 - \rho_1)^k$ and τ_{max_1}.

After 500 or so cycles (roughly corresponding to 2, 5 and 10 sec for instances with 100, 300 and 500 cars, respectively), the first pheromone structure actually influences ants so that the success rate of $ACO(\tau_1, \eta)$ (respectively, $ACO(\tau_1, \tau_2)$) becomes significantly higher than the success rate of Greedy(η) (respectively, $ACO(\tau_2)$).

As a conclusion, note that the second pheromone structure τ_2 allows ants to solve more than half of the runs very quickly (in less than 0.05 sec). The first pheromone structure τ_1 needs more time to guide ants towards better sequences (around 2, 5 and 10 sec for instances with 100, 300 and 500 cars, respectively), but actually improves the solution process. At the end of the solution process, the combination of the two pheromone structures allows ants to solve almost 95% of the runs.

12.6. Comparison of ACO with state-of-the-art approaches

12.6.1. *Considered approaches*

Many different approaches for solving the car sequencing problem, which is a classical benchmarking problem for evaluating new solution approaches, have been proposed. Exact constraint programming approaches [BRA 07, DIN 88, REG 97, VAN 06] are usually limited to small instances and are not able, for example, to solve all instances of the benchmark of Lee [LEE 98] within a reasonable amount of time. As a comparison, our different ACO algorithms are able to solve all these instances in less than 0.01 sec.

Many heuristic approaches have also been proposed. Most of these are based on local search such as [DAV 99, EST 05, GOT 03, LEE 98, MIC 02, NEV 04, PER 04]. We now compare the best of our four algorithms, i.e. $ACO(\tau_1, \tau_2)$, with two of these local search approaches which have shown to be very effective, i.e. IDWalk and VFLS.

12.6.2. *IDWalk*

IDWalk [NEV 04] is a new metaheuristic based on a local search that appears to obtain better results than other metaheuristics (e.g. tabu search and simulated annealing) for solving e.g. the car sequencing problem. As well as the maximum number of moves (MaxMv), this approach introduces only one parameter referred to as Max which determines the maximum number of neighbors that are considered before performing every move.

At each iteration, IDWalk chooses the first non-decreasing neighbor. If all the Max considered neighbors deteriorate the current solution, IDWalk chooses the best one over them. The Max parameter is automatically determined at the beginning of the search by performing a few short walks (of 2000 moves) with different possible values. This value is also reactively adapted during the solution process when the length of the walk reaches some given limits.

In the case of the car sequencing problem, the neighborhood is defined by the set of all sequences that can be obtained by swapping any pair of cars that have different car classes such that at least one car is involved in one or more constraint violations. The car that is involved in constraint violations is chosen with respect to a probability that is proportional to the number of constraints it violates. The initial sequence of cars from which the local search is performed is constructed in a greedy way, using the η heuristic described in section 12.2.

12.6.3. *VFLS*

VFLS (very fast local search) [EST 05, EST 08] is the algorithm that won the ROADEF challenge for the car sequencing problem (among 27 teams from all over the world) [SOL 08]. In addition to capacity constraints, the ROADEF problem contains some extra constraints that are related to car colors and minimizing solvents. The implementation of VFLS considered in this comparison is an adaptation of the challenge winner, where data structures have been optimized to focus on capacity constraints only.

The VFLS algorithm is based on a local search approach similar to that proposed in [GOT 03]. Starting from an initial sequence that is constructed in a greedy way using a heuristic based on utilization rates, at each iteration the algorithm chooses the first neighbor of the current solution that does not increase its cost. The considered neighborhood is defined by a set of five transformations (exchange of two cars, insertion of a car backwards or forwards and mirror and random permutations of subsequences). The probability of choosing each of these transformations is 0.6, 0.13, 0.13, 0.13 and 0.01, respectively.

12.6.4. *Experimental set-up*

We compare the three approaches on the 82 instances of the test suite provided by Perron and Shaw. However, to evaluate scale-up properties, we have grouped these instances into three subsets with respect to the number of cars $|C|$ to be sequenced. The first group contains the 32 instances with 100 cars, the second contains the 21 instances with 300 cars and the third contains the 29 instances with 500 cars.

The three algorithms have been implemented in C or C++, and have been run on the same 2 GHz Pentium 4. (The code for IDWalk and VFLS were kindly supplied by their authors, who also validated the obtained results.) Each algorithm has been run 50 times on each instance.

12.6.5. *Experimental results*

Figures 12.2, 12.3 and 12.4 show the evolution of the success rates with respect to CPU time on instances with 100, 300 and 500 cars, respectively. In the three figures, we note that for very short CPU time limits $ACO(\tau_1, \tau_2)$ is better than IDWalk, which itself is better than VFLS. After 0.1 sec of CPU time, $ACO(\tau_1, \tau_2)$ has solved more than 60% of the runs while VFLS and IDWalk have solved 6% and 25% of the runs, respectively. However, the success rate of VFLS increases more steeply than the success rates of IDWalk and $ACO(\tau_1, \tau_2)$. After a few seconds of CPU time, VFLS has clearly surpassed IDWalk. Finally, at the end of the processing time, VFLS has reached

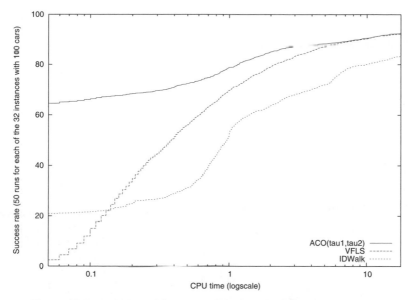

Figure 12.2. *Evolution of the percentage of successful runs with respect to CPU time for ACO(τ_1, τ_2), VFLS and IDWalk on the 32 instances with 100 cars*

the success rate of ACO(τ_1, τ_2) for the instances with 100 and 300 cars, whereas VFLS has outperformed ACO(τ_1, τ_2) for the instances with 500 cars.

The differences in the time complexities of these algorithms is highlighted by the fact that ACO(τ_1, τ_2) is outperformed by VFLS at the end of the processing time for the largest instances with 500 cars. Indeed, if there are $|C| = n$ cars to sequence and $|classes(C)| = k$ different car classes, then the complexity of constructing one sequence by an ant is nk, the complexity of the pheromone laying step is $O(n)$ and the complexity of the evaporation step is $O(n^2)$.

As a comparison, the time complexity of performing one move in both IDWalk and VFLS does not depend on the total number of cars to be sequenced.

Each move is locally evaluated by considering only a subsequence of cars and the time complexity of one move mainly depends on the sizes (q_i) of the gliding subsequences on which the capacity constraints must be checked. In

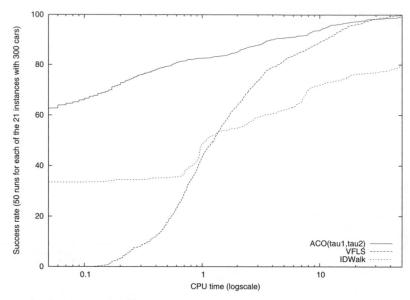

Figure 12.3. *Evolution of the percentage of successful runs with respect to CPU time for ACO(τ_1, τ_2), VFLS and IDWalk on the 21 instances with 300 cars*

the test suite we have considered here, these sizes are bound between 2 and 5 for all instances.

12.7. Discussion

This first illustration of ACO capabilities on a specific CSP has shown us that this approach may obtain competitive results with respect to state-of-the-art solutions for a problem which has been widely studied in the CP community and which was the subject of an international competition in 2005.

Note that using pheromone to identify critical cars gives significantly better results than a dedicated heuristic which has been specifically designed for this problem. The simplicity of the approach can also be highlighted. The program implementing ACO(τ_1, τ_2) has less than 400 lines (including input and output issues).

However, the ACO algorithms described in this chapter have been designed to solve the car sequencing problem and cannot be used to solve other CSPs.

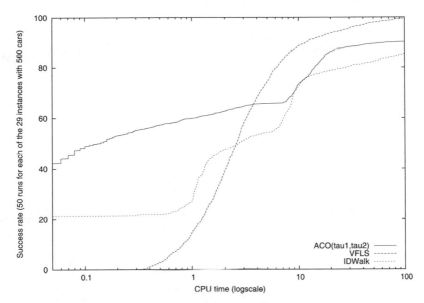

Figure 12.4. *Evolution of the percentage of successful runs with respect to CPU time for ACO(τ_1, τ_2), VFLS and IDWalk on the 29 instances with 500 cars*

The following chapter shows how ACO may also be used to solve any finite domain CSP modeled as a triple (X, D, C).

Chapter 13

Subset Selection with ACO

In the previous chapter, we described an ant colony optimization algorithm for solving a specific constraint satisfaction problem, i.e. the car sequencing problem. This is a rather straightforward application of ACO. Indeed, the car sequencing problem is easily modeled as best Hamiltonian path-finding problems, where ants must visit every vertex in a graph as for the traveling salesman problem. To solve such best Hamiltonian path-finding problems with the ACO metaheuristic, a pheromone trail τ_{ij} is associated with each edge (i, j). This pheromone trail represents the learnt desirability of visiting vertex j immediately after vertex i, and is used to guide ants during their path construction step.

However, many combinatorial problems involve selection rather than ordering or sequencing. Given a set S, some subset $S' \subseteq S$ which satisfies certain properties and/or which optimizes some objective function is to be selected. We refer to such a class of problems as subset selection problems (SSPs). Some well-known examples of SSPs are the maximum clique problem, the multidimensional knapsack problem, the Boolean satisfiablility problem and the constraint satisfaction problem.

Solving an SSP with an ACO algorithm poses the problem of choosing a relevant pheromone structure which will actually guide the search towards the best areas of the search space. Indeed, combinations are subsets of objects and the order in which objects are selected is not significant. It is therefore meaningless to model them as path-finding problems and lay pheromone trails on consecutively visited vertices.

We describe how to solve SSPs with the ACO metaheuristics in this chapter. We first introduce the class of SSPs, which includes constraint satisfaction problems, and provide example members of it in section 13.1. We define the generic ant colony optimization algorithm for this class of problem in section 13.2, and describe two instantiations of this algorithm (corresponding to two different pheromone structures) in section 13.3. We show in section 13.4 how this generic algorithm may be instantiated to solve CSPs, and illustrate the performance of this algorithm on different CSP instances in section 13.5.

13.1. Subset selection problems

SSPs involve finding an optimal feasible subset of objects within an initial set of objects. More formally, an SSP is defined by a triple $(S, S_{\text{feasible}}, f)$ where

- S is a set of candidate objects;
- $S_{\text{feasible}} \subseteq \mathcal{P}(S)$ is a set that contains all feasible subsets of S; and
- $f : S_{\text{feasible}} \rightarrow \mathbb{R}$ is an objective function that associates a real-valued cost $f(S')$ with every feasible subset of objects $S' \in S_{\text{feasible}}$.

The goal of an SSP $(S, S_{\text{feasible}}, f)$ is to find $s^* \subseteq S$ such that $s^* \in S_{\text{feasible}}$ and $f(s^*)$ is maximal. We describe a few classical problems within this framework in the following sections.

13.1.1. *Maximum clique*

The decision problem related to the maximum clique problem is defined by problem 2.2. The goal of the maximum problem is to find the largest clique in a graph. We define the SSP $(S, S_{\text{feasible}}, f)$ such that

- S contains all the vertices of the graph;
- S_{feasible} contains all the cliques of G, i.e. all the sets $S' \subseteq S$ such that every pair of distinct vertices in S' is connected by an edge in the graph; and
- f is the cardinality function.

13.1.2. *Multidimensional knapsack*

This problem is defined by problem 3.1. The goal is to find a subset of objects that maximizes a total profit while satisfying some resource constraints. We define the SSP $(S, S_{\text{feasible}}, f)$ such that

– S is the set of objects;

– S_{feasible} contains every subset that satisfies all the capacity constraints, i.e.

$$S_{\text{feasible}} = \{S' \subseteq S \mid \forall i \in 1, \ldots, m, \sum_{j \in S'} d_{ij} \leq c_i\};$$

– f returns the total profit, i.e.

$$\forall S' \in S_{\text{feasible}}, f(S') = \sum_{j \in S'} p_j.$$

13.1.3. *Maximum Boolean satisfiability*

The decision problem related to the maximum Boolean satisfiablity is the SAT problem defined in problem 2.1. The goal is to find a truth assignment of Boolean variables that satisfies a maximum number of clauses. We define the SSP $(S, S_{\text{feasible}}, f)$ such that

– S contains all Boolean variables;

– S_{feasible} contains all the subsets of S, i.e. $S_{\text{feasible}} = \mathcal{P}(S)$; and

– f returns the number of satisfied clauses, i.e. $\forall S' \in S_{\text{feasible}}, f(S')$ is the number of clauses that are satisfied when all variables of S' are set to True and all others to False.

13.1.4. *Maximum constraint satisfaction*

The goal is to find an assignment of values to variables that satisfies a maximum number of constraints. We define the SSP $(S, S_{\text{feasible}}, f)$ such that

– S contains every label $\langle X_i, v_i \rangle$ pairing a variable X_i with a value v_i from that variable's domain $D(X_i)$;

– S_{feasible} contains all the subsets of S that do not contain two different labels for the same variable, i.e.

$$S_{\text{feasible}} = \{S' \subseteq S \mid \forall(\langle X_i, v_i \rangle, \langle X_j, v_j \rangle) \in S' \times S', X_i = X_j \Rightarrow v_i = v_j\};$$

– f returns the number of satisfied constraints, i.e. $\forall S' \in S_{\text{feasible}}$, $f(S')$ is the number of constraints such that every variable involved in the constraint is assigned a value by a label of S' and the constraint is satisfied by this assignment of values to variables.

CSPs are special cases of maximum constraint satisfaction and can easily be modeled as SSPs.

13.1.5. *Minimum vertex cover*

The goal is to find the smallest subset of the vertices of a graph G that contains at least one vertex of every edge of G. As this is a minimization problem, we may consider the dual problem that involves finding the largest set of vertices such that no edge has its two vertices in this set. We define the SSP $(S, S_{\text{feasible}}, f)$ such that

– S contains all the vertices of the graph;

– S_{feasible} contains all the subsets $S' \subseteq S$ such that for all edges (i, j) of the graph, $i \notin S'$ or $j \notin S'$; and

– f is the cardinality function.

13.1.6. *Maximum common subgraph*

Given two graphs G_1 and G_2, the goal is to find the largest graph which is isomorphic to subgraphs of both G_1 and G_2. We define the SSP $(S, S_{\text{feasible}}, f)$ such that

– S contains each couple of vertices (i, j) such that i is a vertex of G_1 and j is a vertex of G_2; and

– S_{feasible} contains all the subsets of S such that the corresponding induced subgraphs in G_1 and G_2 are isomorphic, i.e. each vertex of one graph is matched to at most one vertex of the other graph and edges are matched, i.e.

$$S_{\text{feasible}} = \{S' \subseteq S \mid \quad \forall((i, j), (k, l)) \in S'^2, i = k \Leftrightarrow j = l \text{ and}$$
$$(i, k) \text{ is an edge of } G_1$$
$$\text{iff } (j, l) \text{ is an edge of } G_2;\}$$

– f is the cardinality function.

13.1.7. *Edge-weighted k-cardinality tree*

This problem is a generalization of the minimum weight spanning tree problem. Given a weighted graph, the goal is to find a minimum weight subtree with exactly k edges. We define the SSP $(S, S_{\text{feasible}}, f)$ such that

– S contains all the vertices of the graph;

– S_{feasible} contains all the subsets $S' \subseteq S$ such that $|S'| \leq k$ and S' is a tree; and

– $f(S') = 0$ if $|S'| \neq k$, and $f(S') = -\sum_{(i,j) \in S'} weight(i,j)$ otherwise.

13.2. Description of Ant-SSP

The solution of an SSP is a subset of objects, and the *order* in which objects are selected when constructing a combination is not significant. It is therefore meaningless to model SSPs as path-finding problems and lay pheromone trails on consecutively visited vertices. Two main pheromone structures may be considered for solving SSPs with ACO.

The first pheromone structure associates a pheromone trail τ_i with each object $i \in S$, so that τ_i represents the learnt desirability of selecting object i. This pheromone structure has been used to solve many different SSPs, for example: multidimensional knapsack problems [LEG 99]; maximum clique problems [SOL 06]; set-covering problems [HAD 00]; constraint satisfaction problems [TAR 05]; edge-weighted k-cardinality tree problems [BLU 02]; and graph-matching problems [SAM 06].

The second pheromone structure associates a pheromone trail τ_{ij} with each pair of different objects $(i,j) \in S \times S$, so that τ_{ij} represents the learnt desirability of selecting both objects i and j in a same subset. This pheromone structure has also been used to solve many different SSPs such as: maximum clique problems [FEN 03]; multidimensional knapsack problems [ALA 07]; constraint satisfaction problems [SOL 02]; edge-weighted k-cardinality tree problems [BLU 02]; and graph-matching problems [SAM 05].

In this chapter, we describe all these different algorithms within a unified framework. We therefore introduce a generic ACO algorithm for SSPs, referred to as Ant-SSP. This algorithm is parameterized by

– the SSP to solve, described by a triple $(S, S_{\text{feasible}}, f)$ (an instantiation of this algorithm for solving CSPs is described in section 13.4);

– a pheromone strategy which determines the pheromone structure on which ants lay pheromone trails, and the way they exploit and reinforce these trails (two pheromone strategies are described in section 13.3); and

– a set of numerical parameters.

The algorithm follows the generic MAX-MIN Ant System framework described in algorithm 12.1. We describe in the following two sections the procedure used by ants to build combinations and the pheromone laying procedure.

13.2.1. *Construction of a combination by an ant*

Algorithm 13.1 describes the procedure used by ants to construct subsets.

Note that the precondition of this procedure imposes that, for each non-empty feasible subset $S' \in S_{\text{feasible}}$, there exists at least one object $o_i \in S'$ such that $S' - \{o_i\}$ is also feasible. Indeed, this precondition is mandatory to ensure that each subset of S_{feasible} (including the optimal solution) may be built in an incremental way, starting from the empty set and at each step adding an object chosen within the set of candidate objects that are consistent with the current subset.

Example 13.1. *Let us consider the edge-weighted k-cardinality tree problem defined in section 13.1.7. For this problem, we have defined S_{feasible} as the set of all trees having a number of vertices that is smaller than or equal to k, so that we can incrementally build a tree with k vertices starting from the empty tree. Had we defined S_{feasible} as the set of all trees having exactly k vertices, this would no longer have been possible.*

Starting from an empty set, objects are iteratively selected within the set *Candidates* (which contains all feasible objects with respect to the objects the ant has chosen so far) using a probabilistic transition rule. More precisely, the probability $p(o_i)$ of selecting $o_i \in Candidates$ when ant k has already selected the subset of objects S_k depends on two factors:

– The *pheromone factor* $\tau_{\text{factor}}(o_i, S_k)$ evaluates the learnt desirability of adding object o_i to subset S_k based on the pheromone trails that have been deposited previously on pheromonal components. The definition of this factor depends on the pheromone strategy, as discussed in section 13.3.

Algorithm 13.1: buildSubset

Input:

an SSP $(S, S_{\text{feasible}}, f)$

a heuristic function $\eta_{\text{factor}} : S \times \mathcal{P}(S) \to \mathbb{R}^+$

a pheromone factor $\tau_{\text{factor}} : S \times \mathcal{P}(S) \to \mathbb{R}^+$

two numerical parameters α and β

Precondition:

$\forall S' \in S_{\text{feasible}}, S' \neq \emptyset \Rightarrow \exists o_i \in S', S' - \{o_i\} \in S_{\text{feasible}}$

Postrelation:

returns a feasible subset of objects $S' \in S_{\text{feasible}}$

1 **begin**

2    $S_k \leftarrow \emptyset$

3    $Candidates \leftarrow S$

4   **while** $Candidates \neq \emptyset$ **do**

5   Choose an object $o_i \in Candidates$ with respect to probability

6      $$p(o_i) = \frac{[\tau_{\text{factor}}(o_i,S_k)]^\alpha \cdot [\eta_{\text{factor}}(o_i,S_k)]^\beta}{\sum_{o_j \in Candidates}[\tau_{\text{factor}}(o_j,S_k)]^\alpha \cdot [\eta_{\text{factor}}(o_j,S_k)]^\beta}$$

7      $S_k \leftarrow S_k \cup \{o_i\}$

8   Remove o_i from $Candidates$

9   Remove from $Candidates$ every object o_j such that $S_k \cup \{o_j\} \not\subseteq S_{\text{feasible}}$

10   **return** S_k

11 **end**

– The *heuristic factor* $\eta_{\text{factor}}(o_i, S_k)$ evaluates the promise of object o_i based on information local to the ant, i.e. the solution it has built so far, S_k. The definition of this factor is dependent upon the problem $(S, S_{\text{feasible}}, f)$. We show in section 13.4 how this factor may be defined to solve CSPs.

As for other ACO algorithms, α and β are two parameters that determine the relative importance of these two factors.

Once each ant has constructed a feasible subset, one or more constructed solutions may be improved by using a problem-dependent form of local search. In some cases local search is applied to all constructed solutions; in other cases it is applied to the best solution of the cycle.

13.2.2. *Pheromone laying step*

Ant-SSP considers an *elitist strategy* where only the best ants in each cycle, i.e. one or more of those whose solutions are no worse than any other ant's solution, deposit pheromone. The amount of pheromone deposited by these best ants depends on the quality of the constructed solution. In many cases, it is inversely proportional to the gap in quality between the constructed solution and the best constructed solution since the beginning of the run S_{best}. Let $\{S_1, \ldots, S_{nbAnts}\}$ be the set of combinations built during the last cycle. The pheromone laying procedure is defined as:

for every combination $S_i \in \{S_1, \ldots, S_{nbAnts}\}$ **do**
    if $\forall S_k \in \{S_1, \ldots, S_{nbAnts}\}, f(S_i) \geq f(S_k)$ **then**
        increase the quantity of pheromone on each pheromone component
        of S_i by
$$\frac{1}{1+f(S_{\text{best}})-f(S_i)}$$

The set of pheromone components associated with a combination S_i depends on the considered pheromone strategy and is described in section 13.3.

13.3. Instantiations of Ant-SSP with respect to two pheromone strategies

The generic algorithm Ant-SSP is parameterized by a pheromone strategy and we now describe two instantiations of this algorithm: Ant-SSP(Vertex) (where pheromone is laid on objects) and Ant-SSP(Clique) (where pheromone is laid on pairs of objects). For each pheromone strategy, we define:

– the pheromone structure associated with an SSP $(S, S_{\text{feasible}}, f)$, i.e. the set of components on which ants may lay pheromone trails;

– the set of pheromone components associated with a combination $S_k \in S_{\text{feasible}}$, i.e. the set of pheromone components on which some pheromone is actually laid when solution S_k is rewarded; and

– the pheromone factor $\tau_{\text{factor}}(o_i, S_k)$ which is associated with an object o_i and a partial solution S_k, and which is used in the probabilistic transition rule.

13.3.1. *The vertex pheromone strategy*

For SSPs, combinations built by ants are subsets of objects. The order in which objects are selected is not significant. Hence, a first pheromone strategy consists of laying pheromone on objects from the best constructed solutions.

In this case, the pheromone structure associates a pheromone trail τ_{o_i} with each object $o_i \in S$. Intuitively, this quantity of pheromone represents the learnt desirability of selecting o_i when constructing a combination.

When rewarding a combination S_k, the set of pheromone components on which pheromone is laid is the set of selected objects in S_k, i.e. $\{\tau_{o_i} \mid o_i \in S_k\}$.

Finally, the pheromone factor in the probabilistic transition rule corresponds to the quantity of pheromone on the considered object, i.e. $\tau_{\text{factor}}(o_i, S_k) = \tau(o_i)$.

13.3.2. *The clique pheromone strategy*

The vertex pheromone strategy implicitly assumes that the desirability of an object is independent of other selected objects. However, in some cases, the desirability of an object may depend on the subset of already selected objects.

Example 13.2. *Let us consider a constraint satisfaction problem that contains two variables x and y that can be assigned either 0 or 1, so that the initial set of objects S contains the labels $\langle x, 0 \rangle$, $\langle x, 1 \rangle$, $\langle y, 0 \rangle$ and $\langle y, 1 \rangle$. Let us now assume that this problem contains the constraint $x \neq y$. In this case, the desirability of selecting either label $\langle y, 0 \rangle$ or label $\langle y, 1 \rangle$ for y depends on the label selected for x (and vice versa).*

Pheromone trails could therefore be used to learn that $(\langle x, 0 \rangle, \langle y, 1 \rangle)$ and $(\langle x, 1 \rangle, \langle y, 0 \rangle)$ are pairs of labels that fit well together. $(\langle x, 0 \rangle, \langle y, 0 \rangle)$ and $(\langle x, 1 \rangle, \langle y, 1 \rangle)$ are less interesting pairs of labels, however.

Hence, a second pheromone strategy for subset selection problems consists of laying pheromone on pairs of objects. In this case, the pheromone structure associates a pheromone trail τ_{o_i, o_j} with every pair of objects $(o_i, o_j) \in S \times S$. Intuitively, this quantity of pheromone represents the learnt desirability of selecting both o_i and o_j within the same subset.

When rewarding a combination S_k, the set of pheromone components on which pheromone is laid is the set of pairs of objects in S_k, i.e. $\{\tau_{o_i o_j} \mid (o_i, o_j) \in S_k \times S_k, o_i \neq o_j\}$. In other words, the edges of the clique of vertices S_k are rewarded.

Finally, the pheromone factor in the probabilistic transition rule depends on the quantity of pheromone on every pair of objects (o_i, o_j) such that o_j is an object that has already been selected in S_k, i.e.

$$\tau_{\text{factor}}(o_i, S_k) = \sum_{o_j \in S_k} \tau_{o_i o_j} \text{ if } S_k \neq \emptyset.$$

When choosing the first object (when $S_k = \emptyset$), the pheromone factor may be set to 1. In this case, the probability of choosing the first object only depends on the heuristic factor.

Note that this pheromone factor can be computed in an incremental way: once the first object o_i has been chosen, for each candidate object o_j the pheromone factor $\tau_{\text{factor}}(o_j, S_k)$ is initialized to $\tau_{o_i o_j}$. Each time a new object o_l is added to the subset, for each candidate object o_j the pheromone factor $\tau_{\text{factor}}(o_j, S_k)$ is incremented by $\tau_{o_l o_j}$.

13.3.3. *Comparison of the two strategies*

The two pheromone strategies were introduced independently from a construction graph and from the walk of an ant in this graph. We now illustrate and compare the two strategies from this point of view. In both cases, the construction graph is a complete non-directed graph which associates one vertex with each object. The walk of an ant is an elementary path in this graph, and the combination associated with this walk is the subset of vertices it has passed through. Table 13.1 provides the current set of objects selected by an ant as vertices visited in a walk of a complete graph at (a), i.e. vertices 1, 2 and 4.

At (b) and (c) of Table 13.1, we define the probability of selecting object 5 and highlight in bold the pheromone components considered by Ant-SSP(Vertex) and Ant-SSP(Clique), respectively. While the pheromone factor in Ant-SSP(Vertex) only depends on the pheromone trail laying on the candidate vertex, the pheromone factor in Ant-SSP(Clique) depends on all pheromone trails laying between the candidate vertex and the current set of objects.

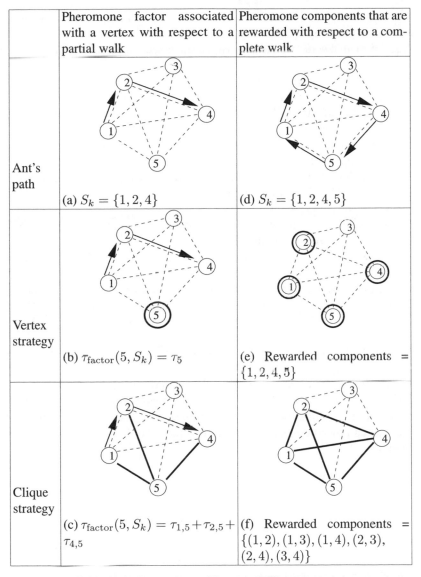

	Pheromone factor associated with a vertex with respect to a partial walk	Pheromone components that are rewarded with respect to a complete walk
Ant's path	(a) $S_k = \{1, 2, 4\}$	(d) $S_k = \{1, 2, 4, 5\}$
Vertex strategy	(b) $\tau_{\text{factor}}(5, S_k) = \tau_5$	(e) Rewarded components = $\{1, 2, 4, 5\}$
Clique strategy	(c) $\tau_{\text{factor}}(5, S_k) = \tau_{1,5} + \tau_{2,5} + \tau_{4,5}$	(f) Rewarded components = $\{(1,2), (1,3), (1,4), (2,3), (2,4), (3,4)\}$

Table 13.1. *Comparison of Vertex and Clique strategies*

The final set of objects selected by an ant, i.e. $\{1, 2, 4, 5\}$ is provided in Table 13.1 at (d). We highlight in bold the pheromone components onto which pheromone will be deposited by Ant-SSP(Vertex) and Ant-SSP(Clique) at (e) and (f), respectively. In the latter case, note that all edges belonging to the clique of visited vertices (and not just the traversed edges) are updated.

Table 13.1 highlights differences in the time complexities of Ant-SSP(Vertex) and Ant-SSP(Clique). Indeed, to construct subsets, Ant-SSP(Vertex) and Ant-SSP(Clique) perform almost the same number of operations. The only difference is in the computation of pheromone factors for the probabilistic transition rule and, as pointed out previously, pheromone factors in Ant-SSP(Clique) may be computed in an incremental way. Each time a new object is selected, the pheromone factor of each candidate object can be updated by a simple addition.

To update the pheromone trails of pheromone components, Ant-SSP(Vertex) and Ant-SSP(Clique) perform a different number of operations. In Ant-SSP(Vertex), the evaporation step requires $\mathcal{O}(card(S))$ operations and the reward of a subset S_k requires $\mathcal{O}(card(S_k))$ operations. In Ant-SSP(Clique), the evaporation step requires $\mathcal{O}(card(S)^2)$ operations and the reward of a subset S_k requires $\mathcal{O}(card(S_k)^2)$ operations.

13.4. Instantiation of Ant-SSP to solve CSPs

To solve a specific SSP with Ant-SSP, we have to define (1) the heuristic factor $\eta_{\text{factor}}(o_i, S_k)$ which evaluates the promise of object o_i with respect to the current solution S_k (used in the probabilistic transition rule) and (2) a local search procedure that may be applied to one or more of the constructed solutions.

13.4.1. *Heuristic factor*

When solving CSPs, variable/value couples which correspond to the assignment of a value to a variable are to be selected. A heuristic factor is therefore defined $\eta_{\text{factor}}(\langle x_i, v_i \rangle, S_k)$ which evaluates the promise of assigning x_i to v_i when the partial assignment S_k has already been built. As the final goal is to minimize the number of violated constraints, the heuristic factor favors the choice of couples introducing less new violations. We have also seen in section 4.3 that better assignments are usually built when assigning the most constrained variables first (the domain of which contains the smallest number of values that are consistent with the current partial assignment).

A heuristic factor which integrates these two criteria can be designed as follows:

if $x_i = minDom(X, S_k)$ **then:**
$$\eta_{\text{factor}}(\langle x_i, v_i \rangle, S_k) = \frac{1}{1 + cost(\{\langle x_i, v_i \rangle\} \cup S_k) - cost(S_k)}$$
else
$$\eta_{\text{factor}}(\langle x_i, v_i \rangle, S_k) = 0$$

where $cost(S)$ is the number of constraints violated by an assignment S and $minDom(X, S_k)$ is a function which returns the non-assigned variable, the domain of which contains the smallest number of consistent values with respect to the partial assignment S_k.

13.4.2. *Local search*

The local search procedure that has been considered in experiments reported in the next section is based on the *min-conflicts* heuristic of [MIN 92]. At each step in the local search, we randomly choose a variable that is involved in one or more violated constraints. We then choose a value for this variable which minimizes the number of conflicts. This repair procedure stops when the number of violated constraints is not improved for a certain number of successive iterations.

13.5. Experimental results

We now report experimental results obtained with Ant-SSP when solving constraint satisfaction problems. We first evaluate and compare the two pheromone strategies and the interest of integrating a local search procedure on randomly generated binary instances. We then compare Ant-SSP with other constraint solvers on instances used for the constraint solver competition which took place in 2006.

13.5.1. *Randomly generated binary instances*

We consider four classes of randomly generated instances of the model-A class [MAC 98]. We only consider feasible instances which have at least one solution. Each set contains twenty different instances, each of them having 100 variables, a uniform domain size of 8 and a connectivity of 0.14 (i.e. the probability of adding a constraint between two variables is equal to 0.14).

The four sets of instances have been generated with different tightness ratio p_2, which determines the number of couples of values which are removed from the relation defining a constraint. The goal here is to exemplify what happens around the phase transition region, which contains the more difficult instances. This phase transition region occurs when the constrainedness κ is equal to 1 [GEN 96]. Hence, the four sets of instances have been generated by setting the tightness ratio p_t to 0.2, 0.23, 0.26 and 0.29, so that the constrainedness κ is equal to 0.74, 0.87, 1.00 and 1.14, respectively.

For all these instances, we have fixed the number of ants *nbAnts* to 30, the weight of the pheromone factor α to 1, the weight of the heuristic factor β to 10, the evaporation rate ρ to 0.01 and the minimal and maximal pheromone bounds $\tau_{\min}$ and $\tau_{\max}$ to 0.01 and 4, respectively. Each algorithm was run five times on each of the twenty instances, for each of the four classes of instances. All runs were performed on a 2 GHz Pentium 4 processor.

Table 13.2 compares different variants of Ant-SSP: with the strategy Vertex, with the strategy Clique and with and without local search.

	Without local search						With local search					
	Ant-SSP(Vertex)			Ant-SSP(Clique)			Ant-SSP(Vertex)			Ant-SSP(Clique)		
p_2	%	#C	Time	%	#C	Time	%	#C	Time	%	#C	Time
0.20	100	90	1.2	100	63	4.8	100	2	0.0	100	2	0.0
0.23	45	1084	19.5	93	849	78.2	91	472	30.8	100	230	31.6
0.26	89	1019	18.1	97	737	66.1	99	365	26.9	100	260	38.7
0.29	100	449	7.8	100	516	45.2	100	27	1.8	100	38	5.4

Table 13.2. *Experimental comparison of different variants of Ant-SSP: each line gives the percentage of runs that have found a solution, the number of cycles (#C) and the CPU time in seconds spent finding a solution (averaged over the successful runs) for Ant-SSP(Vertex) and Ant-SSP(Clique), with and without local search*

Let us first compare Ant-SSP(Vertex) and Ant-SSP(Clique) when local search is not used to improve the combinations found by ants. On the considered instances, Ant-SSP(Clique) is significantly more successful than Ant-SSP(Vertex), especially when considering classes closer to the phase transition region. The number of cycles needed to find a solution is also usually smaller for Ant-SSP(Clique). However, as a cycle of Ant-SSP(Clique) has a higher time complexity than a cycle of Ant-SSP(Vertex), Ant-SSP(Vertex) is significantly quicker than Ant-SSP(Clique).

Table 13.2 also shows that the hybridization of Ant-SSP with a local search procedure significantly improves success rates. Ant-SSP(Clique) combined with local search is therefore able to solve all instances. Note also that the number of cycles needed to find a solution is always decreased when using local search to improve combinations built by ants. However, as this local improvement step also requires time, the global CPU time is not always decreased.

13.5.2. *Results on instances of the 2006 solver competition*

An international CSP solver competition was held in 2006 [VAN 07]. 32 constraint solvers have been experimentally compared for different classes of instances. We have selected a small subset of the 3425 instances used for this competition, i.e. the 230 satisfiable binary instances, the constraints of which are defined in extension. (The only criteria for selecting instances is the simplicity of the parser that must be designed to handle these instances.) The main features of these instances are listed in Table 13.3.

In order to allow a fair comparison of Ant-SSP with those obtained during the competition we have considered similar experimental set-ups, i.e. each algorithm is run once and the CPU time limit is fixed to 30 minutes. However, solutions of the competition were run on a 3 GHz Intel Xeon whereas Ant-SSP was run on a 2.16 GHz Intel Core Duo.

Ant-SSP has been hybridized with local search, and we have chosen a parameter setting for Ant-SSP which favors a quick convergence in order to be able to quickly solve rather easy instances. We have set the number of ants *nbAnts* to 15, the weight of the pheromone factor α to 2, the weight of the heuristic factor β to 8, the evaporation rate ρ to 0.02 and the minimal bound τ_{min} to 0.01. The value of the τ_{max} parameter is dynamically adapted during the solution process with respect to a rule introduced in [STÜ 00]: τ_{max} is set to δ_{avg}/ρ, where δ_{avg} is equal to the average quantity of pheromone laid at each cycle.

As the CPU time limit is rather long (30 minutes) and Ant-SSP is run only once for each instance, we have used the resampling ratio to automatically

Class	# Instances	# Variables	# Values	# Constraints
composed-25-10-20	10	105	10	620
marc	5	$\in [80; 96]$	$\in [80; 96]$	$\in [3160; 4560]$
rand-2-23	5	23	23	253
rand-2-24	3	24	24	276
rand-2-25	6	25	25	300
rand-2-26	4	26	26	325
rand-2-27	5	27	27	351
rand-2-30-15-fcd	20	30	15	$\in [212; 230]$
rand-2-40-19-fcd	20	40	19	$\in [330; 351]$
rand-2-50-23-fcd	20	50	23	$\in [455; 479]$
geom	92	50	20	$\in [339; 498]$
frb30-15	5	30	15	$\in [208; 217]$
frb35-17	5	35	17	$\in [260; 273]$
frb40-19	5	40	19	$\in [308; 326]$
frb45-21	5	45	21	$\in [369; 394]$
frb50-23	5	50	23	$\in [430; 456]$
frb53-24	5	53	24	$\in [470; 476]$
frb56-25	5	56	25	$\in [511; 525]$
frb59-26	5	59	26	$\in [547; 559]$

Table 13.3. *Features of instances of the 2006 competition: each line gives the name of the class, the number of different instances in the class, the number of variables, the size of the domains and the number of constraints*

diversify the search and restart new searches each time a stagnation is detected (within the time limit of 30 minutes):

– each time a combination is recomputed, pheromone trails associated with components of the combination are decreased by multiplying them by 0.9; and

– when the number of recomputed combinations reaches 1000, pheromone trails are reinitialized to $\tau_{\max}$.

Table 13.4 compares the two variants of Ant-SSP with results obtained by solvers of the 2006 competition. For each class of instances, we report the results obtained by the best solver over the 23 solvers of the competition. All these solvers are based on complete tree-search approaches as for that introduced in Chapter 4. More information on these solutions may be found in [VAN 07].

	Best 2006 solver			Ant-SSP (Vertex)		Ant-SSP (Clique)		Tabu	
	nb	time	(solver)	nb	time	nb	time	nb	time
comp-25-10-20	10	**0.06**	(2)	10	1.31	10	8.03	10	0.32
marc	5	**19.95**	(3)	5	26.96	5	27.05	5	28.21
rand-2-23	5	14.82	(1)	5	**1.42**	5	3.15	5	5.76
rand-2-24	3	9.94	(2)	3	**3.22**	3	7.43	3	8.25
rand-2-25	6	52.69	(5)	6	**3.20**	6	7.27	6	6.71
rand-2-26	5	180.86	(2)	5	**3.26**	5	87.71	5	21.13
rand-2-27	4	248.71	(2)	4	**23.45**	4	193.88	4	26.35
2-30-15	20	**0.2**	(1)	20	0.4	20	0.8	20	0.5
2-40-19	20	25.3	(2)	20	**7.0**	20	98.3	20	8.2
2-50-23	14	829.7	(4)	**20**	81.9	17	347.6	**20**	**31.0**
geom	**92**	**1.0**	(1)	91	11.0	91	50.2	**92**	3.6
frb30-15	5	**0.2**	(2)	5	0.4	5	1.3	5	0.5
frb35-17	5	2.1	(2)	5	3.0	5	5.0	5	**0.9**
frb40-19	5	9.4	(1)	5	**7.0**	5	103.5	5	9.1
frb45-21	5	123.4	(2)	5	467.7	5	354.1	5	**43.4**
frb50-23	3	327.2	(2)	3	430.4	3	680.5	**4**	**9.9**
frb53-24	1	74.0	(3)	3	105.7	3	530.8	**4**	**291.6**
frb56-25	0	–	–	2	535.8	2	170.2	**4**	**329.3**
frb59-26	1	413.9	(3)	1	63.6	0	–	**4**	**523.7**

Table 13.4. *Results on instances of the 2006 competition: each line gives, for each approach, the number of instances solved in less than thirty minutes (nb) and the CPU time (averaged over the solved instances on a 3 GHz Intel Xeon for the competition solvers and on a 2.16 GHz Intel Core Duo for Ant-SSP and Tabu). Each line first gives the results of the best solver of the competition for the considered class of instances; the number in brackets gives the best solver (1 corresponds to VALCSP 3.0, 2 to VALCSP 3.1, 3 to Abscon 109 AC, 4 to buggy$_{2-5}$ and 5 to buggy$^s_{2-5}$). Each line gives the results of Ant-SSP(Vertex), Ant-SSP(Clique) and Tabu*

We also compare Ant-SSP with the local search algorithm based on the tabu metaheuristics described in [GAL 97]. We present results obtained with a tabu list length set to 50 and a restart of the local search from a randomly generated combination every million moves (this parameter setting gives the best results on these instances).

Table 13.4 shows that, on these instances, Ant-SSP(Vertex) is able to solve more instances (and is quicker) than Ant-SSP(Clique) (within the CPU time limit of 30 minutes). We also note that Ant-SSP(Vertex) is able to solve more instances than the best solvers of the 2006 competition (except for an instance of the geom which is not solved by Ant-SSP(Vertex)), and is often quicker. Of couse, this result should be considered together with the fact that the solvers of the competition are based on exact approaches: they are able to prove that inconsistent instances do not have solutions, whereas Ant-SSP cannot.

Finally, Table 13.4 shows that Ant-SSP(Vertex) and tabu have very similar performances on the classes comp-25-10-20, marc, rand-2-* and 2-*-*. The two approaches are able to solve all instances of these classes, and CPU times are comparable. However, Ant-SSP(Vertex) has not been able to solve one instance of the geom class, whereas tabu has solved all of them. Moreover, Ant-SSP(Vertex) is clearly outperformed by tabu on the frb instances.

Note that these last instances are very difficult [XU 07], implying that very few solvers are able to solve them. As far as we know, tabu is the best performing approach on these instances.

13.6. Discussion

We have shown in this chapter that ant colony optimization may be used to solve constraint satisfaction problems in a generic way, without specific knowledge of the constraints.

Note that if experiments have only been reported for binary constraints defined in extension, the solving principle may be extended to handle any other type of constraint. The only limitation to handling other kinds of constraints is that relevant data structures must be designed which allow ants to efficiently evaluate the number of new constraint violations due to the addition of a variable/value couple to a partial assignment.

Pheromone is used here to guide the choice of values to variables. We have proposed and compared two different pheromone strategies. The Vertex strategy learns the desirability of assigning a value to a variable independently of the current partial assignment. The Clique strategy learns that with respect to this current partial assignment.

Experimental results show us that a search with the Clique strategy is more often able to find a solution than a search with the Vertex strategy, but it also has a higher time complexity.

If an experimental set-up is considered such that we have limited time to solve each instance (but we may restart new searches as often as needed within this time limit, as is the case for the 2006 solver competition), the Vertex strategy usually obtains better results. This is the case since it may be restarted more often within the same time limit, thus increasing the probability of finding a solution.

Chapter 14

Integration of ACO in a CP Language

In Chapters 12 and 13, we demonstrated how to use ACO to solve two types of constraint satisfaction problems, i.e. the car sequencing problem and binary constraint satisfaction problems. In both cases, the ACO algorithm samples the search space by iteratively building complete assignments in a greedy randomized way. It uses pheromone trails to progressively bias the probability of assigning a value to a variable with respect to the past experience of the colony. Pheromone trails are therefore used as value-ordering heuristics.

This idea may be generalized to solve any kind of constraint satisfaction problem. However, designing ACO algorithms for solving new CSPs implies quite a lot of programming. If procedures for managing and exploiting pheromone are very similar from one program to another, so that they can easily be reused, solving a new CSP implies that procedures for checking constraints must be written. In particular, when choosing a value to be assigned to a variable, the heuristic factor used in the probabilistic transition rule is defined with respect to the number of new constraint violations entailed by this assignment. We therefore have to maintain a data structure which gives the number of entailed constraint violations for each value in the domain of each non-assigned variable.

There exist many constraint programming libraries (e.g. Choco, described in section 7.2) which have been enriched by a large number of constraints. These constraints may be used to describe many different kinds of problems such as planning or resource allocation. Algorithms have been designed for each of these constraints in order to check the consistency of the constraints and to propagate these constraints in order to filter the associated variables.

In this chapter, we show that we can reuse these procedures for solving CSPs with ACO. In section 14.1, we describe a generic framework for integrating ACO in a CP library. This framework is a generalization of the integration of ACO within the CP library ILOG solver which is described in [KHI 08]. We illustrate this integration of ACO within a CP library on the car sequencing problem in section 14.2.

14.1. Framework for integrating ACO within a CP library

The idea is to use a CP library to describe the problem to be solved, but to replace the predefined search procedure by an ACO search where assignments are built according to a greedy randomized procedure biased by a pheromone learning mechanism.

This may be implemented with any CP library (such as Choco or ILOG solver) which provides mechanisms for restarting the search (as a new search must be begun for each new assignment construction) and which allows the programmer to specify their own value selection procedure (as values must be chosen with respect to an ACO probabilistic transition rule).

Algorithm 14.1 describes the ACO-CP procedure which is used to search solutions. This procedure replaces the classical tree search-based procedure used by CP languages. Note that this ACO procedure is no longer exact, contrary to search procedures usually embedded in CP languages. Hence, ACO-CP is not able to prove inconsistency if the problem does not have solutions. Also, it may fail to find a solution to a problem that actually has solutions. In this case, it will return the best assignment found, i.e. the one which assigns the largest number of variables.

ACO-CP basically follows the ACO framework. At each cycle, each ant builds an assignment using pheromone trails as value-ordering heuristics (lines 4 to 7) and then pheromone trails are updated (lines 8 to 13).

In section 14.1.1, we describe the pheromone strategy Φ which is used to learn a value-ordering heuristic. In section 14.1.2 we describe the procedure used to build assignments and in section 14.1.3 we describe the pheromone updating procedure.

Algorithm 14.1: ACO-CP

Input:

A CSP (X, D, C),

A pheromone strategy $\Phi = (S_\Phi, \tau_\Phi, comp_\Phi)$,

A heuristic factor η,

A set of parameters $\{\alpha, \beta, \rho, \tau_{\min}, \tau_{\max}, nbAnts, maxCycles\}$

Postrelation:

Returns a (partial or complete) consistent assignment for (X, D, C)

1 Initialize all trails of S_Φ to $\tau_{\max}$

2 $\mathcal{A}_{\text{best}} \leftarrow \emptyset$

3 **repeat**

   /* Assignment construction step   */

4 | **for** *each* $k \in \{1, \ldots, nbAnts\}$ **do**

5 | | Build a (partial or complete) consistent assignment $\mathcal{A}_k$

6 | | **if** $card(\mathcal{A}_k) \geq card(\mathcal{A}_{\text{best}})$ **then** $\mathcal{A}_{\text{best}} \leftarrow \mathcal{A}_k$

7 | | **if** $var(\mathcal{A}_{\text{best}}) = X$ **then return** $\mathcal{A}_{\text{best}}$

   /* Pheromone updating step   */

8 | Evaporate each trail of S_Φ by multiplying it by $(1 - \rho)$

9 | **for** *each partial assignment* $\mathcal{A}_k \in \{\mathcal{A}_1, \ldots, \mathcal{A}_{nbAnts}\}$ **do**

10 | | **if** $\forall \mathcal{A}_i \in \{\mathcal{A}_1, \ldots, \mathcal{A}_{nbAnts}\}, card(\mathcal{A}_k) \geq card(\mathcal{A}_i)$ **then**

11 | | | increment each trail of $comp_\Phi(\mathcal{A}_k)$ of

   | | | $\dfrac{1}{1 + card(\mathcal{A}_{\text{best}}) - card(\mathcal{A}_k)}$

12 | **if** *a pheromone trail is lower than* $\tau_{\min}$ **then** set it to $\tau_{\min}$

13 | **if** *a pheromone trail is greater than* $\tau_{\max}$ **then** set it to $\tau_{\max}$

14 **until** *maxCycles reached* ;

15 **return** $\mathcal{A}_{\text{best}}$

14.1.1. *Pheromone strategy*

The pheromone strategy denoted by Φ is a parameter of ACO-CP and is defined by a triple $(S_\Phi, \tau_\Phi, comp_\Phi)$ such that:

– S_Φ is the set of components on which ants lay pheromone.

– τ_Φ is a function which defines how pheromone trails of S_Φ are used to bias the search. More precisely, given a partial assignment $\mathcal{A}$, a variable $x_i \notin var(\mathcal{A})$ and a value $v \in D(x_i)$, the function $\tau_\Phi(\mathcal{A}, x_i, v)$ returns the value of the pheromone factor which evaluates the learnt desirability of adding $\langle x_i, v \rangle$ to the partial assignment $\mathcal{A}$.

– $comp_\Phi$ is a function which defines the set of components on which pheromone is laid when rewarding an assignment $\mathcal{A}$, i.e. the function $comp(\mathcal{A})$ returns the set of pheromone components associated with $\mathcal{A}$.

The goal of the pheromone strategy is to learn, from previous constructions, which decisions have allowed ants to build good assignments and to use this information to bias further constructions. The default pheromone strategy, denoted by Φ_{default}, is the same as that used in the Vertex variant of the generic procedure Ant-SSP introduced in Chapter 13:

– ants lay pheromone on variable/value couples, i.e.

$$S_{\Phi_{\mathrm{default}}} = \{\tau_{\langle x_i,v\rangle} | x_i \in X, v \in D(x_i)\}$$

so that each pheromone trail $\tau_{\langle x_i,v\rangle}$ represents the learnt desirability of assigning value v to x_i;

– the pheromone factor is defined by

$$\tau_{\Phi_{\mathrm{default}}}(\mathcal{A}, x_j, v) = \tau_{\langle x_j,v\rangle};$$

– the set of components associated with an assignment is

$$comp_{\Phi_{\mathrm{default}}}(\mathcal{A}) = \{\tau_{\langle x_i,v\rangle} | \langle x_i, v\rangle \in \mathcal{A}\}.$$

For specific problems, it may be preferable to consider other pheromone strategies so that the user may design their own pheromone strategies. In this case, the triple $(S, \tau, comp)$ must be defined. We shall propose and compare two other pheromone strategies for the car sequencing problem in section 14.2.

14.1.2. *Construction of assignments*

At each cycle, each ant k builds a (either partial or complete) consistent assignment $\mathcal{A}_k$ (line 5). We can use the search procedure of a CP library to do this; this allows us to reuse the numerous existing procedures for declaring, checking and propagating constraints. In most CP libraries, the search procedure is based on the simple-backtrack procedure described in section 4.1 and is combined with constraint propagation techniques such as those described in section 4.2.

At each step, the search procedure chooses a non-assigned variable x_i and a value $v_i \in D(x_i)$ (with respect to some ordering heuristics). x_i is then assigned to v_i and constraints are propagated in order to reduce the domains of the variables that are not yet assigned and to trigger new variable assignments (if a domain has been reduced to a singleton) or a failure (if a domain has been reduced to the empty set). This *choose, assign and propagate* step is repeated either until all variables have been assigned (a solution has been found) or propagation has detected a failure (the search must backtrack to the previous choice point).

Most CP libraries provide procedures for implementing randomized restart strategies (as described in section 4.3.3). In this case, the programmer can specify a limit to the number of backtracks. When setting this limit to 1, the search procedure is stopped at the first backtrack so that it builds only 1 assignment. This assignment is partial if constraint propagation has detected a failure; it is complete if all variables have been assigned without detecting a failure (i.e. a solution has been found).

Most CP libraries also allow the programmer to specify variable and value-ordering heuristics which should be used during the search. In ACO-CP, the next variable to assign may be chosen with respect to any predefined ordering heuristic such as the *min domain* heuristic. However, the value-ordering heuristic is defined with respect to ACO. Let $\mathcal{A}_k$ be the partial assignment under construction and x_j be the next variable to assign. The value v to be assigned to x_j is randomly chosen in $D(x_j)$ with respect to probability

$$p(x_j, v) = \frac{[\tau_\Phi(\mathcal{A}_k, x_j, v)]^\alpha \cdot [\eta(\mathcal{A}_k, x_j, v)]^\beta}{\sum_{w \in D(x_j)} [\tau_\Phi(\mathcal{A}_k, x_j, w)]^\alpha \cdot [\eta(\mathcal{A}_k, x_j, w)]^\beta}.$$

The pheromone factor $\tau_\Phi(\mathcal{A}_k, x_j, v)$ is a measure of the past experience of the colony regarding the addition of $\langle x_j, v \rangle$ to the partial assignment $\mathcal{A}_k$. Its definition depends on the considered pheromone strategy Φ, which is a parameter of ACO-CP (this pheromone factor is defined by $\tau_{\langle x_j, v \rangle}$ when considering the default pheromone strategy). The heuristic factor $\eta(\mathcal{A}_k, x_j, v)$ is a parameter of ACO-CP which allows the user to specify value-ordering heuristics. This may be a generic heuristic (such as those introduced in section 4.3) or may be problem-dependent (such as those introduced in section 12.2 for the car sequencing problem).

At each cycle, ACO-CP therefore builds *nbAnts* assignments by using a randomized restart strategy with no backtrack and by replacing the default value-ordering heuristic by a pheromone-based probabilistic transition rule.

This procedure builds partial consistent assignments (as the construction is stopped as soon as propagation detects a failure). The quality of the constructed assignments therefore depends on the number of assigned variables. The goal of the ants is to build the partial assignment that assigns as many variables as possible.

This is quite different from the Ant-SSP procedure which was introduced in Chapter 13, where each ant builds a complete assignment such that all variables are assigned to values. In this case, the constructed assignment may be inconsistent and the quality of a constructed assignment depends on the number of violated constraints. The goal of the ants is therefore to build the complete assignment that violates as few constraints as possible.

14.1.3. *Pheromone updating step*

Once every ant has constructed a partial assignment, pheromone trails are updated according to ACO. They are first decreased by multiplying them by $(1-\rho)$, where $\rho \in [0; 1]$ is the evaporation rate (line 8). They are then rewarded with respect to their contribution to the construction of good assignments, i.e. those with the largest number of assigned variables (lines 9 to 11). The quantity of pheromone laid is proportionally inverse to the gap of sizes between the rewarded assignment $\mathcal{A}_k$ and the best assignment $\mathcal{A}_{\mathrm{best}}$ built since the beginning of the search (including the current cycle).

Note that Ant-CP follows the MAX-MIN Ant System scheme [STÜ 00] so that pheromone trails are bound between τ_{min} and τ_{max} (lines 12 and 13).

14.2. Illustration of ACO-CP on the car sequencing problem

We have described in [KHI 08] an implementation of ACO-CP with the CP library ILOG solver, and have experimentaly validated this framework on the car sequencing problem. In this section, we briefly report some of these results. More details may be found in [KHI 08].

14.2.1. *CSP model*

The car sequencing problem has been described with the CP modeling language of ILOG Solver by using the CSP model introduced in section 3.7. Let us briefly recall that this model associates a variable x_i with each position

i in the sequence of cars and a variable o_i^j with each position i in the sequence of cars and each option j. The domain of x_i variables is the set of car classes whereas the domain of o_i^j variables is $\{0, 1\}$. This model corresponds to the first model proposed in the ILOG Solver user manual for the car sequencing problem.

14.2.2. *Variable ordering heuristic*

We have used a classical sequential variable-ordering heuristic which consists of assigning slot variables in the order defined by the sequence of cars, i.e. $x_1, x_2, x_3, \ldots$ Note that each option variable o_i^j is assigned by constraint propagation when the corresponding slot variable x_i is assigned.

14.2.3. *Pheromone strategies*

As pheromone is at the core of the efficiency of any ACO implementation, we have explored the impact of its structure. As well as the default pheromone strategy Φ_{default} (which associates a trail with every couple (x_i, v) such that x_i is the variable associated with position i and v is a value of $D(x_i)$, i.e. a car class), we have introduced and compared two other strategies denoted Φ_{classes} and Φ_{cars}.

14.2.3.1. *Pheromone strategy Φ_{classes}*

This pheromone strategy was introduced in [GRA 04]. The pheromone structure $S_{\Phi_{\text{classes}}}$ associates a trail $\tau_{(v,w)}$ with every couple of car classes (v, w). This pheromone trail represents the learnt desirability of sequencing a car of class w just after a car of class v or, in other words, of assigning the value w to a variable x_i when x_{i-1} has just been assigned to v.

For this pheromone strategy, the pheromone factor is equal to the pheromone trail between the last assigned car class and the candidate car class (this factor is equal to 1 when assigning the first variable):

$$\tau_{\Phi_{\text{classes}}}(\mathcal{A}, x_k, v) = \tau_{(w,v)} \quad \textbf{if } k > 1 \textbf{ and } \langle x_{k-1}, w \rangle \in \mathcal{A}$$
$$\tau_{\Phi_{\text{classes}}}(\mathcal{A}, x_k, v) = 1 \qquad \textbf{if } k = 1.$$

When updating pheromone trails, pheromone is laid on value couples which have been assigned consecutively:

$$comp_{\Phi_{\text{classes}}}(\mathcal{A}) = \{\tau_{(v,w)} | \exists x_l \in X, \{\langle x_l, v \rangle, \langle x_{l+1}, w \rangle\} \subseteq \mathcal{A}\}.$$

14.2.3.2. *Pheromone strategy* Φ_{cars}

This pheromone strategy corresponds to that introduced in section 12.2. The pheromone structure $S_{\Phi_{\text{cars}}}$ associates a trail $\tau_{(v,i,w,j)}$ with each couple of car classes (v, w) and each $i \in [1; \#v]$ and $j \in [1; \#w]$ where $\#v$ and $\#w$ are the number of cars within the classes v and w, respectively. This trail represents the learnt desirability of sequencing the jth car of class w just after the ith car of class v.

In this case, the pheromone factor is defined:

$$\tau_{\Phi_{\text{cars}}}(\mathcal{A}, x_k, v) = \tau_{(w,j,v,i+1)} \quad \textbf{if } k > 1 \textbf{ and } \langle x_{k-1}, w \rangle \in \mathcal{A}$$
$$\textbf{and } j = card(\{\langle x_l, w \rangle \in \mathcal{A}\})$$
$$\textbf{and } i = card(\{\langle x_l, v \rangle \in \mathcal{A}\})$$
$$\tau_{\Phi_{\text{cars}}}(\mathcal{A}, x_k, v) = 1 \quad \textbf{if } k = 1.$$

When updating pheromone trails, pheromone is laid on car couples which are consecutively sequenced:

$$comp_{\Phi_{\text{cars}}}(\mathcal{A}) = \{\tau_{(v,i,w,j)} | \quad \exists x_l \in X, \{\langle x_l, v \rangle, \langle x_{l+1}, w \rangle\} \subseteq \mathcal{A}_k$$
$$\textbf{and } i = card(\{\langle x_m, v \rangle / m \le l\})$$
$$\textbf{and } j = card(\{\langle x_m, w \rangle / m \le l+1\})\}.$$

14.2.4. *Heuristic factor*

The heuristic factor used in the probabilistic transition rule was introduced in section 12.2 and is based on the sum of option utilization rates:

$$\eta_{\text{DSU}}(\mathcal{A}, x_i, v) = \sum_{o_j \in O} r(v, o_j) \frac{\text{reqSlots}(o_j, n_j)}{card(C) - card(\mathcal{A})}$$

where n_j is the number of cars that have not yet been sequenced and that require option o_j and $\text{reqSlots}(o_j, n_j)$ is the minimum number of positions that allow n_j cars to be sequenced requiring option o_j without violating the capacity constraints of o_j. $\text{reqSlots}(o_j, n_j)$ is defined:

if $n_j \% p_j = 0$ **then**:
$$\text{reqSlots}(o_j, n_j) = q_j \frac{n_j}{p_j} - q_j + p_j$$
else:
$$\text{reqSlots}(o_j, n_j) = q_j \frac{n_j - n_j \% p_j}{p_j} + n_j \% p_j.$$

14.2.5. *Experimental results*

In [KHI 08], we have reported experimental results for the 82 instances of the test suite used in section 12.5. These experimental results have been obtained with the parameter setting: $\alpha = 1$, $\beta = 6$, $\rho = 0.02$, $nbAnts = 30$, $\tau_{\min} = 0.01$ and $\tau_{\max} = 4$.

In particular, we have compared the three different pheromone structures i.e. Φ_{default}, Φ_{classes} and Φ_{cars}. To evaluate the influence of the pheromone on the solution process, we have also considered a strategy without pheromone denoted $\Phi_\emptyset$. In this case, the pheromone structure $S_{\Phi_\emptyset}$ is the empty set, the pheromone factor is constant $(\tau_{\Phi_\emptyset}(\mathcal{A}, x_k, v) = 1)$ and the set of components associated with an assignment to reward is empty $(comp_{\Phi_\emptyset}(\mathcal{A}) = \emptyset)$.

Experimental results reported in [KHI 08] have shown us that, after 3000 cycles, using pheromone increases the success rate from 66.3% for $\Phi_\emptyset$ to 79.4% for Φ_{cars}, 72.6% for Φ_{default} and 68.3% for Φ_{classes}. For these instances, the best pheromone strategy is therefore Φ_{cars}. The default pheromone strategy is poorer than Φ_{cars}, but better than Φ_{classes}.

These experiments have shown us that ACO-CP based on Φ_{cars} exhibits performances that are very similar to those of the algorithm $\text{ACO}(\tau_1, \eta)$ introduced in section 12.2. These two algorithms use the same pheromone strategy and the same heuristic based on utilization rates. They differ mainly in the way they build assignments: ACO-CP builds partial consistent assignments (thus allowing constraint propagation algorithms that have been defined for tree search-based approaches to be used) and $\text{ACO}(\tau_1, \eta)$ builds complete inconsistent assignments.

The time needed to implement these two algorithms is very different. For the ACO-CP variant that uses the default pheromone strategy, the user only has to describe the problem by declaring variables and posting constraints. For the two other variants of ACO-CP which use dedicated pheromone strategies, the user has to specify the pheromone structure S_Φ and the two functions τ_Φ and $comp_\Phi$ (which define the pheromone factor and the pheromone components associated with an assignment to reward).

However, CPU times obtained with ACO-CP are clearly an order higher than those obtained with the ACO algorithm described in section 12.2. For instances with 100 cars, 3000 cycles of ACO-CP are computed in 5 minutes or so. Indeed, using the constraint propagation procedures embedded in a CP library is more time consuming than using *ad hoc* procedures for this problem. This point will be discussed in Chapter 15.

14.3. Discussion

These first experiments on the car sequencing problem have shown us that integrating an ACO search might be designed as a simple extension of a CP library such as ILOG Solver. This integration brings the modeling power of CP languages and the simplicity of a declarative approach to ACO. It is worth noting that, due to the modular nature of CP languages that separates the modeling of the problem from the computation of its solution, the CP model used to describe the problem does not depend on the search technique. Other search methods can be tested or combined without changing the problem description.

First experimental results are very promising. Indeed, classical CP solvers based on exhaustive tree search approaches are still not able to solve all instances of *CSPLib* with 100 and 200 cars within a reasonable amount of time. This is also the case even when using dedicated filtering algorithms, such as those proposed in [BRA 07, REG 97, VAN 06]. All these instances are easily solved by the ILOG solver-based implementation of ACO-CP (whatever the pheromone strategy is). The 70 instances with 200 cars (respectively, 4 instances with 100 cars) are solved in less than a second (respectively, less than a minute). As a comparison, filterings introduced in [BRA 07] for the 'sequence' constraint can solve less than half of these instances in less than 100 sec when they are combined with the default tree search of ILOG Solver on a Pentium 4 sequenced at 3.2 Ghz.

These experiments should of course be tested on other problems to further validate this approach.

Chapter 15

Conclusion

We have shown that ant colony optimization is able to efficiently solve constraint satisfaction problems and may be easily integrated in a constraint programming language. This integration allows us to reuse a constraint-based modeling language that contains many predefined constraints as well as the associated procedures that have been implemented for checking and propagating these constraints.

A key point for the success of constraint programming relies on the efficiency of the embedded constraint solver. Two main issues should be further explored to improve this point.

15.1. Towards constraint-based ACO search

The first results obtained by Ant-CP, which integrates ACO to a CP library, could be improved by using constraint propagation algorithms dedicated to an ACO search. Indeed, the constraint propagation algorithms that are integrated with CP libraries such as Choco or ILOG Solver are designed for a complete tree search which backtracks on previous choices when a failure is detected. They therefore maintain data structures that allow the solver to restore the context of the previous choice point at each backtrack. These data structures are expensive to maintain whereas they are not necessary in the context of an ACO search that never backtracks on its choices.

The same is true of a constraint-based local search language such as Comet, described in section 7.3. Indeed, Comet may be used to implement a constraint-based ACO search. (The name *constraint-based ACO search* emerged from a discussion with Pascal Van Hentenryck and Yves Deville, and comes from the constraint-based local search paradigm which underlies Comet.) Van Hentenryck and Michel have shown in [VAN 05] that the Comet language may be used to implement an ACO algorithm in a declarative way. However, Comet is mainly dedicated to perturbative heuristic approaches which explore the search space by applying transformation operators to existing combinations, as described in Chapter 5. Comet therefore automaticaly maintains data structures that allow the incremental and efficient evaluation of the impact of these transformations on the objective function and on constraint violations.

These data structures may also be utilized during an ACO search, at each step of a combination construction, to incrementally evaluate heuristic factors. However, Comet maintains more information than necessary because choices made during a greedy construction are never modified. Note, however, that the data structures maintained by Comet ease a hybridization of ACO with local search.

The first main issue for an efficient integration of ACO within a constraint programming language is the design of incremental procedures associated with constraints. These procedures must incrementally check constraint violations and update objective functions in the context of a heuristic constructive search where choices are never modified by backtracking (as for complete tree search approaches) or by applying elementary transformation operators (as for perturbative heuristic approaches).

15.2. Towards a reactive ACO search

Constraint programming aims to free the user from programming the search. Ideally, the user simply defines the problem by means of constraints and the search of solutions is automatically ensured by embedded constraint solvers. However, the user often has to help the solver in order to overcome combinatorial explosion.

In complete tree search approaches, key points are therefore (1) to choose relevant ordering heuristics which are able to guide the search and (2) to design a good CP model such that constraint propagation can restrain combinatorial explosion (by adding redundant constraints or by using appropriate global constraints, for example).

In heuristic approaches, a key point is to balance intensification and diversification in order to guide the search towards better combinations while allowing it to escape from suboptimal areas.

In ACO, this balance is mainly achieved through the tuning of pheromone parameters. We have seen that these parameters have a strong influence on the solving process. This is a real hindrance in using ACO to implement a CP search as parameter tuning is rather contradictory with the automatic solving goal of CP. A main issue for the success of an ACO CP approach is therefore to design adaptive ACO approaches which are able to dynamically tune parameters during the solving process. We have seen in Chapter 8 that there exist intensification and diversification measures such as the resampling and similarity ratios. These may be used to dynamically detect stagnation or overdiversification situations.

A first basic adaptive ACO framework was described in Chapter 13. In particular, the resampling ratio is used to prevent early stagnation by decreasing pheromone trails that are associated with combinations that are resampled. It is also used to detect the convergence of the search process and automatically reinitialize pheromone trails in this case. This allows the number of cycles of each ACO run to be dynamically adapted.

This kind of approach should be generalized to tune other parameters, thus leading to a reactive ACO framework which is able to dynamically adapt all parameters with respect to the need for intensification or diversification.

Bibliography

[AAR 89] AARTS E., KORST J., *Simulated Annealing and Boltzmann Machines: A Stochastic Approach to Combinatorial Optimization and Neural Computing*, John Wiley & Sons, Chichester, 1989.

[ALA 07] ALAYA I., SOLNON C., GHEDIRA K., "Optimisation par colonies de fourmis pour le problème du sac-à-dos multi-dimensionnel", *Techniques et Sciences Informatiques (TSI)*, vol. 26, num. 3–4, p. 271–390, 2007.

[ANG 09] ANGUS D., WOODWARD C., "Multiple objective ant colony optimisation", *Swarm Intelligence*, vol. 3, num. 1, p. 69–85, 2009.

[BAK 95] BAKER A., Intelligent backtracking on constraint satisfaction problems: experimental and theoretical results, PhD thesis, University of Oregon, 1995.

[BAL 94] BALUJA S., Population-based incremental learning: a method for integrating genetic search based function optimization and competitive learning, Technical report, Carnegie Mellon University, Pittsburgh, USA, 1994.

[BAT 01] BATTITI R., PROTASI M., "Reactive local search for the maximum clique problem", *Algorithmica*, vol. 29, num. 4, p. 610–637, 2001.

[BAT 08] BATTITI R., BRUNATO M., MASCIA F., *Reactive Search and Intelligent Optimization*, vol. 45 of *Operations Research/Computer Science Interfaces Series*, Springer, 2008.

[BEL 07] BELDICEANU N., CARLSSON M., DEMASSEY S., PETIT T., "Global constraint catalogue: past, present and future", *Constraints*, vol. 12, num. 1, p. 21–62, 2007.

[BES 97] BESSIÈRE C., RÉGIN J.-C., "Arc consistency for general constraint networks: preliminary results", *Proceedings of International Joint Conference on Artificial Intelligence (IJCAI)*, p. 398–404, 1997.

[BES 02] BESSIÈRE C., MESEGUER P., FREUDER E., LARROSA J., "On forward checking for non-binary constraint satisfaction", *Artificial Intelligence*, vol. 141, num. 1, p. 205–224, 2002.

[BES 03] BESSIÈRE C., VAN HENTENRYCK P., "To be or not to be... a global constraint", *Proceedings of International Conference on Principles and Practice of Constraint Programming (CP)*, vol. 1118 of *LNCS*, Springer, p. 789–794, 2003.

[BIS 97] BISTARELLI S., MONTANARI U., ROSSI F., "Semiring-based constraint satisfaction and optimization", *Journal of the ACM*, vol. 44, num. 2, p. 201–236, 1997.

[BLU 02] BLUM C., "Ant colony optimization for the edge-weighted k-cardinality tree problem", *Proceedings of GECCO 2002*, p. 27–34, 2002.

[BLU 04] BLUM C., DORIGO M., "The hyper-cube framework for ant colony optimization", *IEEE Transactions on Systems, Man, and Cybernetics - Part B*, vol. 34, num. 2, p. 1161–1172, 2004.

[BOY 07] BOYSEN N., FLIEDNER M., "Comments on solving real car sequencing problems with ant colony optimization", *European Journal of Operational Research*, vol. 182, num. 1, p. 466–468, 2007.

[BRA 07] BRAND S., NARODYTSKA N., QUIMPER C.-G., STUCKEY P. J., WALSH T., "Encodings of the sequence constraint", *13th International Conference on Principles and Practice of Constraint Programming (CP)*, vol. 4741 of *LNCS*, Springer, p. 210–224, 2007.

[BRÉ 79] BRÉLAZ D., "New methods to color the vertices of a graph", *Communications of the ACM*, vol. 22, num. 4, p. 251–256, 1979.

[BUL 99] BULLNHEIMER B., HARTL R. F., STRAUSS C., "An improved ant system algorithm for the vehicle routing problem", *Annals of Operations Research*, vol. 89, p. 319–328, 1999.

[CHE 91] CHEESEMAN P., KANELFY B., TAYLOR W. M., "Where the *really* hard problems are", *International Joint Conference on Artificial Intelligence (IJCAI)*, Morgan Kaufmann, Sydney, Australia, p. 331–337, 1991.

[CHU 98] CHU P., BEASLEY J., "A genetic algorithm for the multidimensional knapsack problem", *Journal of Heuristics*, vol. 4, p. 63–86, 1998.

[CLA 96] CLARK D. A., FRANK J., GENT I. P., MACINTYRE E., TOMOV N., WALSH T., "Local search and the number of solutions", *International Conference on Principles and Practice of Constraint Programming (CP)*, vol. 1118 of *LNCS*, Springer-Verlag, p. 119–133, 1996.

[COL 90] COLMERAUER A., "An introduction to Prolog III", *Communications of the ACM*, vol. 33, num. 7, 1990.

[COO 71] COOK S. A., "The complexity of theorem-proving procedures", *STOC '71: Proceedings of the Third Annual ACM Symposium on Theory of Computing*, ACM, p. 151–158, 1971.

[COR 90] CORMEN T. H., LEISERSON C. E., RIVEST R. L., *Introduction to Algorithms*, MIT Press, 1990.

[CRA 03] CRAENEN B. G., EIBEN A., VAN HEMERT J., "Comparing evolutionary algorithms on binary constraint satisfaction problems", *IEEE Transactions on Evolutionary Computation*, vol. 7, num. 5, p. 424–444, 2003.

[DAS 99] DASGUPTA D., *Artificial Immune Systems and their Applications*, Springer-Verlag, 1999.

[DAV 95] DAVENPORT A., "A comparison of complete and incomplete algorithms in the easy and hard regions", *Proceedings of CP'95 Workshop on Studying and Solving Really Hard Problems*, p. 43–51, 1995.

[DAV 99] DAVENPORT A. J., TSANG E. P., "Solving constraint satisfaction sequencing problems by iterative repair", *Proceedings of the First International Conference on the Practical Applications of Constraint Technologies and Logic Programming (PACLP)*, p. 345–357, 1999.

[DEB 01] DEBRUYNE R., BESSIÈRE C., "Domain filtering consistencies", *Journal of Artificial Intelligence Research*, vol. 14, p. 205–230, 2001.

[DEN 90] DENEUBOURG J.-L., ARON S., GOSS S., PASTEELS J. M., "The self-organizing exploratory pattern of the Argentine ant", *Journal of Insect Behavior*, vol. 3, p. 159–168, 1990.

[DIM 96] DIMITRIOU T., IMPAGLIAZZO R., "Towards an analysis of local optimization algorithms", *Proceedings of Symposium on Theory of Computing*, p. 304–313, 1996.

[DIN 88] DINCBAS M., SIMONIS H., VAN HENTENRYCK P., "Solving the car-sequencing problem in constraint logic programming", *European Conference on Artificial Intelligence (ECAI)*, p. 290–295, 1988.

[DOR 92] DORIGO M., Optimization, learning and natural algorithms (in Italian), PhD thesis, Department of Electronics, Politecnico di Milano, Italy, 1992.

[DOR 96] DORIGO M., MANIEZZO V., COLORNI A., "Ant system: optimization by a colony of cooperating agents", *IEEE Transactions on Systems, Man, and Cybernetics - Part B: Cybernetics*, vol. 26, num. 1, p. 29–41, 1996.

[DOR 97] DORIGO M., GAMBARDELLA L. M., "Ant colony system: a cooperative learning approach to the traveling salesman problem", *IEEE Transactions on Evolutionary Computation*, vol. 1, num. 1, p. 53–66, 1997.

[DOR 04] DORIGO M., STÜTZLE T., *Ant Colony Optimization*, MIT Press, 2004.

[EST 05] ESTELLON B., GARDI F., NOUIOUA K., "Ordonnancement de véhicules: une approche par recherche locale à grand voisinage", *Actes des premières Journées Francophones de Programmation par Contraintes (JFPC)*, p. 21–28, 2005.

[EST 08] ESTELLON B., GARDI F., NOUIOUA K., "Two local search approaches for solving real-life car sequencing problems", *European Journal of Operational Research (EJOR)*, vol. 191, num. 3, p. 928–924, 2008.

[FEN 03] FENET S., SOLNON C., "Searching for maximum cliques with ant colony optimization", *Applications of Evolutionary Computing, Proceedings of EvoWorkshops 2003: EvoCOP, EvoIASP, EvoSTim*, vol. 2611 of *LNCS*, Springer-Verlag, p. 236–245, 2003.

[FEO 89] FEO T., RESENDE M., "A probabilistic heuristic for a computationally difficult set covering problem", *Operations Research Letters*, vol. 8, p. 67–71, 1989.

[FON 99] FONLUPT C., ROBILLIARD D., PREUX P., TALBI E., "Metaheuristics – advances and trends in local search paradigms for optimization", *Fitness Landscape and Performance of Meta-heuristic*, p. 255–266, Kluwer Academic Press, 1999.

[FRE 92] FREUDER E., WALLACE R., "Partial constraint satisfaction", *Artificial Intelligence*, vol. 58, p. 21–70, 1992.

[FRE 97] FREUDER E. C., "In pursuit of the Holy Grail", *Constraints*, vol. 2, num. 1, p. 57–61, 1997.

[GAL 97] GALINIER P., HAO J.-K., "Tabu search for maximal constraint satisfaction problems", *International Conference on Principles and Practice of Constraint Programming (CP)*, vol. 1330 of *LNCS*, Springer, p. 196–208, 1997.

[GAR 79] GAREY M., JOHNSON D., *A Guide to the Theory of NP-Completeness*, Freeman, 1979.

[GEN 94] GENT I. P., WALSH T., "Easy problems are sometimes hard", *Artificial Intelligence*, vol. 70, num. 1–2, p. 335–345, 1994.

[GEN 96] GENT I., MACINTYRE E., PROSSER P., WALSH T., "The constrainedness of search", *14th National Conference on Artificial Intelligence (AAAI)*, 1996.

[GEN 98] GENT I., Two Results on Car-sequencing Problems, Technical report (http://www.apes.cs.strath.ac.uk/apesreports.html), APES, 1998.

[GEN 99] GENT I., WALSH T., CSPLib: a benchmark library for constraints, Report , APES-09 1999, 1999, http://csplib.cs.strath.ac.uk/.

[GEN 02] GENT I., PROSSER P., "An empirical study of the stable marriage problem with ties and incomplete lists", *Proceedings of ECAI 2002: 15th European Conference on Artificial Intelligence*, IOS Press, p. 141–145, 2002.

[GLO 93] GLOVER F., LAGUNA M., "Tabu search", *Modern Heuristics Techniques for Combinatorial Problems*, p. 70–141, Blackwell Scientific Publishing, Oxford, Royaume-Uni, 1993.

[GOM 01] GOMES C., SELMAN B., "Algorithm portfolios", *Artificial Intelligence*, vol. 126, num. 1–2, p. 43–62, Elsevier Science Publishers Ltd., 2001.

[GOT 03] GOTTLIEB J., PUCHTA M., SOLNON C., "A study of greedy, local search and ant colony optimization approaches for car sequencing problems", *Applications of Evolutionary Computing*, vol. 2611 of *LNCS*, Springer, p. 246–257, 2003.

[GRA 59] GRASSÉ P.-P., "La reconstruction du nid et les coordinations inter-individuelles chez bellicostitermes natalensis et cubitermes. La théorie de la stigmergie: essai d'interprétation du comportement des termites constructeurs", *Insectes sociaux*, vol. 61, p. 41–81, 1959.

[GRA 04] GRAVEL M., GAGNÉ C., PRICE W., "Review and comparison of three methods for the solution of the car-sequencing problem", *Journal of the Operational Research Society*, vol. 56, num. 11, p. 1287–1295, 2004.

[GUN 01] GUNTSCH M., MIDDENDORF M., SCHMECK H., "An ant colony optimization approach to dynamic TSP", *Proceedings of GECCO 2001*, p. 860–867, 2001.

[GUN 02] GUNTSCH M., MIDDENDORF M., "Applying population based ACO to dynamic optimization problems", *Proceedings of Ants 2002*, vol. 2463 of *LNCS*, Springer, p. 97–104, 2002.

[HAD 00] HADJI R., RAHOUAL M., TALBI E.-G., BACHELET V., "Ant colonies for the set covering problem", *Proceedings of ANTS 2000*, p. 63–66, 2000.

[HAN 03] HANDA H., "Hybridization of estimation of distribution algorithms with a repair method for solving constraint satisfaction problems", *Genetic and Evolutionary Computation (GECCO)*, vol. 2723 of *LNCS*, Springer, p. 991–1002, 2003.

[HOF 69] HOFFMAN E., LOESSI J., MOORE R., "Constructions for the solution of the m queens problem", *Mathematics Magazine*, vol. 42, num. 2, p. 66–72, 1969.

[HOG 96] HOGG T., "Refining the phase transition in combinatorial search", *Artificial Intelligence*, vol. 81, num. 1–2, p. 127–154, 1996.

[HOG 98] HOGG T., "Exploiting problem structure as a search heuristic", *International Journal of Modern Physics C*, vol. 9, p. 13–29, 1998.

[HOP 73] HOPCROFT J., KARP R., "An $n^{5/2}$ algorithm for maximum matchings in bipartite graphs", *SIAM Journal of Computing*, vol. 2, num. 4, p. 225–231, 1973.

[JAG 01] JAGOTA A., SANCHIS L., "Adaptive, restart, randomized greedy heuristics for maximum clique", *Journal of Heuristics*, vol. 7, num. 6, p. 565–585, 2001.

[JON 95] JONES T., FORREST S., "Fitness distance correlation as a measure of problem difficulty for genetic algorithms", *Proceedings of International Conference on Genetic Algorithms*, Morgan Kaufmann, Sydney, Australia, p. 184–192, 1995.

[JUS 02] JUSSIEN N., LHOMME O., "Local search with constraint propagation and conflict-based heuristics", *Artificial Intelligence*, vol. 139, num. 1, 2002.

[KAU 02] KAUTZ H., HORVITZ E., RUAN Y., GOMES C., SELMAN B., "Dynamic restart policies", *18th National Conference on Artificial intelligence*, American Association for Artificial Intelligence, p. 674–681, 2002.

[KEN 95] KENNEDY J., EBERHART R., "Particle swarm optimization", *Proceedings of IEEE International Conference on Neural Networks*, p. 1942–1948, 1995.

[KHI 08] KHICHANE M., ALBERT P., SOLNON C., "Integration of ACO in a constraint programming language", *6th International Conference on Ant Colony Optimization and Swarm Intelligence (ANTS'08)*, vol. 5217 of *LNCS*, Springer, p. 84–95, 2008.

[KIS 04] KIS T., "On the complexity of the car sequencing problem", *Operations Research Letters*, vol. 32, p. 331–335, 2004.

[LAR 01] LARRANAGA P., LOZANO J., *Estimation of Distribution Algorithms: A New Tool for Evolutionary Computation*, Kluwer Academic Publishers, 2001.

[LAU 78] LAURIÈRE J.-L., "ALICE: a language and a program for solving combinatorial problems", *Artificial Intelligence*, vol. 10, p. 29–127, 1978.

[LEE 98] LEE J. H., LEUNG H.-F., WON H.-W., "Performance of a comprehensive and efficient constraint library using local search", *11th Australian JCAI*, LNAI, Springer-Verlag, 1998.

[LEG 99] LEGUIZAMON G., MICHALEWICZ Z., "A new version of ant system for subset problem", *Proceedings of Congress on Evolutionary Computation*, p. 1459–1464, 1999.

[LOU 02] LOURENCO H., MARTIN O., STÜTZLE T., "Iterated local search", *Handbook of Metaheuristics*, p. 321–353, Kluwer Academic Publishers, 2002.

[MAC 98] MacIntyre E., Prosser P., Smith B., Walsh T., "Random constraints satisfaction: theory meets practice", *CP98, LNCS 1520*, p. 325–339, Springer Verlag, Berlin, Allemagne, 1998.

[MCK 81] McKay B., "Practical graph isomorphism", *Congressus Numerantium*, vol. 30, p. 45–87, 1981.

[MER 99] Merz P., Freisleben B., "Fitness landscapes and memetic algorithm design", *New Ideas in Optimization*, p. 245–260, McGraw Hill, 1999.

[MIC 02] Michel L., van Hentenryck P., "A constraint-based architecture for local search", *17th ACM SIGPLAN Conference on Object-Oriented Programming, Systems, Languages, and Applications (OOPSLA)*, ACM Press, p. 83–100, 2002.

[MIN 92] Minton S., Johnston M., Philips A., Laird P., "Minimizing conflicts: a heuristic repair method for constraint satisfaction and scheduling problems", *Artificial Intelligence*, vol. 58, p. 161–205, 1992.

[MLA 97] Mladenović N., Hansen P., "Variable neighborhood search", *Compositions in Operations Research*, vol. 24, p. 1097–1100, 1997.

[MOR 01] Morrison R. W., Jong K. A. D., "Measurement of population diversity", *5th International Conference EA 2001*, vol. 2310 of *LNCS*, Springer-Verlag, p. 31–41, 2001.

[NEV 04] Neveu B., Trombettoni G., Glover F., "ID Walk: A candidate list strategy with a simple diversification device", *International Conference on Principles and Practice of Constraint Programming (CP)*, vol. 3258 of *LNCS*, Springer Verlag, p. 423–437, 2004.

[PAP 94] Papadimitriou C., *Computational Complexity*, Addison Wesley, 1994.

[PAR 86] Parello B., Kabat W., Wos L., "Job-shop scheduling using automated reasoning: a case study of the car sequencing problem", *Journal of Automated Reasoning*, vol. 2, p. 1–42, 1986.

[PEL 99] Pelikan M., Goldberg D., Cantú-Paz E., "BOA: The bayesian optimization algorithm", *Proceedings of the Genetic and Evolutionary Computation Conference GECCO-99*, vol. I(13–17), p. 525–532, 1999.

[PER 04] PERRON L., SHAW P., "Combining forces to solve the car sequencing problem", *Integration of AI and OR in Constraint Programming for Combinatorial Optimization Problems (CP-AI-OR)*, vol. 3011 of *LNCS*, Springer, p. 225–239, 2004.

[RÉG 94] RÉGIN J.-C., "A filtering algorithm for constraints of difference in CSPs", *Proceedings of 12th Conference of American Association of Artificial Intelligence*, vol. 1, American Association of Artificial Intelligence, p. 362–367, 1994.

[REG 97] REGIN J.-C., PUGET J.-F., "A filtering algorithm for global sequencing constraints", *International Conference on Principles and Practice of Constraint Programming (CP)*, vol. 1330 of *LNCS*, p. 32–46, Springer-Verlag, 1997.

[RES 03] RESENDE M., RIBEIRO C., "Greedy randomized adaptive search procedures", *Handbook of Metaheuristics*, p. 219–249, Kluwer Academic Publishers, 2003.

[ROS 96] ROSÉ H., EBELING W., ASSELMEYER T., "Density of states - a measure of the difficulty of optimisation problems", *Proceedings of PPSN'96*, LNCS 1141, Springer Verlag, p. 208–217, 1996.

[ROS 06] ROSSI F., VAN BEEK P., WALSH T., Eds., *Handbook of Constraint Programming*, Elsevier, 2006.

[SAM 05] SAMMOUD O., SOLNON C., GHÉDIRA K., "Ant algorithm for the graph matching problem", *5th European Conference on Evolutionary Computation in Combinatorial Optimization*, vol. 3448 of *LNCS*, Springer Verlag, p. 213–223, 2005.

[SAM 06] SAMMOUD O., SORLIN S., SOLNON C., GHÉDIRA K., "A comparative study of ant colony optimization and reactive search for graph matching problems", *6th European Conference on Evolutionary Computation in Combinatorial Optimization (EvoCOP 2006)*, vol. 3906 of *LNCS*, Springer, p. 234–246, 2006.

[SEL 94] SELMAN B., KAUTZ H., COHEN B., "Noise strategies for improving local search", *Proceedings of the 12th National Conference on Artificial Intelligence*, AAAI Press/The MIT Press, Menlo Park, USA, p. 337–343, 1994.

[SHI 95] SHIEX T., FARGIER H., VERFAILLIE G., "Valued constraint satisfaction problems: hard and easy problems", *International Joint Conference on Artificial Intelligence (IJCAI)*, MIT Press, Cambridge, Etats-Unis, p. 631–637, 1995.

[SHM 95] SHMOYS D. B., "Computing near-optimal solutions to combinatorial optimization problems", *DIMACS Series in Discrete Mathematics and Theoretical Computer Science*, vol. 20, p. 355–397, 1995.

[SID 01] SIDANER A., BAILLEUX O., CHABRIER J.-J., "Measuring the spatial dispersion of evolutionist search processes: application to Walksat", *5th International Conference EA 2001*, vol. 2310 of *LNCS*, Springer-Verlag, p. 77–90, 2001.

[SMI 96] SMITH B., "Succeed-first or fail-first: a case study in variable and value ordering heuristics", *3rd Conference on the Practical Applications of Constraint Technology PACT'97*, p. 321–330, 1996.

[SOC 08] SOCHA K., DORIGO M., "Ant colony optimization for continuous domains", *European Journal of Operational Research*, vol. 185, num. 3, p. 1155–1173, 2008.

[SOL 00] SOLNON C., "Solving permutation constraint satisfaction problems with artificial ants", *Proceedings of ECAI'2000*, IOS Press, p. 118–122, 2000.

[SOL 02] SOLNON C., "Ants can solve constraint satisfaction problems", *IEEE Transactions on Evolutionary Computation*, vol. 6, num. 4, p. 347–357, 2002.

[SOL 06] SOLNON C., FENET S., "A study of ACO capabilities for solving the maximum clique problem", *Journal of Heuristics*, vol. 12, num. 3, p. 155–180, Springer, 2006.

[SOL 08] SOLNON C., CUNG V.-D., NGUYEN A., ARTIGUES C., "The car sequencing problem: overview of state-of-the-art methods and industrial case-study of the ROADEF'2005 challenge problem", *European Journal of Operational Research*, vol. 191, num. 3, p. 912–917, 2008.

[STA 95] STADLER P., "Towards a theory of landscapes", *Complex Systems and Binary Networks*, vol. 461, Springer Verlag, p. 77–163, 1995.

[STÜ 00] STÜTZLE T., HOOS H., "MAX-MIN Ant System", *Journal of Future Generation Computer Systems, special issue on Ant Algorithms*, vol. 16, p. 889–914, 2000.

[STÜ 02] STÜTZLE T., DORIGO M., "A short convergence proof for a class of ant colony optimization algorithms", *IEEE Transactions on Evolutionary Computation*, vol. 6, num. 4, p. 358–365, 2002.

[STÜ 04] STÜTZLE T., HOOS H., *Stochastic Local Search: Foundations and Applications*, Morgan Kaufman, 2004.

[TAR 05] TARRANT F., BRIDGE D., "When ants attack: ant algorithms for constraint satisfaction problems", *Artificial Intelligence Review*, vol. 24, num. 3–4, p. 455–476, 2005.

[VAN 97] VAN HENTENRYCK P., MICHEL L., DEVILLE Y., *Numerica: A Modelling Language for Global Optimization*, MIT Press, 1997.

[VAN 02] VAN HEMERT J., BÄCK T., "Measuring the searched space to guide efficiency: the principle and evidence on constraint satisfaction", *Proceedings of the 7th International Conference on Parallel Problem Solving from Nature*, vol. 2439 of *LNCS*, Berlin, Springer-Verlag, p. 23–32, 2002.

[VAN 04] VAN HEMERT J., SOLNON C., "A Study into ant colony optimization, evolutionary computation and constraint programming on binary constraint satisfaction problems", *Evolutionary Computation in Combinatorial Optimization (EvoCOP 2004)*, vol. 3004 of *LNCS*, Springer-Verlag, p. 114–123, 2004.

[VAN 05] VAN HENTENRYCK P., MICHEL L., *Constraint-based Local Search*, MIT Press, 2005.

[VAN 06] VAN HOEVE W., PESANT G., ROUSSEAU L.-M., SABHARWAL A., "Revisiting the sequence constraint", *12th International Conference on Principles and Practice of Constraint Programming (CP)*, vol. 4204 of *LNCS*, Springer, p. 620–634, 2006.

[VAN 07] VAN DONGEN M., LECOUTRE C., ROUSSEL O., "Results of the second CSP solver competition", *Proceedings of Second International CSP Solver Competition*, p. 1–10, 2007.

[WAL 72] WALTZ D., Generating semantic descriptions from drawings of scenes with shadows, Report num. AI-TR-271, MIT Artificial Intelligence Laboratory, 1972.

[WAL 96] WALLACE R., "Analysis of heuristics methods for partial constraint satisfaction problems", *International Conference on Principles and Practice of Constraint Programming (CP)*, vol. 1118 of *LNCS*, Springer, p. 308–322, 1996.

[XU 07] XU K., BOUSSEMART F., HEMERY F., LECOUTRE C., "Random constraint satisfaction: Easy generation of hard (satisfiable) instances", *Artificial Intelligence*, vol. 171, num. 8-9, p. 514–534, Elsevier Science Publishers Ltd., 2007.

[YAN 06] YANG Q., SUN J., ZHANG J., WANG C., "A hybrid siscrete particle swarm algorithm for hard binary CSPs", *Advances in Natural Computation*, num. 4222LNCS, Springer, p. 184–193, 2006.

[ZIN 07] ZINFLOU A., GAGNÉ C., GRAVEL M., "Crossover operators for the car sequencing problem", *7th European Conference on Evolutionary Computation in Combinatorial Optimization (EvoCOP)*, vol. 4446 of *Lecture Notes in Computer Science*, p. 229–239, 2007.

[ZLO 04] ZLOCHIN M., BIRATTARI M., MEULEAU N., DORIGO M., "Model-based search for combinatorial optimization: a critical survey", *Annals of Operations Research*, vol. 131, p. 373–395, 2004.

Index